LYNDON B. JOHNSON

LYNDON B. JOHNSON

SCOTT BARBOUR, *Book Editor*

DAVID L. BENDER, *Publisher*
BRUNO LEONE, *Executive Editor*
BONNIE SZUMSKI, *Editorial Director*
STUART B. MILLER, *Managing Editor*
JAMES D. TORR, *Series Editor*

GREENHAVEN PRESS, INC.
SAN DIEGO, CALIFORNIA

Every effort has been made to trace the owners of copyrighted material. The articles in this volume may have been edited for content, length, and/or reading level. The titles have been changed to enhance the editorial purpose.

No part of this book may be reproduced or used in any form or by any means, electrical, mechanical, or otherwise, including, but not limited to, photocopy, recording, or any information on storage and retrieval system without prior written permission from the publisher.

Library of Congress Cataloging-in-Publication Data

Lyndon B. Johnson / Scott Barbour, book editor.
    p.   cm. — (Presidents and their decisions)
    Includes bibliographical references (p.) and index.
    ISBN 0-7377-0499-3 (pbk. : alk. paper) — ISBN 0-7377-0500-0
(lib. : alk. paper)
    1. Johnson, Lyndon B. (Lyndon Baines), 1908–1973. 2. United
States—Politics and government—1963–1969—Decision making.
I. Barbour, Scott, 1963– . II. Series.

E846 .L94 2001
973.923'092—dc21   00-028333
                                                                        CIP

Cover photo: © CORBIS
Lyndon Baines Johnson Library 29, 34
National Archives 39, 158, 177

Series Design: LiMiTeD Edition Book Design, Linda Mae Tratechaud

©2001 Greenhaven Press, Inc.
P.O. Box 289009, San Diego, CA 92198-9009

PRINTED IN THE U.S.A.

CONTENTS

grams left many blacks worse off than before Johnson became president.

CHAPTER 3: ESCALATING THE VIETNAM WAR

Chapter 4: De-Escalating the War and Withdrawing from the Presidential Race

FOREWORD

"**T**HE PRESIDENCY OF THE UNITED STATES IS OFTEN DE-
scribed as the most powerful office in the world,"
writes Forrest McDonald in *The American Presidency: An
Intellectual History.* "In one sense this description is accurate," he says, "for even casual decisions made in the White
House can affect the lives of millions of people." But Mc-
Donald also notes that presidential power "is restrained by
the countervailing power of Congress, the courts, the bureaucracy, popular opinion, the news media, and state and
local governments. What presidents do have is awesome
responsibilities combined with unique opportunities to
persuade others to do their bidding—opportunities en-
hanced by the possibility of dispensing favors, by the mys-
tique of presidential power, and by the aura of monarchy
that surrounds the president."

The way various presidents have used the complex
power of their office is the subject of Greenhaven Press's
Presidents and Their Decisions series. Each volume in the
series examines one particular president and the key decisions he made while in office.

Some presidential decisions have been made in a relatively brief period of time, as with Abraham Lincoln's sus-
pension of the writ of habeus corpus at the start of the
Civil War. Others were refined as they were implemented
over a period of years, as was the case with Franklin Delano Roosevelt's struggle to lead the country out of the
Great Depression. Some presidential actions are generally
lauded by historians—for example, Lyndon Johnson's support of the civil rights movement—while others have been
condemned—such as Richard Nixon's efforts to cover up
the Watergate scandal.

Most of the truly history-making presidential decisions, though, remain the subject of intense scrutiny and historical debate. Many of these were made during a time of war or other crisis, in which a president was forced to risk either spectacular success or devastating failure. Examples include Lincoln's much-scrutinized handling of the crisis at Fort Sumter, the first conflict of the Civil War, and Harry Truman's controversial decision to use the atomic bomb in order to end World War II.

Each volume in the Presidents and Their Decisions series devotes a full chapter to each of the president's key decisions. The essays in each chapter offer a range of perspectives on the president and his actions. Some provide background on the political, social, and economic factors behind a particular decision. Others critique the president's performance, offering a negative or positive appraisal. Essays have been chosen for their concise and engaging presentation of the facts, and each is preceded by a straightforward summary of the article's content.

In addition to the articles, the books include extensive material to help the student researcher. An opening essay provides both a brief biography of the president and an overview of the events that occurred during his time in office. A chronology also helps readers keep track of the dates of specific events. A comprehensive index and an annotated table of contents aid readers in quickly locating material of interest, and an extensive bibliography serves as a launching point for further research. Finally, an appendix of primary historical documents provides a sampling of the president's most important speeches, as well as some of his contemporaries' criticisms.

Greenhaven Press's Presidents and Their Decisions series will help students gain a deeper understanding of the decisions made by some of the most influential leaders in American history.

LYNDON B. JOHNSON:
A BIOGRAPHY

L YNDON JOHNSON'S PRESIDENCY BEGAN WITH TRAGEDY.
On November 22, 1963, at 12:30 p.m., President John
F. Kennedy was assassinated in Dallas, Texas. Two hours
later, at 2:30 p.m., Johnson took the presidential oath
aboard Air Force One with his wife, Lady Bird, and
Kennedy's widow, Jackie Kennedy, by his side.

The next five years, the Johnson years, would see their
own share of tragedy. Johnson's presidency occurred against
the backdrop of a tumultuous era. The years 1963 to 1968
saw the continuation and increasing militancy of the civil
rights movement, race riots in many cities nationwide, the
assassinations of Martin Luther King Jr. and Robert
Kennedy, escalation of the Vietnam War and a growing antiwar movement, the student movement, and dramatic cultural shifts that included the sexual revolution and widespread
experimentation with psychedelic drugs and alternative
lifestyles. All of these events and forces impacted Johnson
and his presidency and were in turn influenced by him.

Many of the decisions Johnson made during his presidency had an enormous impact on the mood of the nation, on the course of events, and even on the shape of history. Johnson's domestic agenda—including his War on
Poverty—resulted in a record-breaking onslaught of new
legislation designed to help poor people and improve living conditions for Americans. As president, Johnson
signed three major civil rights bills—the Civil Rights Act of
1964, the Voting Rights Act of 1965, and the Civil Rights
Act of 1968. The most momentous act of Johnson's presidency, however, was his decision to escalate America's involvement in the Vietnam War. This decision ensured that

Johnson's presidency, which began with tragedy, would end with tragedy as well.

Lyndon's Parents

Lyndon Baines Johnson was born on August 27, 1908, in a farmhouse on the Pedernales River in the rural Hill Country of Texas. He was the first of five children, two boys and three girls, born to Samuel Ealy Johnson Jr. and Rebekah Johnson. After Lyndon came Rebekah (1910), Josefa (1912), Sam Houston (1914), and Lucia (1916).

Sam Johnson was a large, robust man who enjoyed drinking, gambling, and vulgar talk with his friends. Throughout Lyndon's childhood, Sam worked alternately as a real estate agent and a farmer, moving his family in and out of nearby Johnson City between farming stints. He was successful at neither enterprise, but was especially ill-suited for farming. At one point Sam's attempt at farming got the family so deep in debt they never recovered, but the extended Johnson clan buffered the family from serious hardship.

Samuel's major influence on Lyndon stemmed not from his farming and real estate dealing, but from his involvement in state politics: He served in the Texas House of Representatives from 1904 to 1908 and again from 1918 to 1924. Samuel was a Democrat who sided with the farmers against the moneyed interests. He opposed monopolies, supported taxes on large corporations, and advocated for improved education and the eight-hour workday. He also combated discrimination. In 1918, following World War I, the Senate passed a bill, aimed specifically at Germans, authorizing imprisonment of anyone using disloyal language at any time. Johnson later told Doris Kearns, author of *Lyndon Johnson and the American Dream*, "My father stood right up against that situation. . . . He got up on the floor of the House of Representatives and made a wonderful speech pleading for tolerance and common sense. He was a great civil libertarian. . . . At the same time, he fought the Ku Klux

Klan and defended civil liberties on all levels."[1] Samuel Johnson's tendency to defend the underdog, strive to improve society, and seek social justice would all be inherited by Lyndon Johnson and played out in his political life.

In contrast to her husband, Lyndon's mother, Rebekah Baines, was an educated, sophisticated woman who enjoyed poetry and literature and condemned drinking, swearing, and gambling. She had been raised by Joseph Wilson Baines, who had been a schoolteacher, a lawyer, and a newspaperman. He had acquired a significant fortune by means of practicing law and renting land to tenant farmers, and he was well-known for his piety, honesty, and principles. When he lost his fortune in 1904, Rebekah was forced to grow accustomed to a less lavish lifestyle and to work. However, this adjustment was minor compared to the one she experienced after marrying Samuel Johnson and moving with him to the Pedernales Valley. As biographer Robert A. Caro puts it,

> Rebekah's father had created a niche in the Hill Country, and had raised a daughter who fitted into that niche: a college graduate, a lover of poetry, a soft-spoken, gentle, dreamy-eyed young lady who wore crinolines and lace—and broad-brimmed, beribboned hats with long veils. . . . Now, overnight, at the age of twenty-six (Sam was almost thirty), she was out of the niche—a fragile Southern flower suddenly transplanted to the rocky soil of the Pedernales Valley.[2]

In her new life, she was forced to endure the hard work of rural homemaking, isolation, and the difficulty of trying to fit in with the Johnson clan, whom she perceived to be socially inferior.

Some biographers have suggested that Rebekah's and Samuel's differences created a tense atmosphere, into which their firstborn son arrived. Doris Kearns has suggested that Rebekah, displeased by her husband's vulgarity and baseness, was determined to instill refinement and poise in her son. She allowed his hair to grow long and curly, dressed him in fine outfits, taught him to read at an early age, and enrolled him in dance and violin lessons. Kearns writes,

> The image of Rebekah Baines Johnson that emerges . . . is that of a drastically unhappy woman, cut off from all the things that had once given her pleasure in life, stranded in a cabin on a muddy stream with a man she considered vulgar and brutish, a frustrated woman with a host of throttled ambitions, trying, through her first-born son, to find a substitute for a dead father, an unsuccessful marriage, and a failed career.[3]

Throughout his earliest years, Johnson was caught between his mother's desire for him to be cultured and refined and his fathers insistence that he not be made into a "sissy."

Young Lyndon

Lyndon is remembered as being a precocious, mischievous child who was exceptionally bright for his age. Throughout his childhood, he was extremely resistant and defiant toward all forms of authority, frequently disobeying his parents and teachers. He exhibited many of the traits that would stay with him throughout his life, including a frantic need for attention and admiration, a fiercely competitive, aggressive, ambitious spirit, a natural tendency to lead (even among older boys), an outgoing, verbose personality style, and—even as a preteen—an insatiable interest in politics. He soon put aside his violin and dance lessons in favor of outdoor pursuits.

Johnson's defiance toward his parents and other authority figures intensified as he grew older. He was extremely disobedient in school, although he received fair grades because he was smart and could talk his way out of trouble. At home he often refused to do his chores, and would instead force his younger siblings to do them. In town he would seek sympathy (and food) from adults by exaggerating the severity of the family's economic plight.

In May 1924, at the age of fifteen, Johnson graduated from high school. He decided not to go to college, a decision that disappointed his parents. Instead, he went west in a Model T Ford with a group of friends, eventually ending up in California, where Lyndon worked as a clerk in a law office and as an elevator operator.

Johnson returned to Texas in the fall of 1925, but he was still not willing to go to college. He lived at home and worked a road construction job that his father obtained for him. Finally, in February 1927, he gave in to the pressure to attend college. Robert Dallek, the author of a two-volume biography of Johnson, provides a concise description of Johnson's character traits as he emerged from childhood and adolescence: "Ambition, strivings for prominence, resentment against established authority and power, identification with the underdog, idealism, grandiosity, adaptability to changing circumstances—all, in one degree or other, were elements of LBJ's personality."[4] They would remain Johnson's defining characteristics throughout his life.

College and Teaching

Johnson attended Southwest Texas State Teachers College in San Marcos, Texas. In September 1928 he received his elementary school teaching certificate and took a job as principal and teacher at a Mexican-American grade school in Cotulla, a small town sixty miles north of the Mexican border, near San Antonio. His students were poor, had limited English skills, and were accustomed to being generally neglected by the educational system. Johnson brought the full force of his personality to bear on the school. He forbade his students from speaking Spanish, believing that their failure to learn English would keep them from succeeding in life. He was a stern disciplinarian, spanking boys and verbally berating girls who showed disrespect to him or who spoke Spanish on school grounds. He used half of his first paycheck to buy volleyballs, basketballs, and softball bats and gloves for the school. He organized debating contests, declamation contests, and spelling bees. In short, he applied his domineering personality to the task of pushing the students to rise above their impoverished environment.

In Cotulla, for the first time in his life Johnson was in a position of genuine authority and leadership—and he relished the experience. It not only satisfied his grandiosity, but his need for attention and affection as well. Despite his overzealousness and strictness, Johnson was enormously well-liked by the students and their parents. As Caro writes, "No teacher had ever really cared if the Mexicans learned or not. This teacher cared.... And he received in return for his energy and his interest and his beneficence a rich measure of the gratitude and respect he had always craved."[5] Johnson got a taste of the adoration that can come with leadership.

The experience also deepened Johnson's commitment to serve the interests of the underdogs and the underprivileged. While he may not have been sensitive to their distinctive cultural experience, Johnson was clearly fond of his students and sincere in his efforts to help them. The same ideals and sentiments that motivated him in Cotulla would later find expression in his antipoverty and civil rights efforts. As Dallek states: "The year in Cotulla sensitized Johnson to the deprivation suffered by what would later be called America's 'invisible poor.' It also encouraged him to believe that people in a position of authority or power could open avenues of opportunity to the disadvantaged that would serve not only themselves but society as a whole."[6]

Johnson returned to San Marcos in May 1929 and completed his studies in August 1930, with a B.S. degree in education and history. While in school, Johnson was involved in politics both on and off campus. In July 1930, he made an impromptu speech at a rally for a local candidate for the state railroad commission. Although the speech itself was unimpressive, Johnson made a favorable impression on Welly Hopkins, a candidate for the state Senate, who gave Johnson a job as his campaign manager. Johnson's success in this role led to another position as campaign manager for Edgar Witt, a candidate for lieutenant governor, which was also successful.

In the fall of 1930, Johnson taught government and speech briefly at Pearsall, a town near Cotulla, but in October he accepted a better job teaching speech and debate at Sam Houston High School in Houston. Johnson took to this job with his characteristic fervent energy and dedication. However, in November 1931, partly on the basis of his demonstrated success at managing the campaigns of Hopkins and Witt, he was offered a job as secretary to newly elected congressman Richard Kleberg. On December 2, 1931, Johnson departed Texas for Washington, D.C.

Johnson in Washington

Richard Kleberg came from a wealthy family and had little interest in work. Consequently, Johnson essentially ran his office. He took to the task with the same obsessive energy that he applied to his previous jobs. He worked extremely long hours—day and night—seven days a week, in an effort to learn the ropes and respond to the concerns of Kleberg's constituents. He drove his staff with his typical domineering zeal. As Dallek writes, two of Johnson's subordinates recalled that "he was so demanding and occasionally so overbearing and abusive that they periodically wanted to quit. Receiving a personal phone call or taking a work break to drink coffee or smoke a cigarette was forbidden. Even going to the bathroom was frowned upon."[7]

At this time Johnson began his practice of forcing his subordinates, especially his more educated and refined ones, to accompany him to the bathroom to take dictation as he sat on the toilet defecating. Some commentators have dismissed this habit as simply evidence of Johnson's rural roots and informal style. Others have characterized it as an effort to humiliate and exert control over his subordinates—especially men with pretensions of superior grooming, education, or social class. Johnson would continue this practice up to and throughout his years in the White House.

As Kleberg's secretary, Johnson learned a great deal about the political process and began to build a political power base for himself. He had a tremendous influence over Kleberg's political actions; for example, he pressured Kleberg to support Franklin Delano Roosevelt's (FDR) New Deal programs, which were designed to ease the effects of the Great Depression. Johnson also became speaker of the Little Congress, an organization for congressional secretaries that held debates under the rules of the House of Representatives. After quietly orchestrating his victory, Johnson transformed the Little Congress from a social organization to a political institution of some import.

Lady Bird

In September 1934, while in Austin, Texas, on business, Johnson met Claudia Alta (Lady Bird) Taylor. Taylor, four years Johnson's junior, was the daughter of an ambitious businessman and an emotionally frail woman who had died when Taylor was six years old. The moniker Lady Bird was given her by a black nursemaid who had said she was "as purdy as a lady bird."[8] Those who knew her described her as outwardly restrained but possessing an inner strength. At the time she met Lyndon, she had recently completed college, earning a Bachelor of Arts degree in 1933 and a Bachelor of Journalism in 1934.

Johnson was immediately attracted to Lady Bird. The day after meeting her, he took her on a date, where he told her all about his life and asked her probing questions. Lady

Bird was both repulsed and intrigued by this treatment. Within twenty-four hours, Johnson had proposed to her, although Taylor neither accepted nor declined this offer. Johnson returned to Washington and continued to court her long-distance. He returned to Austin in November and kept up the pressure until Taylor agreed to marry him at the spur of the moment on the seventeenth, just ten weeks after they had met.

Adjusting to married life was a challenge for Lady Bird. Not only was she inexperienced at keeping house, she was unprepared for Lyndon's personality style. Lyndon treated his new wife in a manner not unlike his conduct toward his subordinates in the office. He required her to serve him coffee and bring him his daily newspaper in bed, lay out his clothes, and refill his cigarette lighters and pens and place them in the appropriate pockets of his clothes. His demands extended to her person. As Dallek writes, "He also managed her dress and appearance, insisting that she wear high-heeled instead of flat-heeled shoes, that she lose some weight, change her hairstyle, wear brighter colors, and take more care with her makeup."[9] In addition, he embarrassed her in public by ordering her, for example, to change her stockings or bring him a slice of pie.

The NYA

In 1935, partly because of the connections he had made as Kleberg's secretary, Johnson was appointed by FDR to head the Texas office of the National Youth Administration (NYA), a New Deal program designed to help young people remain in school or receive job training. Johnson's decision to accept the position was partly political. Serving as the state director of a national program would help him to create a base of support in his efforts to serve in Congress as a representative of Texas. However, the position also appealed to his idealism and his desire to help the poor and promote equality of opportunity for all Americans.

As the youngest state director of the NYA, Johnson brought the same obsessive enthusiasm to the task as he had to his previous positions. Again he drove his staff to work sixteen- to eighteen-hour days, seven days a week. Again he dominated and bullied his staff. And again he inspired them. As Dallek writes, "He inspired them with a sense that they were making history—that they were reaching out to desperate young people whose lives would be profoundly affected by what the NYA did."[10] Johnson proved to be an enormously successful administrator, and his agency helped thousands of young people stay in school and gain employment.

Congressman Johnson

The opportunity to run for Congress presented itself in February 1937, when the representative of Johnson's home district, James B. Buchanan, died unexpectedly. Johnson borrowed $10,000 from Lady Bird's father and announced his candidacy. Competing with eight other candidates, Johnson ran on a platform of absolute support for FDR's New Deal, including a controversial plan to enlarge the Supreme Court, known as court-packing. Johnson campaigned with the same vigor he brought to all of his endeavors. In the end, he won with 28 percent of the vote.

During his first years in Congress, Johnson fulfilled his promise to support FDR's New Deal by voting with the president on almost every piece of legislation in the House. In return, Johnson received federal aid to support his efforts to improve the Hill Country by renovating schools, fighting polio, and installing fire alarms, among other projects. Johnson's primary interest during these years was rural electrification. He initiated large public works projects to build dams on the Pedernales River in order to bring electricity to farmers and other rural residents. In doing so, Johnson not only gained the support of many of his constituents, but also the financial support of Herman

Brown, the owner of Brown and Root, the contracting firm that won many of the dam-building contracts. Johnson's alliance with Brown would continue throughout his legislative career. In a clearly unethical, albeit not atypical, relationship, Johnson received significant financial support for his political campaigns in return for various extremely lucrative government contracts.

In 1941, with the financial backing of Brown and Root, Johnson sought a seat in the U.S. Senate, which was vacated due to the death of Morris Sheppard. In an elaborately choreographed campaign, Johnson did surprisingly well against popular Texas governor W. Lee (Pappy) O'Daniel, going into the election with a small lead in the polls. Twenty-four hours after the polls closed, Johnson was ahead by over 5,000 votes, with 90 percent of the votes counted. However, as Bruce J. Schulman, author of *Lyndon B. Johnson and American Liberalism*, explains, O'Daniel was able to capitalize on Johnson's relative lack of experience with Texas balloting and "steal" the election:

> Stolen elections were not unusual in southern politics, in Texas politics especially. In many areas of the state, political machines controlled the balloting and could deliver large sums of votes to the highest bidder. If your candidate fell behind, the machine could "find" a few more votes. It was crucial, however, not to report your precincts too soon; otherwise, the opposing side knew your total and could maneuver to beat it. In the 1941 race, both candidates had made such arrangements with political bosses around Texas. But the overly confident and inexperienced LBJ erred and reported his total too early. O'Daniel's forces furnished just enough additional votes to tip the election.[11]

Johnson planned to run against O'Daniel again six months later when the current term ended, but World War II intervened.

After the Japanese attack on Pearl Harbor on December 7, 1941, Johnson took a leave of absence to assume active naval duty. He worked in noncombat roles, including inspecting shipyards and serving as a liaison to New Zealand. In June 1942, he rode along on an air raid mission against Japanese forces in the region of Lae, New Guinea. He originally boarded a B-26 bomber called the *Wabash Cannonball*, but deplaned to urinate. When he returned his seat was taken, so he boarded a different B-26 called the *Heckling Hare*. The mission was extremely dangerous. The U.S. planes came under attack by Japanese Zeros before reaching their targets. The *Wabash Cannonball*, the plane Johnson had nearly flown in, was quickly shot down, killing all aboard. The *Heckling Hare* came under fire, lost power in one engine, and was hit on both wings. The pilot skillfully avoided being shot down and even shot down one enemy plane before returning to base without having completed the mission.

General Douglas MacArthur awarded Johnson a Silver Star medal for his service on the *Heckling Hare*, while the rest of the crew received no medals. Johnson, knowing he did not deserve the award, went so far as writing a letter turning it down. However, he never sent the letter and made political use of the medal throughout his career.

Senator Johnson

Johnson returned to Washington and Congress in July 1942, where he continued to support FDR on most issues. He decided to try his luck in the 1948 Senate race. In the primary, he trailed the conservative Texas governor Coke Stevenson with 34 percent to Stevenson's 40 percent. This outcome resulted in a tight runoff in which each candidate controlled the ballot boxes in separate regions. Eventually Johnson won by 87 votes due to the results of a small town in south Texas, where Johnson won 202 votes and Stevenson received one. Stevenson contested these highly dubious results in federal court, but Johnson's legal advisers took the case to the Supreme Court for an immediate ruling in their favor, clearing the way for Johnson's election to the Senate. Johnson was given the ironic nickname "Landslide Lyndon" due to his narrow victory.

The Senate suited Johnson's personality style perfectly. The House of Representatives had been too large, consisting of 435 members, for Johnson to deal with each colleague on an individual basis. In the Senate, which at that time contained 96 members, Johnson could and did get to know every member intimately. As Schulman writes,

> The United States Senate was the ideal playing field for a man of Johnson's talents, a master of the face-to-face contact. He could please, tease, cajole, trade, deal, threaten—grab a man by his lapels, speak right into his face, look into his heart, and convince him that he had always wanted to vote the way LBJ was asking.[12]

It was in the Senate that Johnson perfected his persuasive conversation technique known as "the Treatment," by which he overpowered his colleagues in one-on-one discussions. Syndicated columnists Rowland Evans and Robert Novak provide perhaps the most vivid description of the Treatment:

> The Treatment could last ten minutes or four hours. . . . Its tone could be supplication, accusation, cajolery, exuberance, scorn, tears, complaint, the hint of threat. It was all of these together. It ran the gamut of human emotions. Its velocity was breathtaking, and it was all in one direction. Interjections from the target were rare. Johnson anticipated them before they could be spoken. He moved in close, his face a scant millimeter from his target, his eyes widening and narrowing, his eyebrows rising and falling. . . . Mimicry, humor, and the genius of analogy made The Treatment an almost hypnotic experience and rendered the target stunned and helpless.[13]

Johnson quickly rose to the position of minority leader of the Senate. In 1955, when Democrats attained the majority, he became majority leader. By placing himself in these leadership roles, Johnson achieved increased visibility as a national leader, paving the way for his eventual run for the presidency. Throughout his years in the Senate (1948–1960), Johnson maintained a moderate stance, careful not to alienate the conservative administration of Dwight Eisenhower, on the one hand, or his northern liberal supporters on the other. He was also careful not to identify himself too strongly with Southern leaders while simultaneously not upsetting the status quo on racial issues.

Johnson continued to walk a fine line on the issue of civil rights. While he favored programs to assist poor blacks, he had opposed laws outlawing segregation since his arrival in Congress in 1937. On the other hand, he supported the Supreme Court's 1954 decision in *Brown v. Board of Education*, which declared segregated schools unconstitutional. In addition, despite significant pressure from his southern colleagues, he refused to sign the "Southern Manifesto," a document vowing opposition to school desegregation. In 1957, for the first time, he decided to support a civil rights law. The law that eventually passed was weak, but Johnson considered it an important first step toward equality. Perhaps more importantly, at least to Johnson, it helped to establish Johnson's image on the national scene as a supporter of African Americans.

As 1960 approached, Johnson considered running for president. He had doubts about his health, having suffered a heart attack in 1955, and about whether a southerner could win the presidency. He did not campaign or enter the primary election. Instead, he expected that he would be nominated at the Democratic national convention due to the absence of any better candidates. In retrospect, Johnson's excessive confidence appears absurd when one considers that his main opponent was Senator John F.

Kennedy. Johnson clearly under-appreciated Kennedy's popularity. As Schulman explains, Johnson "referred to Kennedy as 'the boy'. . . . He never conceived of 'the boy' as a serious rival."[14] Contrary to Johnson's expectations, Kennedy easily won the nomination. He offered Johnson the vice presidency, and Johnson reluctantly accepted.

Vice President Johnson

The transition from majority leader of the Senate to the office of the vice presidency was difficult for Johnson. It involved giving up one of the most powerful positions in the world for a position with virtually no power at all. It also involved placing himself in a position subordinate to a man nine years his junior—a man he had previously led in the Senate. Johnson attempted unsuccessfully to transform the office into a position of real power. For example, he drafted an executive order giving the vice president authority over various areas of national government and requiring the vice president to receive copies of all important presidential documents. Kennedy never signed the order, however, and Johnson was forced to settle into a role of mostly symbolic importance. He later admitted that he hated it.

As vice president, Johnson oversaw the nation's space program and chaired the President's Committee on Equal Employment Opportunity (PCEEO), which was established to enforce an executive order banning racial discrimination by government contractors. He also served as an ambassador overseas, traveling to various countries, including Vietnam and the Soviet Union. In Vietnam, Johnson got a firsthand introduction to the problem that would confront him years later as president—the problem that many commentators credit for the ruin of his presidency.

President Johnson

Johnson's tenure as vice president came to a sudden end on November 22, 1963, when Kennedy was assassinated in

Dallas, Texas. Following Kennedy's assassination, Johnson faced the formidable task of leading the nation through a period of profound grief and shock. Kennedy was a young, vibrant president, and his violent death traumatized the nation. Johnson's many years of political experience enabled him to manage this period of transition graciously. Some Kennedy supporters—particularly Kennedy's brother Robert—believed Johnson was too quick to take over. But most observers agree that Johnson, while eager to be president, was primarily motivated by a genuine desire to ensure continuity and unity in the nation.

Johnson's political experience also helped him to understand that taking the office of the president in the wake of an assassination of a popular president was different from being elected. He instinctively knew that success for himself and the liberal establishment lay not in bringing his own agenda to the White House, but in continuing the efforts begun by Kennedy. He asked all of Kennedy's staff to remain, and he pledged to fulfill the objectives of Kennedy's "New Frontier"—a set of liberal domestic and foreign policy reforms, including expanded foreign aid, a tax cut, and civil rights, education, and health care legislation—which had been largely stalled in Congress.

Johnson announced his commitment to the Kennedy agenda in one of his most memorable speeches. On November 27, five days after the assassination, Johnson spoke before a joint session of Congress. Starting with the words, "All I have I would have given gladly not to be standing here today," Johnson went on to praise Kennedy, describe the nation's sense of loss at his death, and vow to carry on his agenda. Echoing the words JFK uttered in his inaugural address, "Let us begin," Johnson declared, "Let us continue."[15]

Once in office, Johnson established a rigorous work schedule, just as he had in all previous positions. Johnson worked a two-shift day. The first shift began at 6:30 or 7:00

A.M. and lasted until 2:00 P.M., when Johnson would take a vigorous walk or swim. Then he would put on pajamas and take a nap until 4:00 P.M., when he would shower and dress for the next shift, which lasted until midnight or 2:00 A.M.

Along with his obsessive work habits, Johnson brought his particular personality style to the White House. He spent hours on the telephone and required his staff to have telephones installed in their bathrooms so they could be reached at all times. He interrupted meetings to take breaks, moving the whole meeting to the swimming pool, where he would strip naked and take a swim, expecting others present to do likewise. He would require his staff to continue conversations with him as he sat on the toilet or took a shower.

Interestingly, he treated his own staffers with less deference than the Kennedy staff, who remained in the White House after Kennedy's death. Doris Kearns attributes this disparate treatment to Johnson's insecurity vis-á-vis the Kennedy staff, which was composed of east-coast intellectuals whom he considered extremely adept political thinkers:

> With his own men, Johnson commanded, forbade, insisted, swaggered, and swore. Verbal tirades and fits of temper became an integral part of his image. On occasion, it seemed as if Johnson *needed* to make his staff look ridiculous; that he was strengthened by his exposure of the inadequacies of others. In addition, Johnson's outbursts with his own men helped him to deal with the Kennedy men from a position of strength. His modesty and deference could command their loyalty, but he wanted their respect as well, the respect due a strong man.[16]

Johnson's tendency to equate political success with masculine strength is well-documented. As Schulman notes, "Johnson invariably described meeting political defeat as having one's pecker cut off and derided JFK's reputation as a playboy by boasting that he had 'slept with more women by accident than Kennedy ever had on purpose.'"[17]

In the year following Kennedy's death, Johnson strove to fulfill his promise to enact the former president's agenda. He ushered Kennedy's $11 billion tax cut bill through Congress. Kennedy's staff had been working quietly on a poverty program but had planned to wait until after the 1964 elections to unveil it. Johnson embraced the concept, expanded it, and pushed ahead with it. In his state of the union address for 1964, he announced an "all-out war on human poverty."[18] The Economic Opportunity Act of 1964, which passed in the Spring of that year, embodied this effort.

Johnson also pushed Kennedy's civil rights agenda forward. Immediately after taking office, Johnson met with civil rights leaders and vowed his commitment to their cause. The result of his effort was the passage of the Civil Rights Act of 1964, which guaranteed equal opportunity in employment and banned segregation in public accommodations, such as hotels and restaurants. Southern opponents of the bill attempted a filibuster in the Senate. Rather than water down the bill to appease the Southerners, Johnson sought "cloture," which involved getting two-thirds of the Senate to vote to stop the debate—an unprecedented feat. Passage of the Civil Rights Bill was a monumental legislative triumph that perhaps only Johnson, the master legislator, could have accomplished. This act was by far the strongest civil rights bill ever passed—and was considered by many to be the first genuine one.

President in His Own Right

Soon after coming to office, Johnson began to set his sights on the 1964 election. He believed that the office of the presidency was not entirely his until he had been placed there by the people. Until that happened, he was merely the caretaker of Kennedy's legacy. His intense need for admiration drove him to seek victory by a large margin. Indeed, with Minnesota senator Hubert Humphrey as his running mate, he beat the extreme right-wing conservative Barry Goldwater by a margin of 60.8—the largest margin achieved by a president in U.S. history. This time, unlike the 1948 Senate race, the moniker "Landslide Lyndon" contained no irony. Johnson interpreted his large victory as a mandate to pursue his own agenda of liberal reform.

Lyndon B. Johnson and his family watch the 1964 presidential election returns broadcast live on television. Johnson beat opponent Barry Goldwater in a landslide victory.

Johnson's domestic agenda was captured by the slogan "Great Society," which he began using in his speeches in 1964. This phrase was used broadly to refer to Johnson's liberal domestic agenda. More specifically, it described primarily his civil rights and antipoverty programs, but also his legislation to reform education, health care, environmental laws, cultural institutions, and economic policy.

Once elected president in his own right, Johnson turned his attention to creating his Great Society by pushing his legislation through Congress. Blessed with a Democratic majority in Congress, Johnson achieved unprecedented success. He was helped in this endeavor by his intimate familiarity with every detail of the congressional system, both formal and informal, and his gift at making it work in his favor. He used the Treatment on his staff and members of Congress, relentlessly following the progress of every bill. In the end, Congress approved 69 percent of his bills in 1965, compared to 27 percent of Kennedy's bills in 1963. Among the measures that passed were the Medicare program; increases in funding for primary, secondary, and higher education; the creation of the Department of Housing and Urban Development; voting rights for minorities; an immigration bill eliminating racial quotas; a highway beautification bill; air and water pollution bills; the establishment of the Department of Transportation; and a minimum wage increase. Johnson's success at getting legislation passed is undeniable.

However, Johnson's success at marshalling bills through Congress was not followed up by successful implementation of the new programs. In order to ensure their passage, many of the bills, including the Elementary and Secondary Education Act, Medicare, and highway beautification, contained compromises that diluted their ability to effect significant change. Perhaps more importantly, Johnson did not devote as much energy to managing the implementation of programs as he did to the passage of legislation. Once the bills were passed, the creation and administration of programs was largely ignored.

Perhaps the most controversial component of the Great Society was the War on Poverty, an assortment of programs created under the Economic Opportunity Act. This attack on poverty included Head Start, an early education program; the Job Corps, a job-training program for poor, inner-city youths; and the Community Action Program (CAP), an effort to mobilize poor communities for change. The CAP was perhaps the most controversial aspect of the War on Poverty. The program largely bypassed local leaders and called for the "maximum feasible participation" of the poor themselves. Local leaders resented being left out of the equation and resisted the "maximum feasible participation" clause. Fearing political backlash, Johnson backed down, and control of the programs was turned over to local officials.

Another factor that limited the effectiveness of the Great Society was the fact that most of the programs Johnson created were inadequately funded. This problem only became worse as the nation found itself deeper and deeper into the Vietnam War. Johnson believed that he could afford to create his Great Society at home and fight a war overseas without raising taxes. Many historians contend that this strategy spelled doom for Johnson's presidency. History has taught that a leader can have guns *or* butter—war or domestic wealth—but not both. Johnson sought guns *and* butter, and the results were tragic. Although historians debate the ultimate effectiveness of the Great Society, all agree that it did not come close to living up to its promises. All agree that Vietnam deserves much of the blame.

Civil Rights

When Johnson signed the landmark Civil Rights Act of 1964, he believed he had put the issue of civil rights to rest for at least two years. But the course of events would soon demand his involvement. In early 1965, civil rights leaders, including Martin Luther King Jr., staged voting rights demonstrations in Selma, Alabama. Local law enforcement officials attacked the protesters in a violent confrontation that would later be known as "Bloody Sunday." Johnson eventually sent federal troops to protect the demonstrators.

In the wake of these events, Johnson called for legislation to guarantee blacks the right to vote. In a dramatic speech delivered on March 15, 1965, Johnson took the bold move of adopting the rallying cry of the civil rights movement, stating "We shall overcome" repeatedly throughout his speech. Many civil rights leaders were amazed by this show of support for their cause. Martin Luther King Jr. reportedly cried while watching the speech on television. The law that resulted from Johnson's efforts, the Voting Rights Act, was signed into law on August 6, 1965. It was an effective law, forbidding local leaders from imposing unduly restrictive requirements for voter registration.

The Voting Rights Act did not signal the end of Johnson's work on civil rights. Events continued to demand his attention. Riots in Watts, a ghetto in South Central Los Angeles, in August 1965, and other cities during the following three summers, vividly communicated that all was not well in the black community. Despite the removal of overt barriers to employment and public accommodations, blacks continued to experience poverty and feelings of disaffection. Indeed, following the passage of the Civil Rights Act of 1964, the nature of the civil rights movement changed, becoming more militant, shying away from legal remedies in favor of direct action, and demanding equality of results rather than simply equality of opportunity.

Johnson was dismayed by the rioting. He considered it a personal betrayal; African Americans, for whom he had done so much, had turned against him. Despite feeling slighted, however, Johnson remained sympathetic. While he condemned the rioters and the militant activists who called for radical solutions, he continued to support poverty programs and civil rights legislation. Moreover, he adopted the prevailing liberal view that the riots were a response to black poverty, which stemmed from the disruption of the black family, a legacy of slavery. The necessary governmental response to such structural inequity, according to the liberal view, was not simply to remove barriers to opportunity, which had been the traditional approach. Instead, government needed to take action to ensure equality of results. Thus dawned the era of "affirmative action." Johnson voiced his allegiance to this philosophy in a speech at Howard University on June 4, 1965:

> You do not take a person who, for years, has been hobbled by chains and liberate him, bring him up to the starting line of a race and then say, "you are free to compete with all the others," and still justly believe that you have been completely fair.
>
> Thus it is not enough just to open the gates of opportunity. All our citizens must have the ability to walk through those gates.
>
> This is the next and the more profound stage of the battle for civil rights. We seek not just freedom but opportunity. We seek not just legal equity but human ability, not just equality as a right and a theory but equality as a fact and equality as a result.[19]

Consistent with the affirmative action approach, the Equal Employment Opportunity Commission, created in 1965, began to establish and enforce integration targets and guidelines for racial equality in business and education institutions.

Johnson continued to champion civil rights in the manner he knew best: legislation. He sought the passage of new civil rights bills in 1966 and 1967, which focused mostly on removing discriminatory barriers to housing, but was unsuccessful. In April 1968, Martin Luther King Jr. was assassinated in Memphis, Tennessee. Riots broke out in 130 cities, killing 46 people and causing over $100 million in damages. In the wake of these events, Congress passed Johnson's civil rights bill in 1968.

On the issue of civil rights, Johnson faced criticism

President Johnson signs the 1968 Civil Rights Bill, which made discrimination in the sale or rental of housing illegal.

from both the right and the left. Many white conservatives, particularly southerners, opposed Johnson's attempts to legislate equality, especially as the focus of the movement shifted from equality of opportunity to equality of results, as riots erupted in the cities, and as the movement became increasingly strident and violent. On the left, many radicals believed Johnson did not go far enough to transform the unjust structure of American society that kept minorities oppressed. These criticisms aside, Johnson's achievements on civil rights were probably his most significant triumphs and were applauded by all but the most radical black activists. Steven F. Lawson, a history professor at the University of Carolina at Greensboro, writes, "Most commentators have agreed that the passage of three pieces of legislation in 1964, 1965, and 1968 provide ample testimony of the President's political skills and humanitarian instincts."[20]

Vietnam: Historical Background

In order to fully appreciate the predicament Johnson faced in Vietnam, it is necessary to understand the history of U.S. involvement in that Southeast Asian nation. Following World War II, Vietnam remained a French colony, despite FDR's support for decolonization. In 1945, when Ho Chi Minh, a Vietnamese Marxist rebel, declared Vietnam independent from France, U.S. president Harry Truman provided financial assistance to help France fight Ho Chi Minh's forces. Faced with an aggressive and determined foe, France required steadily increasing American aid. After Truman, Dwight Eisenhower continued the U.S. policy in support of France. It was Eisenhower who first articulated the domino theory, the belief that if one country fell to communism, the other countries of Southeast Asia would fall one by one.

In 1954, the French suffered a major defeat at Dien Bien Phu and were on the verge of losing their colony. Eisenhower considered sending U.S. troops to Vietnam, but could not garner enough support for this policy. Instead, Vietnam was divided in two, with Ho Chi Minh controlling the North and U.S.-supported Ngo Dinh Diem controlling the South. The nation was scheduled to be reunified after elections in 1956. However, as the time approached it was evident that Diem would lose, and elections were cancelled. Ho Chi Minh's supporters in the South, dubbed the Vietcong (Vietnamese Communists), began an insurrection against the Diem regime.

When Kennedy took office in 1961, he declared his commitment to prevent the Communist takeover of South Vietnam, just as his predecessors had done. To this end, he sent supplies, financial aid, and advisers to support Diem. Eventually, the United States could not in good conscience support Diem, due to his tyrannical leadership style and his oppression of the Buddhist majority. Kennedy secretly authorized the Vietnamese leader's execution. Diem was murdered three weeks before Kennedy's 1963 assassination.

Thus, when Johnson took the reigns at the White House, the United States had 16,000 U.S. troops in Vietnam and an eighteen-year history of involvement in the region. Moreover, the U.S. policy, from Truman to Eisenhower to Kennedy, had been unwavering opposition to a Communist takeover of the nation. In the context of the Cold War, this policy was absolutely conventional. Johnson's adherence to this policy placed him squarely in line with his predecessors and the majority of contemporary foreign policy experts. Nevertheless, by conforming to the conventional wisdom, Johnson would come to be known as the president responsible for one of the most tragic foreign policy debacles in the nation's history—a disaster that would come to be commonly known as "Lyndon Johnson's war."

Vietnam: Escalation

Johnson's escalation of the conflict began gradually, in response to several discrete incidents. On August 2, 1964, the U.S. destroyer *Maddox* was fired on by North Vietnamese naval forces in the Gulf of Tonkin, near North Vietnam. Two nights later, the *Maddox* and another destroyer reported being fired on again, although this report has never been substantiated. In response, Johnson authorized a bombing raid over North Vietnam. He also submitted the Gulf of Tonkin Resolution to Congress, a document requesting presidential authorization to "take all necessary measures to protect American troops and prevent further aggression in Vietnam." The resolution was overwhelmingly supported by both houses of Congress.

The next incident occurred on February 6, 1965, when the U.S. Air Force base in Pleiku came under attack, killing eight U.S. servicemen and wounding over one hundred others. Johnson ordered another bombing raid. Soon after the attack, Johnson decided to initiate a sustained bombing campaign—Rolling Thunder—which began on February 13. However, Johnson did not inform Congress or the American public that he had changed his policy from bombing in response to attacks on U.S. troops to sustained bombing. Over the next couple of months, Johnson increased the number of troops in Vietnam to 50,000 and authorized their use in active combat—all without telling the American people. By the middle of June, the number of troops in Vietnam had reached 82,000.

In June 1965, Johnson was informed that bombing raids had neither impeded the North's fighting capability nor diminished their morale. His military leaders requested vastly increased troops and equipment, and the majority of his foreign policy advisers agreed that South Vietnam would collapse without these additional resources. Johnson was extremely distressed by this news, but he was determined not to lose the war. In late July, after numerous meetings and much deliberation, he authorized an increase of 50,000 troops, promised to send 50,000 more by the end of the year, and authorized U.S. troops to function independently of Vietnamese leadership. He also agreed to initiate bombing in the South as well as increase bombing in the North. Thus Johnson "Americanized" the war. As with his previous steps toward escalation, Johnson minimized the seriousness of the measures he was undertaking, deliberately misleading the public about the extent—and potential cost—of his policies.

American military strategy in Vietnam after July 1965 was one of attrition. U.S. forces attempted to wear down the enemy through sustained bombing from the air and searching out and destroying Vietcong and North Vietnamese forces on the ground. It was believed that superior U.S. firepower and resources would thin out the enemy troops, destroying their ammunition and infrastructure, and undermining their morale. By 1967 it was clear that this strategy was an utter failure. Despite heavy losses, the Vietcong were easily able to replace lost men. They were also at a distinct advantage on the ground due to their adeptness at fighting in the jungles, swamps, and rice paddies of their homelands and to their reliance on a network of tunnels in which they evaded air raids and launched guerrilla attacks.

Johnson's "Credibility Gap"

Just as Johnson misled the public about his escalation of U.S. involvement in the war, he exaggerated the success of American forces. As the truth emerged regarding the actual course of the war, Johnson's credibility came under increasing scrutiny. As Schulman writes, "Charges about his honesty had vexed Johnson throughout his career, but the credibility gap only became damaging, only lost Johnson the support of middle America, when the emerging truth of the debacle in Vietnam belied Johnson's bold promises and confident reports. For deception lay at the heart of LBJ's Vietnam strategy."[21]

Johnson's "credibility gap" stoked the fires of antiwar protesters. Comprised mostly of student members of the New Left, a left-wing radical movement that disdained the middle-of-the-road liberalism epitomized by Johnson, they protested the war in large numbers, staging a march on the Pentagon in October 1967. The counterculture movement was also sweeping the nation at this time, and many protesters were young people of draft age who, besides being politically opposed to violent U.S. intervention in a foreign land, had a personal stake in their activism. The protesters routinely made their presence known when Johnson made public appearances by chanting, "Hey, hey, LBJ! How many kids did you kill today?" Johnson felt hurt and betrayed by these words and the sentiment behind them.

Johnson's credibility gap came into full focus in the wake of one event: the Tet offensive. On the eve of the Vietnamese New Year (Tet), North Vietnam launched an all-out attack on numerous fronts throughout the South, including the U.S. Embassy in Saigon. Because the Vietcong were out in the open, rather than in the jungles and swamps, American forces were able to engage them successfully and inflict heavy casualties. Tet was a tactical failure for the North and was effectively a victory for U.S. troops. However, Americans had been led to believe that the enemy had been significantly weakened and that the fall of North Vietnam was imminent. The fact that the North was able to launch such a massive attack was evidence to the contrary, severely undermining public support for the war. Johnson could no longer pretend that the war was anything other than what it was: a stalemate.

Several Viet Cong soldiers lie dead in the street as women and children look on. President Johnson's decision to escalate the war in Vietnam has been widely criticized.

Vietnam: Withdrawal
In the wake of Tet, military leaders called for more troops. Johnson's foreign policy advisers, on the other hand, for

the first time began to tell the president the war was hopeless. Johnson took their advice. On March 31, 1968, he appeared before the nation to announce a decrease in the bombing and outline the initial steps toward peace. During the same speech, Johnson made an announcement that shocked all but his wife and a few of his closest aides: "I will not seek and will not accept the nomination of my party for another term as president."

Much speculation surrounds Johnson's decision not to run for reelection. Because he announced the decision in the context of the speech on Vietnam, most commentators focus on the war as the motive. Some suggest that Johnson believed he would have a better chance of achieving peace if he was free of the image of a campaigning politician. Others wonder if this move was Johnson's attempt to project an image of a selfless man able to sacrifice his own career for the good of the nation. Behind both of these arguments lie the facts that Johnson was faring poorly in the polls and primaries and that his longtime nemesis, Robert Kennedy, had recently entered the race, making his odds of victory slim. Finally, Johnson's health was certainly a factor. Heart disease made it unlikely that the president would have survived another four years of the stressful office. Whatever the reason, Johnson retired to his Texas ranch in 1969. He died there of a heart attack on January 22, 1973, one day prior to the announcement of a peace treaty in Vietnam.

Johnson's Legacy

Johnson's resignation brought an end to a lifelong political career that had brought him from the dusty Hill Country of Texas to the most powerful office in the world. As president, Johnson made numerous decisions that had wide-ranging consequences for American society and the world. While he did not realize his vision of a Great Society, he orchestrated the passage of numerous new laws and the creation of various programs and institutions designed to reduce poverty and promote equality, thus enlarging the role of government as an instrument of social change. Some praised this accomplishment while others condemned it for contributing to the modern era of "big government."

On civil rights, Johnson managed the passage of three major civil rights bills that substantially changed the structure of race relations in America. Some criticize Johnson for moving too slowly, but the historical consensus holds that Johnson was truly dedicated to the cause of civil rights and racial equality, and that he did as much as politically feasible to further the cause.

Johnson's most fateful decisions centered on Vietnam. His decision to greatly escalate U.S. involvement in the war in July 1965 set the nation on a course that can only be described as tragic. At the height of the war, a half a million troops were stationed in Vietnam, and by the war's end in 1973, over 58,000 American soldiers had died there. Johnson's decision to expand the war in a deceptive fashion also proved disastrous. By misleading the public and the Congress about the true dimensions of the war, Johnson set the stage for his own downfall. Finally, Johnson's decision to wage war while continuing to push ahead with his domestic agenda proved unrealistic. The nation could not afford both guns and butter. So as the war became bogged down, fewer and fewer dollars were available for Johnson's beloved social programs, many of which consequently proved as unsuccessful as the Vietnam War effort. By attempting to have both guns and butter, Johnson was left with neither.

Notes

1. Doris Kearns, *Lyndon Johnson and the American Dream*. New York: Harper and Row, 1976, p. 37.

2. Robert A. Caro, *The Years of Lyndon Johnson: The Path to Power*. New York: Alfred A. Knopf, 1982, p. 52.

3. Kearns, *Lyndon Johnson and the American Dream*, p. 24.

4. Robert Dallek, *Lone Star Rising: Lyndon Johnson and His Times, 1908–1960*. New York: Oxford University Press, 1991, p. 61.

5. Caro, *The Years of Lyndon Johnson*, p. 168.

6. Dallek, *Lone Star Rising*, p. 80.

7. Dallek, *Lone Star Rising*, p. 101.

8. Dallek, *Lone Star Rising*, p. 113.

9. Dallek, *Lone Star Rising*, p. 119.

10. Dallek, *Lone Star Rising*, p. 131.

11. Bruce J. Schulman, *Lyndon B. Johnson and American Liberalism: A Brief Biography with Documents*. Boston: Bedford, 1995, p. 26.

12. Schulman, *Lyndon B. Johnson and American Liberalism*, p. 42.

13. Rowland Evans and Robert Novak, *Lyndon B. Johnson: The Exercise of Power*. New York: New American Library, 1966, p. 104.

14. Schulman, *Lyndon B. Johnson and American Liberalism*, p. 54.

15. Lyndon B. Johnson, Address before a joint session of Congress, November 27, 1963.

16. Kearns, *Lyndon Johnson and the American Dream*, p. 176.

17. Schulman, *Lyndon B. Johnson and American Liberalism*, p. 68.

18. Lyndon B. Johnson, Annual message to the Congress on the State of the Union, January 8, 1964.

19. Lyndon B. Johnson, "To Fulfill These Rights": Commencement address at Howard University, June 4, 1965.

20. Steven F. Lawson, "Civil Rights," in Robert A. Divine, ed., *The Johnson Years, Volume One: Foreign Policy, the Great Society, and the White House*. Lawrence: University Press of Kansas, 1987, p. 93.

21. Schulman, *Lyndon B. Johnson and American Liberalism*, p. 147.

CHAPTER

1

THE GREAT
SOCIETY

A Failure of National Will Undermined the Great Society

John A. Andrew III

John A. Andrew III contends that Johnson's Great Society had mixed results. Andrew concedes that Johnson's decisions contributed to the Great Society's failures, including the president's tendency to underestimate the costs of poverty programs while overstating their potential benefits. However, Andrew argues that various social, political, and economic forces beyond Johnson's control also impacted the Great Society. Finally, perhaps the greatest impediment to success, according to Andrew, was the American public's lack of will in the face of overwhelming social problems. Andrew is a professor of history at Franklin and Marshall College in Lancaster, Pennsylvania. He is the author of *The Other Side of the Sixties: Young Americans for Freedom and the Rise of Conservative Politics* and *Lyndon Johnson and the Great Society*, from which the following essay is excerpted.

L YNDON JOHNSON ANNOUNCED IN MARCH 1968 THAT HE would not run for reelection. He left the White House in January 1969 after five years as president, his Great Society not only stalled but under attack. In the ensuing years Republicans, conservatives, and even liberals have criticized Great Society legislation as misguided, flawed, dangerous, and often a total failure. One survey of newspaper articles found a pattern of critical commentary

Excerpted from *Lyndon Johnson and the Great Society*, by John A. Andrew III. Copyright ©1998 by John A. Andrew III. Reprinted by permission of Ivan R. Dee, Publisher.

from 1968 to 1988. At first complaints focused on administrative and fiscal concerns. After the mid-1970s they shifted to blame Great Society legislation for the economic problems of that decade, and by the 1980s they argued that the legislation itself had caused most of the social problems then plaguing American society. In the process, critics drew little distinction between Great Society legislation and later legislative efforts to expand, contract, or refine LBJ's programs.

In these later years the liberalism so politically attractive and powerful in the mid-sixties fell victim to internal doubts as well as conservative attacks. The 1960s now seem an unusual decade, one that may not (some say should not) be repeated ever again. And the years from 1964 to 1966, when the bulk of the Great Society legislation became law, appear even more unique. They represent a liberal interlude unmatched in the twentieth century, except perhaps for the mid-1930s, and unlikely to recur in the foreseeable future. After 1966 the Congress became more conservative, more preoccupied with punishing "disorderly" individuals than with eradicating the causes of their discontents.

This change in the national mood is the first thing to remember in assessing the Great Society. To assume that whatever happened after the Great Society stemmed from its legislation is to confuse chronology with causation. Critics argue that LBJ's "wrongheaded" legislative initiatives and excessive use of federal funds bear the responsibility for deteriorating urban conditions and rising welfare rolls (to take just two examples). They would be at least as correct to argue that later problems were due to underfunding, the narrow scope of Great Society legislation, or the law of unintended consequences. The dramatic shift in American social life between the mid-1960s and the mid-1980s has yet to be fully understood. . . .

To assess each of the major themes of the Great Society

in detail would require at least another book. In the years since 1968, not only has our understanding of the problems it addressed become more complex, federal efforts to address them have become far more complicated. Debates have often focused as much on ideology and political posturing as they have on substantive matters. A brief glance at the intervening years, however, can help put the efforts of the Great Society in perspective.

Civil Rights and Race

Few would object that civil rights was a compelling success story. Passage of the 1964 Civil Rights Act and the Voting Rights Act of 1965, along with later civil rights legislation, changed the patterns of race relations and political power in the United States in a way not likely to be reversed. When the debate turned from civil rights to race in the late sixties, the white public reacted sharply. Although the effect was to blame the Great Society, legislative initiatives had less to do with this backlash than the changing cultural ethos. Black Power was an indigenous outpouring of militancy that substituted the rhetoric of race for that of civil rights. Its major impact was to bring the Great Society to a screeching halt as white support for racial change evaporated in the face of riots and continued demonstrations. The dissolution of the civil rights coalition symbolized the deterioration of the consensus upon which the Great Society rested.

As much as racial militancy antagonized whites, the shift in the proof of discrimination—from unequal treatment, with its emphasis on opportunity, to unequal impact, with its focus on outcome—created a racial wedge that frustrated efforts to reinvigorate the earlier idealism of civil rights. This results-based emphasis, popularly known as affirmative action, ran contrary to provisions in the 1964 Civil Rights Act and represented frustration at that act's inability to remedy racial discrimination quickly.

Supreme Court decisions in *Griggs v. Duke Power Co.* (1970) and *Swann v. Charlotte-Mecklenburg County School District* (1971) reinforced affirmative action as the appropriate remedy for continued discrimination. The *Griggs* case embraced the unequal-impact theory, and the *Swann* case held that school busing to achieve racial integration was constitutional.

This shift in emphasis from opportunity to results, as well as the increased racial militancy and urban riots of the late sixties, provoked not only obstinate white resistance to further civil rights legislation but a conviction that the movement had gone too far. In the years after 1970, as Republican administrations came to power largely on the strength of white votes, and as the Republican party gained strength in the white South, racial antagonisms simmered throughout the country. By the 1990s race, not civil rights, clearly characterized the issue of discrimination. Both sides often talked past, not at, each other. With that in mind, in 1997 President Bill Clinton called for a national dialogue on race.

Poverty

Despite this continuing conundrum of race, without question the most controversial assessments of the Great Society lie in the area of antipoverty legislation. Specifically, did the Great Society alleviate poverty? Or did the legislation merely give the poor a sense that relief was a "right" and thereby inflate the welfare rolls? There are probably as many answers as there are questions. We do know that from 1965 to 1969 the number of people officially in poverty declined, from about 17 percent of the population to approximately 12 percent. But was this the result of antipoverty legislation or economic growth? Certainly economic growth accounted for a portion of the shift, but only about 3 percent according to most estimates. Then, when the economy turned sour in the 1970s and 1980s, much of that growth was lost. The point is that government transfer programs, not economic growth, removed many individuals from poverty. Conservative arguments that free-market economics could cure poverty proved hallucinatory.

"CHARGE!"

Central in criticism of the antipoverty effort is the Community Action Program and its Community Action Agencies. Intended to increase local decision-making and facilitate the "maximum feasible participation" of those most affected by new programs, the CAPs and CAAs proved problematic precisely because they threatened real change. They challenged existing power structures and aroused opposition from entrenched political interests, many of them tied to the Democratic party. Their potential for change was real because they promised to empower the powerless. Along with Legal Services, they exposed a fundamental flaw in Great Society antipoverty legislation. Where it promised to alleviate problems, it hoped to do so simply by increasing the size of the pie. The provision of services replaced systemic or structural change. The left attacked LBJ for this limited vision; the right opposed him for having it in the first place.

Among the most significant influences on the poverty issue have been the changing nature of the American economy since the 1960s and the shifting perception of the problem. New technologies have flourished and older industries have decayed or disappeared. This has eliminated a "safety valve" for unskilled or semiskilled workers, or workers with limited educational experience, who previously found employment in the mass-production industries so important since the late nineteenth century. Once workers lost their post-scarcity visions, the politics of scarcity returned with a vengeance, and working-class Americans believed that what helped one group hurt another. They quickly lost all enthusiasm for change. As economic conditions worsened during the ensuing decades, social policy unraveled.

Coupled with this development was a significant shift in the focus of antipoverty discussions. As Michael Katz has argued, at the beginning of the decade the focus was on the white poor in rural areas. After 1964 it shifted to concentrate on African Americans in the cities. This injected race into the debates and significantly altered public support for antipoverty measures. It also obscured the reality that most social welfare spending, such as Social Security, was not limited to the poor, and it directed attention away from an underlying characteristic of poverty, its transitory nature. . . .

Administration

Quite apart from Great Society policies themselves is the question of their implementation. In almost every case political compromises were necessary to pass legislation. This is how the American political system works, but in time some of those compromises revealed legislative flaws. As Hugh Davis Graham has pointed out, too often delivery agencies significantly altered the intent and operation of the original legislation to promote their own agendas. Through "iron triangles" and the use of clientele capture, the very objects of Great Society reforms all too often seized control of the process to block significant change and enhance their own interests. Tied to this was the unwieldy structure of the federal government, which defied the handling of problems that cut across portions of the bureaucracy.

LBJ recognized this and appointed a businessman, Ben Heineman, to head a Task Force on Government Organization and suggest solutions. It recommended strengthening the executive office of the presidency, unifying departments and agencies into "superdepartments," and decentralizing regional administration. Due to report in late 1967, its major recommendations did not become public until the Nixon years.

Lyndon Johnson himself exacerbated many of these problems, often failing to develop advance support for his program among Democrats or the public at large. He not only attacked structural problems through reforms that left existing institutions intact, he implied that the public could support his legislative initiatives without fear of pain or of themselves being changed. Without a politically mobilized constituency, once the middle class retreated from its commitment to helping others, political support for Great Society programs evaporated. Add to this LBJ's penchant for secrecy, and what emerged was a policy mix that avoided public debate and was almost guaranteed to mislead and invite cynicism. LBJ, in short, mistook lack of debate for consensus government. It was, David Broder aptly noted, "hand-me-down government carried to its ultimate expression, with bounties, benefits, and, of course, directions issuing from the top." Writing his memoirs a few years later, the former president admitted as much:

I tried to make it possible for every child of every color to grow up in a nice house, eat a solid breakfast, to attend a decent school and to get a good and lasting job. I asked so little in return, just a little thanks. Just a little appreciation. That's all. But look at what I got instead. Riots in 175 cities. Looting. Burning. Shooting. . . . Young people by the thousands leaving the university, marching in the streets, chanting that horrible song about how many kids I had killed that day. . . . It ruined everything.

Defenders of the Great Society had a different perspective. Richard Goodwin, one of its chief architects, claimed that it did not fail but was abandoned. The experiments of the first two years fell victim to the war in Vietnam, which induced divisiveness and budgetary difficulties. By the 1967 budget, almost 75 percent of funds were designated for war or war-related programs, with only 12.2 percent targeted for health, education, and welfare. After his first term, Richard Nixon abandoned most efforts at reform in an effort to save himself from the ravages of Watergate.

The Great Society failed to grow, as Johnson had hoped, into a "beautiful woman." LBJ had anticipated that his legislation would be "more permanent even than the New Deal." That it was not reflects the failure of Lyndon Johnson as much as (if not more than) the failure of a legislative program. Too often Johnson deliberately understated the continuing costs of new programs and requested only modest funding, hoping that once under way neither Congress nor the public would desert them. This led him to begin more programs than the bureaucracy, the public, or the budget could digest at one time. It also led him to overpromise, to insist that each new endeavor was not only essential but represented *the* solution to complex and perplexing problems. But laws are not an end in themselves. As White House aide Joseph Califano admitted, "We did not recognize that government could not do it all."

Budget Director Charles Schultze summarized this view in the fall of 1966 when he confessed that *"we are not able to fund adequately the new Great Society programs."* But expectations continued to rise. "This leads," Schultze admitted, "to *frustration, loss of credibility, and even deterioration* of State and local services. . . . *Backlog, queuing,* and *griping* build up steadily." Without extensive debate, the public never understood just how complex or interrelated the problems were. While voters overwhelmingly approved LBJ's initiatives in 1965 and 1966, few understood that they represented a beginning rather than the final word. The Great Society, one writer noted, was an aspiration rather than a blueprint. It died when Americans replaced hope with cynicism.

Critics of the Great Society, however, often neglect its popularity and its bipartisanship. Despite controversies, debates, or political and ideological polarization, polls continue to indicate strong public support for these legislative objectives. A Harris Poll in the late 1970s revealed that 82 percent of respondents backed medical care for the aged (98 percent by the 1980s), 90 percent favored federal aid to education, and 95 percent supported the Voting Rights Act. Other polls in the 1980s produced similar results, with respondents supporting level or increased expenditures for these and other programs. Even 76 percent supported the food stamp program, which critics charged promoted welfare dependency. This suggests that the Great Society's objectives were widely accepted, if specific proposals to reach them sparked debate. Republican support for many Great Society measures reflects that acceptance. On several key measures—voting rights, water pollution, Medicare, education, manpower development, truth in packaging, auto safety—significant numbers of Republicans joined Democrats to pass legislation. Only a few bills—the creation of HUD (Housing and Urban Development), housing, antipoverty, highway beauty, Model Cities—attracted limited Republican support. From the perspective of the mid-1990s, however, it is clear that many of those Republicans were moderates or even liberals, the likes of which have since failed at reelection, left the party, or died.

No National Will

Republicans' support for this legislation, and their replacement by individuals more narrowly committed to an ideological conservatism, reflects another element of the Great Society years that goes beyond legislative specifics to a broader essence. That is the question, defined best by Marshall Kaplan and Peggy Cuciti, of a "national community." Before the polarization of the late 1960s and backlash politics, the "me decade" of the 1970s, or the naked selfishness of the 1980s, a commitment to a broader national community pervaded the country. Now so very "sixties," and depicted as the embodiment of the Woodstock Generation, this commitment muted divisions of class and race. It recognized, Kaplan and Cuciti concluded, "responsibility for improving the position of the least advantaged and for shaping the quality of the physical and social environments, its willingness to experiment and to be evaluated and finally its trust in government as the lever for achieving desired change."

Apart from changing priorities, shifting political fortunes, and the movement of the American political spectrum to the right, one other factor helps explain the mixed results of Great Society legislation. Lloyd Ohlin, an architect of community action, summed it up best: "I think we learned the enormous resistance of these institutions to change, their tremendous capacity to resiliently absorb protest, aggression against them, attempts to change their goals or directions, and the internal distribution of power and responsibility within them. Wrong analysis, wrong prescription, wrong results." The Great Society did not solve the problems it identified and addressed, often for the reasons Ohlin suggested. But also missing, despite the rhetoric of a "war" on poverty or the creation of "model" cities, was the national will to win the battles and solve the problems whatever the cost. Much of this failure seems rooted not in the Great Society or the personality of Lyndon Johnson but in the national character. Americans remain more concerned to separate the "deserving" from the "undeserving" poor than to eliminate poverty. Americans are willing to sacrifice as individuals (the Peace Corps, VISTA, Teach for America) but not as a community. The majority remain committed to a belief that all change should be moderate at best.

Embedded in American culture, at least since World War II, is a conviction that economic growth can solve most problems painlessly. If only we could find the correct policies for fine-tuning the economy, it would produce abundance for all. Assured of its future, the middle class would then allocate resources to the poor. We are a middle-class society, and this is both a strength and a weakness. On the one hand a broad middle class reflects the economic success of American capitalism. At the same time the mythic vision of that class leads it to credit itself for its success, and fear of failing prompts it to embrace miserly visions for those less fortunate when the economy slows. By the late 1970s this had led, in the words of civil rights activist Vernon Jordan, to a "new minimalism," which meant "fewer rights and freedoms for those on the bottom half of our social ladder."

When all is said and done, perhaps the biggest failure of Lyndon Johnson's Great Society, a failure shared by the public and critics alike, was its lack of understanding and appreciation for the challenges it confronted. Once Americans saw the scope of the task, its complexity and costs overwhelmed them. The problems remained, the debates continued; but with the consensus frayed, the economy in decline, and the social fabric apparently unraveling, the national will atrophied. In the words of the advocate John Gardner, "I see a society learning new ways as a baby learns to walk. He stands up, falls, stands again, falls and bumps his nose, cries, tries again—and eventually walks. Some of the critics now sounding off about the Great Society would stop the baby after his first fall and say, 'That'll teach you. Stick to crawling.'"

JOHNSON'S DECISIONS ON VIETNAM AND THE ECONOMY UNDERMINED HIS GREAT SOCIETY

DORIS KEARNS

Although Johnson was extremely successful at marshalling his Great Society legislation through Congress in 1964 and 1965, he was less successful at implementing and administering the new programs between 1966 and 1968. According to Doris Kearns, the failures of the Great Society resulted largely from Johnson's decision in 1965 to escalate the war in Vietnam, which drew his attention away from domestic programs. The Great Society was also hurt by Johnson's decision not to raise taxes to head off inflation in 1966. Finally, Johnson lost the support of Congress and the public by understating the cost of the Vietnam War. Kearns, who was a staff assistant to Johnson during his administration, is a former Harvard professor and a Pulitzer Prize–winning biographer. The following essay is excerpted from her book *Lyndon Johnson and the American Dream*.

"I FIGURED WHEN MY LEGISLATIVE PROGRAM PASSED THE Congress," Johnson said in 1971, "that the Great Society had a real chance to grow into a beautiful woman. And I figured her growth and development would be as natural and inevitable as any small child's. In the first year, as we got the laws on the books, she'd begin to crawl. Then in the second year, as we got more laws on the books, she'd begin to walk, and the year after that, she'd be off and running, all the time growing bigger and healthier and fatter. And when she grew up, I figured she'd be so big and beautiful that the American people couldn't help but fall in love with her, and once they did, they'd want to keep her around forever, making her a permanent part of American life, more permanent even than the New Deal.

"But now Nixon has come along and everything I've worked for is ruined. There's a story in the paper every day about him slashing another one of my Great Society programs. I can just see him waking up in the morning, making that victory sign of his and deciding which program to kill. It's a terrible thing for me to sit by and watch someone else starve my Great Society to death. She's getting thinner and thinner and uglier and uglier all the time; now her bones are beginning to stick out and her wrinkles are beginning to show. Soon she'll be so ugly that the American people will refuse to look at her; they'll stick her in a closet to hide her away and there she'll die. And when she dies, I, too, will die."

The commentary is authentic Johnson, truth mingled with censure and regret; the metaphors, uniquely his—the girl-woman, simultaneously his creation, his gift, and his own life—emerging from the inward structure of the mind. It omits, however, the fact that his progeny's growth had been halted, not in 1969, but some years before, during his own Presidency—and not by Richard Nixon, but by Lyndon Johnson himself, as the consequence of his escalatory policy in Vietnam and his economic policy at home.

Nor was the Great Society—as Johnson pictured it in his metaphor—a single entity to be judged a success or failure, dead or alive. It was, in fact, a medley of programs— between 1965 and 1968, five hundred social programs were created—administered with varying degrees of success. Some of these programs—e.g., Medicare and voting rights—succeeded admirably in achieving their objectives; others accomplished far less than was originally hoped—e.g., Model Cities and federal aid to education; still others proved self-defeating—e.g., community action.

Johnson's Administrative Problems

Some of Johnson's administrative problems stemmed from the incoherent structure of the federal government. As Chief Executive, he was expected to obtain concerted action from a sprawling feudal government comprised of hundreds of autonomous fiefdoms, each with its own clientele, traditions, and loyalties. In domestic affairs, the conditions that made for presidential supremacy in foreign affairs were not present. In dealing with controversial issues of health, education, poverty, and manpower, the President could not invoke his office as a symbol of national unity in the same way as he could in matters of war and peace; nor could he point to the widespread consensus of attitudes that underlay his conduct in foreign policy. And his only constitutional grant of authority in domestic affairs was to "take care that the laws be faithfully executed," but even this does not grant independent authority; it only gives him authority to look over other people's shoulders. . . .

In the early months of his administration Johnson shaped a public image of himself he could not sustain over time. Presenting himself to the people as a master technician, a consensual leader who could produce something for everyone without cost to anyone, he created expectations that only a consummate administrator could have satisfied. To say this is not to suggest, as several observers have done, that Johnson was simply ill-suited, because of his legislative background, for the administrative aspects of the Presidency. The job of administering the Great Society was essentially political in nature, involving Johnson in many of the same challenges he had brilliantly mastered in the Senate, in the NYA [National Youth Administration], in the Little Congress [a discussion group for congressional legislative secretaries], and even in college, by developing a flow of detailed information, concentrating in his hands a maximum supply of carrots and sticks with which to reward allies and punish enemies, deciding when and where to intervene.

Admittedly, the scope of the task was far larger, but the President did possess substantial tools for tracking his subordinates' behavior and could have organized his government to provide others, just as he could have expanded the mixture of resources—top-level appointments, White House endorsements, presidential publicity for selected programs, invitations to White House functions, backing on the Hill, budget allocations—which he already had at his disposal for rewarding energetic bureaucrats and sanctioning recalcitrant ones. The point is not that Johnson was incapable of becoming a consummate administrator—that remains an open question—but that he never really tried. His priorities were elsewhere. The skills and resources he might have invested in shaping the bureaucracy to meet the Great Society's goals were channeled, instead, into the war in Vietnam. . . .

The key to the successful passage of the Great Society legislation in 1964–1965 was the constant attention Lyndon Johnson focused on his legislative program. Through nightly memos, Tuesday breakfasts, and Cabinet meetings, he imposed his priorities on the system; and his energy was transmitted to hundreds of key individuals in both the executive and the legislative branches.

This same combination of commitment, energy, and attention could have been focused on questions of administration in 1966–1968. Johnson could have mobilized the members of his White House staff and his Cabinet to provide frequent reports on the implementation of Great Society programs. He could have devised a collective forum—reconstituting the Cabinet meeting or creating a new institution—for discussing administrative problems. He could have reached below his Secretaries to energize lower-level bureaucrats and to keep his Cabinet members on their toes. He could have structured a system of participation within individual agencies so that those responsible for administering the departmental rules and regulations were involved in the process of drawing them up. The principle of involving participants in a process—which he had practiced so successfully on Capitol Hill—had as much force in the bureaucracy as it did in the legislature.

"There's Money Enough To Support Both Of You—Now, Doesn't That Make You Feel Better?"

©1967 by Herblock for *The Washington Post.*

None of these actions would have been easy to carry out in a bureaucratic system that for years had exercised considerable autonomy, free from presidential control. Still, a concerted presidential effort—with the commitment of substantial blocks of time—might have made a difference. But time was the one resource Johnson failed to give to his administrative role. Indeed, as the months went by, consumed more and more by the war in Vietnam, Johnson saw the heads of his domestic agencies less and less. Gradually, an atmosphere developed in which the domestic Cabinet members stopped asking for private meetings, assuming the President was too busy to concern himself with their business, as if their business were no longer his.

In contrast to the systematic way in which he had involved himself in the legislative process, faultlessly preparing his every word and deed, Johnson carelessly delegated the administrative tasks of the Great Society to the members of the White House staff. Worse than noninvolvement was Johnson's sporadic need to reassert control by arbitrarily inserting himself, directly and deeply, into the operation of a particular program. Often provoked by a congressional complaint or a newspaper story, these raids drained the entire system. Demanding instant reports, spot checks on field operations, and sudden meetings with program heads, Johnson created one crisis after another, each lasting no more than one or two days and often totally disappearing once the President's attention returned—as it always did—to Vietnam. . . .

Johnson's Failure to Prevent Inflation

The diversion of Johnson's attention from domestic concerns took place in a period when the problems of the Great Society were no longer simply problems of administration but the erosion of Johnson's consensus and the disappearance of those economic conditions of national life that had made the enactment of the Great Society possible.

The beginnings of the Great Society coincided with the happy realization that federal budget revenues were rising faster than projected expenditures for ongoing programs and allowed Johnson to avoid difficult choices between constituents and programs. The first phase of the Great Society promised something for everyone, and the promises continued even as Johnson escalated the war in July, 1965. His cardinal rule in his conduct of the war was to keep it as painless and concealed as possible. Deliberately avoiding new taxes, he drew upon existing revenues to finance his bombs and his troops. But the painless phases of the Great Society and Vietnam came to an abrupt end as the rising costs of the war combined with increased consumer demand and rising expenditures for the Great Society to produce inflation.

Consumer demand had risen sharply in 1965 in response to the Tax Reduction Act of 1964. Business had spent heavily on new plants and equipment to meet this rising demand. At the same time the government was increasing its expenditures for programs of social reform. Still, all these demands were being met until the economy ran into the sudden and sharp expansion of defense requirements. Together with the other expansions, the defense costs pushed total demand beyond the speed limits at which production could be expanded. Something had to give. Prices started to move up in 1965. As living costs rose, workers sought higher wages. These in turn raised the costs of production. Faced with higher production costs and strong markets, producers sought to raise their prices still further. This was the chain reaction that resulted in the wage-price spiral known as inflation.

Johnson was warned by Gardner Ackley, the Chairman of the Council of Economic Advisers, in December, 1965, that unless expenditures could be contained, a significant tax increase would be necessary to prevent an intolerable degree of inflationary pressure. But the President was in no mood to listen to such warnings at the moment when the American people were enjoying all the favorable consequences of the boom: profits were soaring, consumer living standards were improving dramatically, poverty was declining sharply, and the goal of 4 percent unemployment was finally being reached. While listening to Ackley's concerns, he flatly refused to consider a tax increase, sticking to his initial position that the American nation could afford guns and butter alike. This decision not to recommend a general tax increase in 1966 was the critical decision that set the economic system into a prolonged period of chaos. . . . By refusing to administer counterinflationary measures in the early stages, Johnson allowed the economy to heat up to the point where even drastic measures could have little impact.

Nor was Johnson willing to impose wage and price controls. . . . In the absence of either wage and price controls or a tax increase, the Great Society became the sacrificial lamb of the rising inflation. In early 1965 Johnson had projected that the Great Society would get fatter and fatter with each passing year, and in some respects his projection came true: In 1965 the combined expenditures for education, community development and housing, manpower, health, and welfare totaled $7.6 billion or 6.4 percent of the federal budget. In 1970 the figure was $29.7 billion or 15.1 percent of the budget, representing a quadrupling of outlay. But this increase was less substantial than it appeared because of the rise in prices between 1965 and 1970. And the total increase must be placed alongside the increase in the Defense Department budget in that same period from $46 to $77 billion, an amount greater than the total combined expenditures for all the new human resource programs put together.

Yet all along, the precise costs of the war were kept from the Congress and the American people. Budget Director Charles Schultze remembered that in the spring of 1966 both the President and Secretary McNamara clearly knew that Vietnam spending for fiscal year '67 would be considerably higher—by $6 billion—than the $10 billion allotted for it. Still, they refused to admit how much defense spending would rise, limiting their public statements to vague pronouncements. . . .

If Johnson had hoped to save the Great Society by moving step by step, his secrecy had just the opposite effect. When the inflation set in, in the absence of a wartime mood of sacrifice, the centers of power in the Congress responded with a conventional call to cut the budget. Succumbing to their pressure, Johnson sent word to his agencies: hold the line on budget requests. So just at the time when, according to Johnson's original scenario, the Great Society should have been entering its second phase—in which the good programs were to be expanded and the bad ones scuttled—the program administrators were told to tighten their belts and adopt a program of austerity. And Johnson the benefactor was forced to starve his own programs. . . .

Observing Johnson's immense growth in civil rights, it is possible—in the absence of Vietnam—to imagine an equally impressive growth in any number of areas. But Vietnam *was* there; indeed, at the very moment when new and imaginative thinking was essential, Johnson's mind was elsewhere. Many times, Johnson later recalled, he consciously and deliberately decided not to think another thought about Vietnam. Nonetheless, discussions that started on poverty or education invariably ended up on Vietnam. If Johnson was unhappy thinking about Vietnam, he was even less happy not thinking about it. Away from Westmoreland, McNamara, and Rostow, separated from his maps and his targets, he felt anxious, He found himself unwilling, and soon unable, to break loose from what had become an obsession. . . .

Relations with Congress

Johnson's obsession with the war inevitably damaged his relations with the Congress, contributing to the frantic pace the Great Society tried to sustain, even after the first year of amazing output. Determined to show that the war had not diminished the Great Society, Johnson relentlessly pushed the Congress to prove his case by producing one law after the next. Before one bill on a particular subject could be implemented, a new bill on the same subject had been proposed. Before the standards for the Water Quality Act of 1965 had been developed, the Clean Water Restoration Act of 1966 had been passed and Water for Peace Act had been proposed, diverting both congressional and bureaucratic attention at a time when focus on administrative questions was essential. Under siege about Vietnam, Johnson interpreted pleas made by the congressional leadership to concentrate on questions of implementation as a disguised attempt to sabotage the Great Society.

The more defensive Johnson became about the war, the more he demanded sole credit for the laws the Congress had passed. He violated his own principle of sharing publicity and credit in order to create a base of goodwill for the future. "There were a lot of us," one Senator later said, "who broke our backs on some of these bills, but Lyndon claimed he did it all himself. And you don't make friends that way." By constantly referring to "my Medicare bill," "my housing bill," and "my education bill," Johnson created congressional ill-will that exacerbated the difficulties the Great Society already faced.

But Johnson's faltering touch with the Congress was most clearly revealed in his tortuous struggle over the question of taxes. After hesitating for nearly two years to recommend a tax increase, Johnson finally asked the Congress for a 6 percent surcharge in September, 1967, but the price of the legislation—as Johnson had feared all along— was a crippling reduction in domestic programs.

"You have to go on TV," Wilbur Mills notified the President in 1967, and explain that "because of Vietnam we must cut domestic spending and pass a tax increase, and if you take this position you can count on me to go with you all the way. . . . I also want some commitments made in executive sessions of the Ways and Means Committee on major slashes in domestic spending." The skillful trader, his bargaining position enfeebled, now had to give up what he wanted to get what he needed. . . .

[The President's] request for the tax increase produced only wrangling on the Hill. For eighteen long months, while the economy slid into more and more trouble, the bill remained trapped in the Ways and Means Committee and Johnson was unable to spring it free. It was not until after he had withdrawn from the presidential race in 1968 and after the gold market collapsed that Johnson finally secured the passage of the surcharge.

In the beginning Johnson had expected that economic arguments alone would be sufficient to persuade both the liberals and the conservatives to join with him on the tax increase. But this assumption failed to account for the depth and the bitterness of the issues that separated liberals from conservatives on the question of taxes. While the conservatives linked their support of the tax increase to a demand that Johnson wrap the tax in the American flag and use the resources gained from it to prosecute the war in Vietnam, the liberals conditioned their acceptance on the promise that funds be used solely for domestic purposes without a single penny going to the war. . . .

Loss of Public Support

Fumbling with the Congress, Johnson also fumbled with the American people. "The [prince]," Machiavelli warned, "must arrange to commit all his cruelties at once, so as not to have to recur to them every day. . . . For injuries should be done all together, so that being less tasted, they will give less offence." By refusing to ask for a tax increase early on, Johnson failed to prepare the public for the sacrifices the war would entail. On the contrary, everything he said and did in the early days of his administration promised a painless war and a profitable peace. Nothing creates more bitterness than promises made and not kept. When life got tough on the American people, when the war and the inflation began to intrude upon their daily lives, they aimed their frustration at the President. Between 1964 and 1968 Johnson's support rating dropped 36 percentage points....

Fundamentally Johnson's failure with the public was one of purpose, not technique. His difficulties as a public leader were rooted in the choice he made in 1965 to commit American troops to an undeclared war in Vietnam while continuing to build the Great Society and while keeping the full extent of America's commitment from the public, the Congress, and even members of the executive branch.

JOHNSON'S COMMUNICATION STYLE UNDERMINED HIS GREAT SOCIETY

HUGH SIDEY

Hugh Sidey writes that while Johnson was adept at getting his Great Society bills through Congress, he was unable to generate enthusiasm for his agenda among the public. Because Johnson was not attuned with the age in which he lived, Sidey maintains, the president failed to develop rapport with the American people and inspire them to pursue his goals with him. This communications problem, according to Sidey, was a chief cause of the Great Society's failures. Sidey is a long-time Washington journalist who covered the White House during the Johnson administration. He is currently Washington contributing editor for *Time* magazine.

THE GREAT SOCIETY WAS IN JOHNSON'S HEART, BUT ONLY vaguely in his mind. An accidental President. A great, raw man of immense girth wandering as a stranger in the Pepsi generation. Coarse, earthy—a brutal intrusion into the misty Kennedy renaissance that still clung to the land. Lyndon Johnson roamed the country in a green suit ("the Jolly Green Giant") in the age of muted gray. He was an avuncular figure who eschewed the seashore when the ads beckoned all America to seek the sand and surf. He

Reprinted with permission from Atheneum Books, a division of Simon and Schuster, from *A Very Personal Presidency*, by Hugh Sidey. Copyright ©1968 by Hugh Sidey.

had never skied in his life, and he hunted from the air-conditioned interior of a white Lincoln Continental. His golf was poor. Amid the great crush of culture, he knew neither Beatles nor Brahms. His artist was Norman Rockwell. He detested megalopolis and suburbia with equal passion. When media became the message, he still had a dust-bowl idiom. Quiet understatement and muted self-depreciation were the rage, so he had the Presidential seal emblazoned on cowboy boots, his rancher's jacket, cuff links, cigarette lighters and discardable plastic drinking cups. He proclaimed seriously one day that he was "the most popular Presidential candidate since Franklin Roosevelt."

Those who knew him had a certain admiration for this defiance. But not many knew him that well. Communication with his nation became a towering problem. In fact, long before the Vietnam war had stalled the Great Society financially, it had faltered in Johnson's own rhetoric. While he filled a fat legislative logbook and constructed through the use of his executive powers a commendable framework for his dream, he failed to implant it in the hearts of his countrymen. He could not talk the language or gain rapport with the age in which he came to power. It was one of Washington's fascinations to speculate on why Johnson, who had spent thirty-six years in the city and had learned better than any other man how to find his way through the corridors of power, had failed to adopt some of the sophistication and awareness that swirled about him in the capital. He had the intelligence for it. He also had the time. Yet he never would drop his hostility to this world. The more successful he became, the more defiance he showed. The more power he gained, the more he ignored the changing national customs. While he felt secure in his legislative world, he lost touch in an important way with the nation, and it happened long before he had a chance of being President. The result, as 1968 came, was that the impact of the Great Society was less than it should have been, even considering the Vietnam war.

His legislative achievement was shattering, and in the Johnson mind, still gripped by his Senate experience, little else mattered.

Legislative Success

The $11.5-billion income-tax reduction measure was the lynch-pin of the new economics and provided the stimulus that sent the economy soaring to new records. Congress approved the Civil Rights Act of 1964 in the summer, a measure designed by Kennedy which covered public accommodations, hiring practices and voting rights. It was considered by some to be the strongest and most significant legislation of its kind in the century. Other important bills that were fundamental building blocks in the Great Society came tumbling from the Hill with astonishing ease, considering the stalemate that had developed between Kennedy and Congress. The Economic Opportunity Act of 1964, Johnson's poverty program, which also came from Kennedy blueprints, established ten coordinated programs designed to root out the causes of poverty.

There was a Mass Transit Act, a Water Research Act, a Wilderness Act. Johnson invited every single member of Congress to the White House at least twice in that year in an elaborate program of togetherness. When the year was over, *Congressional Quarterly,* a reliable scorekeeper of legislative activity, found that 57.6 percent of Johnson's legislative requests had been approved, the highest proportion of Presidential requests approved in ten years. That was nothing compared with what was to come.

Johnson's massive victory over Barry Goldwater swept a great new majority into the House, a ready-made machine for Lyndon Johnson. His margin in the House was 295 to 140. In the Senate, LBJ had a 68-to-32 edge.

The President submitted twice as many bills in 1965 as he had in 1964 and 68.9 percent of them were passed, bringing the Johnson assessment that this was "the greatest outpouring of creative legislation in the history of this nation." Though 1966 was not as prolific a year as 1965, the White House claimed when the Eighty-ninth [Congress] ended that the President had gotten 90 percent of the major requests. The legislation, indeed, had come like a freshet. There was Medicare, Federal aid to elementary and secondary education, help for higher education, a farm bill, creation of new Departments of Housing and Urban Development and Transportation, another civil-rights measure—this one voting rights—Social Security increases, housing, an immigration bill abolishing old quotas, a program of aid for Appalachia, truth in packaging, demonstration cities, rent supplements, the clean-rivers measure.

Just about any record that could be conceived of had been broken by Johnson. In the fall of 1966 Larry O'Brien, the chief custodian of legislative matters, could single out the field of education. "No less than twenty-four major pieces of education legislation were enacted in the past three years alone. These laws not only removed from our political debate sterile arguments over church-state relationships, they also ended the old repetitive and largely empty rhetoric of States Rights versus Federal Control. These laws, and others like them, signaled the birth of a new and more creative Federalism."

So much legislation was piled up that in the winter of 1966–67, while surveying his loss of four Senate seats and forty-seven House seats (plus his own precipitous slide from 80-percent approval to 44-percent), Johnson could honestly point out that the heart of the Great Society was passed. His legislative thrust in 1967 was toward consolidation, better administration and funding the programs that already had been passed. The four-year total, as tallied by the White House, was 226 major proposals passed out of 252 requests, for an astounding score of 92 percent.

Johnson's Failure to Ignite the Masses

But the Great Society as it stood when Johnson looked over his handiwork was not a total concept. It was a series of individual programs and ideas, most of which were commendable but which did not make a recognizable whole. Some of the promise of the Great Society could be detected, but the impact was hard to measure. Contained in the bills were the ingredients of the quality life which Johnson had sketched at Ann Arbor. There were attacks on the pollution of our environment, determined thrusts for equal rights and for better educational systems. There was a multitude of programs designed to relieve urban ills, and running through most of them was the realization that more initiative must come from state and local governments and that private capital must be induced to enter the arena. The old concept of the dole was all but abandoned in these schemes. Rent supplements—the idea of direct payments to families for housing, to vary as their earning power changed—was one of the most forward-looking plans devised in Washington in two decades. In Johnson's legislation there was emphasis on beauty and on culture. Men and women were encouraged to learn more, to improve their skills. There was the realization that more attention needed to be focused on children and youth to prevent odious problems later in their lives. The President subscribed, at least philosophically, to the plan to upgrade rural life so that migration to the urban areas would be retarded, thus preventing the inordinate growth of ghetto problems. Vice President Humphrey came up with the formula that $1 million spent in the countryside would save $20 million later in megalopolis. Johnson had endorsed the dignity of man and the pursuit of excellence. Yet something was missing.

There was no national sense of belonging to a new wave or of participating in a great social experiment. There was a minimum of excitement both in Washington and in the country. The great national energy was only partially roused. It was one of Johnson's bitterest disappointments. He wanted desperately to be a modern Franklin Roosevelt, focusing unrest and fragmented energies into a new crusade. He talked about building the Great Society on the foundations of the New Deal. He sometimes compared the Job Corps camps with the old CCC [Civilian Conservation Corps] camps and the Neighborhood Youth Corps with the New Deal's National Youth Administration. . . .

One of Johnson's obvious problems was that igniting people is a far harder task in time of great prosperity than in depression, when desperation dispels caution. The wealth of the United States and its effect on people were almost incalculable. Johnson got a taste when in 1966 he flew to Detroit for the traditional Labor Day rally. In times past, a President used to fill Cadillac Square with tens of thousands of cheering laborers. All that Johnson drew was a few thousand in Cobo Hall. Later Walter Reuther explained that many of the men owned boats or lake cottages and certainly all of them had automobiles. Labor Day had become a real holiday for them. The last thing that Detroit auto workers wanted to do was come downtown to hear a political speech. . . .

Facts and Statistics vs. the Power of Ideas

When he should have educated the population, Johnson preached to them. When he should have galvanized them with his language, he bored them with endless statistics. Johnson had a box-score mentality that he had brought down from the Senate. The measure of the success of a Majority Leader was the number of bills he passed. What the bills meant, what happened to the programs embodied in the measures, was not a primary concern of the Majority Leader. But the most important task of the President is to take an idea from the printed legislative page and turn it into a functioning part of national life. This is leadership, that mysterious executive talent which is made

The Rhetoric of the Great Society

Johnson presented the lofty goals of the Great Society in a speech delivered at the University of Michigan. The speech was written by Richard Goodwin.

For a century we labored to settle and to subdue a continent. For half a century we called upon unbounded invention and untiring industry to create an order of plenty for all of our people.

The challenge of the next half century is whether we have the wisdom to use that wealth to enrich and elevate our national life, and to advance the quality of our American civilization.

Your imagination, your initiative, and your indignation will determine whether we build a society where progress is the servant of our needs, or a society where old values and new visions are buried under unbridled growth. For in your time we have the opportunity to move not only toward the rich society and the powerful society, but upward to the Great Society.

The Great Society rests on abundance and liberty for all. It demands an end to poverty and racial injus-

up of many intangible factors. Yet when Johnson assessed his record, both in private and in public, it inevitably came out in numbers of bills passed and numbers of dollars spent. His evaluation of the splendid achievements of the Eighty-ninth Congress too often dealt not with the thrust of the legislation toward national betterment but with a grand total of 200 major measures submitted and 181 passed for a batting average of .905. In Nashville he told a crowd that his record in education legislation was unexcelled. Then he summed it up thus: "We've passed more bills, spent more money, reached more people, pro-

tice, to which we are totally committed in our time. But that is just the beginning.

The Great Society is a place where every child can find knowledge to enrich his mind and to enlarge his talents. It is a place where leisure is a welcome chance to build and reflect, not a feared cause of boredom and restlessness. It is a place where the city of man serves not only the needs of the body and the demands of commerce but the desire for beauty and the hunger for community.

It is a place where man can renew contact with nature. It is a place which honors creation for its own sake and for what it adds to the understanding of the race. It is a place where men are more concerned with the quality of their goals than the quantity of their goods.

But most of all, the Great Society is not a safe harbor, a resting place, a final objective, a finished work. It is a challenge constantly renewed, beckoning us toward a destiny where the meaning of our lives matches the marvelous products of our labor.

Lyndon Johnson, Remarks at the University of Michigan, May 22, 1964.

vided more comprehensive efforts in three years than in the rest of history." There was a lot of truth in that, yet it was only part of what was needed.

His view of the Kennedy record, because it lacked impressive statistics, was not very flattering. Kennedy had passed the Test Ban Treaty and he had formed the Peace Corps. That was about it, as Johnson saw things.

There were brilliant and important exceptions to this tunnel vision. Civil rights were in Johnson's heart as well as on his legislative list, and he talked about them with profound effectiveness. Before a joint session of Congress a few days after Kennedy's death he said, "We have talked long enough in this country about equal rights. . . . It is time now to write the next chapter—and to write it in the books of law." He did that, but he did not stop there. He took a moving message to the people whenever he had the chance, standing firm even before Southern audiences. He directed his scorn on the Ku Klux Klan. "My father fought them many long years ago in Texas and I have fought them all my life because I believe them to threaten the peace of every community where they exist. I shall continue to fight them because I know their loyalty is to a hooded society of bigots. . . ."

Debating the Meaning of Progress

There was movement in the nation after four years. The amount and its meaning in the country were severely debated.

There were 5.8 million undergraduates attending college—an increase of 1.8 million in that time. Four million older Americans received hospital treatment through Medicare, and more than five million received physicians' services. The Federal statistics showed that people were rising above the poverty line 2.5 times faster than in the previous four years—more than 5.7 million lifted above the line in those four years. Two million children took part in Headstart. The educational gap between Negro and white narrowed some.

Yet the outlines of progress were very dim, if for no other reason than that the great national debates centered on Vietnam and violence in our national life, and it was very hard to assign credit for advances. While the White House quite rightly pointed with pride to the longest economic expansion in our entire history, this prosperity, a very vital force in all of Johnson's programs, was essentially the product of the free-enterprise system and the strong private sector of the economy. The guaranteed annual wage which Ford Motor Company granted its employees in the fall of 1967 probably was as intense a blow against Johnson's ancient enemies of poverty, ignorance and disease as any new program the government launched in the Detroit area in four years.

Again, because of the immense and continually expanding wealth of the nation, one is frustrated in calibrating the forces. The President's talented aide Joe Califano, a genial attorney who had been stolen from Robert McNamara's staff, pointed out that more and more resources were going into the troubled areas. In 1960 Federal aid to the poor totaled $9.9 billion. In 1968 it was $30 billion. In 1960 the Federal government spent $6.6 billion for health; four years later it was over $22 billion. And in four years a million Americans were trained for useful jobs through previously nonexistent Federal programs. These statistics were quickly forgotten, however, when crime and violence continued their upward spiral, an epidemic of riots swept the nation and such responsible people as Pat Moynihan and Richard Nixon warned of terrorism and a possible race war. . . .

A Communications Problem

The term Great Society had virtually faded from Johnson's official vocabulary as he approached the summer of 1968. Johnson looked a visitor in the eye and confessed, "I've got a communications problem." How that problem came about is essential to the understanding of how the Great Society, a splendid infant, was orphaned.

For a long while the thoughtful men of Washington had rejected the careless journalistic assessment that Lyndon Johnson was a consummate politician. The more accurate appraisal suggested that he was superb in the close quarters of the Senate cloakroom (as long as there was a pliable President like Dwight Eisenhower around) but in national politics he was abysmal. He could make a deal with another man, but he could rarely inspire an audience.

He proved this in 1960 in his clumsy effort to get the nomination. He relied on the fumbling efforts of his Senate cronies. When Tom Dodd promised him Connecticut or Clinton Anderson assured him New Mexico was sewed up, he erroneously assumed it was fact. His in-house operatives such as Bobby Baker, the ambitious young man who counted his Senate votes for him, were equally inept. They fed Johnson fraudulent tallies of the delegates because they (include John Connally, who later became Texas Governor) knew nothing of the hard-scrabble politics beyond the cozy quarters of the Capitol. In Los Angeles in 1960 Johnson was overwhelmed by Kennedy, who actually had won the nomination weeks before. The Johnson campaign for the Vice Presidency was no better. His schedules made no sense, his speech subjects were infrequently pertinent. The twenty-six-year-old Bill Moyers tried desperately to insert some order into the chaos and managed to a remarkable degree to carry the Johnson convoy through to a sensible conclusion. All of that, however, was lost on Johnson, who went into the 1964 Presidential campaign as haphazardly as ever. He had no idea, for instance, what political polls were for beyond flaunting them when they were good. And in 1964 the news was so good that LBJ's natural exuberance led him to create huge charts of his favorable ratings and stretch them across the White House East Room; then he would bring guests into this lovely statistical panorama, seize a classroom pointer and romp down the line, chortling over his 83's . . . 72's . . . 69's . . . 78's. His campaign dashes around the country were unplanned, as were his speeches, but it didn't matter because Goldwater was spreading fear. Johnson used the same format in 1966. And then, finally, it began to matter. Once again he roamed the country at his whim. He didn't bother to announce where he was going. His speech subjects did not fit his locations. He paid minimum attention to the local candidates he came to help—he was more interested in reviving his own lagging Gallup ratings. The off-year elections of 1966 were a disaster by anyone's standards. He lost forty-seven seats in the House and four Senate seats. At last it began to dawn not only on the President but on a great many of his exhausted patrons that there was something wrong. It was essentially communication.

From the start of his Presidency, Johnson's language rarely fitted his actions. Certainly his rhetoric did not fit the age. When he meticulously followed carefully prepared texts such as the Ann Arbor charter for the Great Society, his messages carried through. But on his own he was a rambling evangelist of thirty years ago. His oratory had the flamboyant personal style of the Texas county-fair political circuit, devoid of much meaning, but long and loud. . . .

The Importance of Speech in Presidential Leadership

It perhaps is easy to overemphasize the role of language in the Presidency. Indeed, it was fashionable for a while in the Kennedy era to scoff at eloquence. Men who had been around the Capitol for several decades would tell you that in the end the only thing which mattered was what actions a President took, not how he talked or looked. Good language was lumped with "style," a mildly contemptuous term for what middle-aged writers and politicians claimed was Kennedy's only virtuosity. This was an erroneous judgment. Perhaps in an earlier age Presidential speech was less vital, but in Johnson's time language had become an integral part of a President's business. What he said and how were elements of leadership. The clear and cogent statement of ideals and ideas is perhaps a President's greatest challenge and can be his greatest power. Teddy Roosevelt was ahead of his time by about fifty years when he summed up the Presidency as a "bloody pulpit."

The Johnson who immediately entered the American living rooms on the printed page or through electronics was a confusing figure, certainly not compatible with the Great Society he was trying to sell. That society was a challenge. Yet Johnson insisted, like FDR, on making promises. He painted grim pictures of despair whose dimensions often went far beyond the actual state of affairs in this wealthy nation. He often missed his mark, focusing on the rural shack dweller when the symbol of this age was the ghetto dweller. He described himself as the great benefactor who would ease burdens through unexplained economic wizardry that would spend more and save more at the same time. It was Lyndon Johnson's improbable world.

THE GREAT SOCIETY'S WELFARE PROGRAMS HARMED THE POOR

CHARLES MURRAY

Charles Murray is Bradley Fellow at the American Enterprise Institute, a libertarian think tank in Washington, D.C. He is the author of several books on social policy, including *Losing Ground: American Social Policy, 1945–1980*, from which the following essay was excerpted. Murray writes that the United States experienced a revolution in social policy between 1950 and 1980; Johnson's Great Society was the "reform period" of this revolution. According to Murray, the social policies of the Great Society were based on the belief that all poor people were victims of America's flawed social and economic system. As such, the poor were not to blame for their poverty. In this way, Murray contends, the stigma was removed from poverty, welfare, and unemployment, paving the way for massive welfare dependency and worsening poverty among inner-city blacks in the ensuing years.

HISTORICALLY, THE UNITED STATES HAS BEEN A NATION OF people who were either poor or the children of poor parents. Only in the last half of the twentieth century has a large proportion of the middle class become so far removed from poverty that the lack of money became horrifying in itself.

Few of the American poor defined their lives in terms

Excerpted from *Losing Ground: American Social Policy, 1950–1980*, by Charles Murray. Copyright ©1984 by Charles Murray. Reprinted by permission of BasicBooks, a member of Persus Books L.L.C.

of their poverty. Neither did society. The "poor" were a varied lot with complex status distinctions to be drawn. There were the genteel poor who had lost their money but not their manners. There were the poor people who were called "trash"—not just without money, but also uncouth and generally unpleasant company. There were the immigrant poor who, at the same time they were climbing out of poverty, maintained elaborate status structures even in the most crowded tenements. And there were the farmers. Forty-two percent of the population lived on farms in 1900, and most of them were cash-poor. But, from the time of Jefferson down through the years, the farmers were widely seen as (or saw themselves to be) the backbone of the nation and on a considerably higher moral plane than the effete rich.

Status distinctions among the poor began with the assumption that people are responsible for their actions and, specifically, responsible for taking care of themselves and their families as best they could. Missouri farmers and New York immigrants might have had wildly different status distinctions in other respects, but in both communities, and everywhere that poor people lived together, the first distinction was made on this basis. A person might work hard and be poor; that was the way of the world. Poverty had nothing to do with dignity. A person might be out of a job once in awhile because of hard times. That too was the way of the world, and a temporary situation. But a person who was chronically unable to hold onto a job, who neglected children and spouse, was a bum and a no-good, consigned to the lowest circle of status.

Once it was assumed that the system is to blame when a person is chronically out of work and that the system is even to blame when a person neglects spouse and family, then the moral distinctions were eroded. The first casualty inevitably was the moral approbation associated with self-sufficiency. In the 1950s, the reason for "getting people off welfare" was to keep them from being a drag on the good people—meaning the self-sufficient people—and to rescue them from a degrading status. It was not necessary to explain *why* it was better to be self-sufficient; it was a precondition for being a member of society in good standing. In the late 1960s, with the attack on middle-class norms and the rise of the welfare rights movement, this was no longer good enough. Self-sufficiency was no longer taken to be an intrinsic *obligation* of healthy adults.

Among the people who held this view, the next casualty of the assumption that "the system is to blame" was the distinction between the deserving poor and the undeserving poor. Blame is the flip side of praise. To praise the poor who are self-sufficient is to assign to them responsibility for their upstandingness. But if one family is responsible for its success, the next family bears at least a measure of responsibility for its failure. It was much less complicated simply to treat "the poor" as a homogeneous group of victims.

It must be remembered that the shift in opinion was localized. A survey in 1967 showed that 42 percent of Americans still thought poverty reflected "lack of effort," another 39 percent thought that lack of effort had at least something to do with it, and only 19 percent blamed poverty on "circumstances beyond control." But what the mass of Americans thought did not shape the reform period [1964–1967]. In academic and policy-making circles, the conversion was nearly unanimous. The very term "deserving poor" was laughed out of use—witness the reaction of political columnists and cartoonists to the use of "truly needy" by the Reagan administration.

Only the poor were homogenized. In the day-to-day life of the rest of society, the elite, like the broad middle class, continued as always to differentiate the clever from the dull, the upright from the outlaw, the industrious from the indolent, But when it came to the poor, all must be victims. They were not permitted to be superior to one another.

If the poor were all victims, then policy had to be changed. First of all, welfare had to be cleansed of its stigma. Welfare historically had been a blot on the recipient's reputation; to be on welfare was to be inferior to one's neighbors who were not on welfare. But if it was not the welfare recipient's fault that welfare was needed, the stigma was wrong and unfair.

The portrayal and administration of the welfare system changed dramatically to fit the new wisdom. The key administrative changes for AFDC [Aid to Families with Dependent Children] were directives against investigations of eligibility and court decisions easing restrictions on eligibility. In addition, OEO [Office of Economic Opportunity] took a more direct stand against stigma. As early as 1965, it was sending emissaries to spread the word that it was morally permissible to be on welfare. Community Action grants provided the wherewithal for booklets, speeches, and one-on-one evangelizing by staff workers. Welfare was to be considered a right, not charity.

The government's efforts were reinforced by the National Welfare Rights Organization, founded in 1966 and led by George Wiley. By 1967, the NWRO was large enough to hold its first annual convention in Washington. The innovative aspect of the welfare rights movement was not that poor people were organizing. Poor people had been marching on Washington since the town was built. But the age-old slogan was missing. No longer, as always before, did the protesters proclaim that "We don't want charity, we want jobs." In the last half of the 1960s the NWRO demonstrators were not demonstrating so much for jobs as for the right to long-term, unfettered, generous charity.

[Frances Fox] Piven and [Richard A.] Cloward cite evidence that the efforts of the community organizers were successful in reducing the stigma. Such results are plausible. One of the major sources of the stigma attached to welfare was the middle class. For poor people who aspired to be like them in respectability, the appearance of in-the-flesh representatives of the middle class saying that welfare was their due must have had a telling effect. One may visualize, for example, the situation of parents in a slum who have taught their offspring to believe it is shameful to accept welfare. Then the children come home reporting that the supervisors on the Summer Job program, or the organizers of the Community Development project, or the lawyers down at the Legal Services storefront office are saying that such notions are all wrong. Welfare is a right. The parents are dupes. The irony is that parents who have taught their children that welfare is shameful tend to be the kind of people who also teach their children to treat lawyers and supervisors and organizers as role models. How do the parents now convincingly reply, "I don't care what those people [the very people you are supposed to admire] said, it's still wrong . . ."?

Getting rid of the stigma of welfare was a deliberate goal. But another effect was not; it just happened as a logical consequence of denying that people are responsible for their condition: Because the system is to blame, all people on welfare are equally deserving of being given a hand. No one could disqualify himself on moral grounds from eligibility for public assistance—whether or not he was ready to help himself. There was no longer a mechanism for stamping someone unworthy. On the contrary, many of the social-service programs required as a condition of eligibility that the participants be failures. It could not be otherwise. Programs to rehabilitate drug addicts have to be restricted to drug addicts; programs to employ the hardcore unemployed must be restricted to the hard-core unemployed; and so on.

Theoretically, the social service and educational programs could have gotten around this selectivity by providing other programs aimed at those who were especially "worthy"—those who were giving their all and needed just

Evaluating the War on Poverty

Mark I. Gelfand contends that any evaluation of Johnson's antipoverty programs will most likely depend on the appraiser's ideological perspective.

Was the War on Poverty indeed a failure? No other question is more likely to be asked and less likely to be answered satisfactorily. Can we distinguish between the impact of the War on Poverty programs and influences exerted by other policies and programs? Is it reasonable, putting aside the admittedly overblown rhetoric of the mid-1960s, to set any time limit for the successful completion of the struggle to eliminate poverty? By what standards is the war to be judged?

How, for example, does one treat a 1979 study on hunger released by the Field Foundation? In 1967 the foundation sponsored medical teams that helped uncover the prevalence of inadequate diets in the rural South; a decade later the foundation underwrote a follow-up survey on the federal response. The report's major conclusion: "There is nowhere the same evidence of gross malnutrition" witnessed earlier. Infant mortality had declined by about 33 percent; there had been a 50 percent drop in malnutrition-related deaths. Impressive statistics, but the good news they tell is diminished by another, less positive figure: "The current food aid

a little more help to escape from poverty for good. But the mindset was too strong. "Elite" was fast becoming a dirty word in the mid-1960s among whites; "elitism" would soon be a form of bigotry to rank with racism and, later, sexism and ageism. Blacks were especially sensitized. Long ago, W.E.B. Du Bois had urged special emphasis on "the talented tenth" among blacks, and the approach had since

programs have never reached more than 60 percent of the people who need them."

This refrain of "better but" is to be encountered in nearly every appraisal of the antipoverty program. The conclusions drawn are most likely to be a function of the evaluator's philosophical inclinations. Conservatives are prone to stress the shortcomings, label the whole effort a failure, and demand a rollback of federal intervention." Radicals are likely to employ similar characterizations but call for greater federal control of the economy (or, alternatively, more community autonomy) in the pursuit of real equality. Liberals tend to concede the limits of the gains, place the blame on inadequate resources, and urge more social welfare programs and more money. When they join the social scientists in the debate, historians will probably divide along the ideological camps already established.

If that is all historians do, they will be gravely misallocating their energy. Larger questions are presented by the War on Poverty than simply its hits and misses—issues regarding the relationship of the government to its citizens and the structure and strategy of politics, matters of great interest to Lyndon Johnson.

Mark I. Gelfand, "The War on Poverty," from Robert A. Divine, ed., *The Johnson Years, Volume One: Foreign Policy, the Great Society, and the White House.* Lawrence: University Press of Kansas, 1987.

become identified with a compliance with middle-class values (at best), Tom-ism (more likely), and general lack of militance at a time when power to the people was in vogue.

The unwillingness to acknowledge moral inequality was a hallmark of Great Society social programs and persisted throughout the 1970s. It was not just that the squeaky hinges (the failures) got the oil. Administrators of programs made Kafkaesque rules to avoid revealing that some poor people are brighter or of better character or more industrious than others.

One case in point, the "magnet schools," may be used to illustrate the general phenomenon. The purpose of the magnet schools was to lure white middle-class students back into urban school systems by setting up inner-city schools that were open to enrollment from throughout the city and were provided with special resources in a specific area—science, or the arts, or simply a strenuous college-prep program. The theory was that the magnet schools would not only reduce white flight among those who saw an opportunity in the magnet school; they would also break the back of the stereotypes that contributed to white flight from urban schools in general. It was one of the more plausible of the educational innovations of the time.

Some of the vocational schools and elementary schools achieved positive results. But administrators of the high schools with an academic program soon ran up against a dilemma. Inner-city public education was so bad that only a few black students had adequate preparation to enter and successfully complete the curriculum in the magnet school. What should be done? One solution would have been to proceed as planned. The gifted black students who were in the program, even if they were fewer than had been hoped, would have a high-quality education they would not have gotten otherwise, and the white students (and their parents) would see what black students could do, given the opportunity. But few of the magnet schools took this course.

The common solution was rather to impose a racial quota to ensure that "enough" black students got into the magnet school. The results were as one would predict: To fill the quota, black students with inadequate skills were admitted. Then the school had either to flunk the students who could not keep up (unthinkable) or to soften the standards. But softening the standards destroyed the attractions of the magnet school for the white parents it was supposed to entice. And the stereotypes that the magnet schools were to dispel were reinforced. The white students went away with incontrovertible evidence from personal experience that even the brightest black students (for that is what they were *supposed* to be) were not competitive with white students.

The magnet schools story has numerous analogs among other programs of the time. Social programs were initiated with the professed purpose of creating successes from failures. But to create a success, an indispensable element is praise for accomplishment. And if praise for the ones who succeed is to be detailed, emphatic, and credible, it soon becomes necessary to distribute blame as well. Praise is meaningless without the assumption that the people who succeeded are in some practical way *better* than the people who failed, and this the administrators of the programs and the ideologues of the new wisdom were unwilling to confront head-on. To see some as better was perceived as denying that the failures were victims.

Arguably the most insidious single change affecting status relationships within the poor community had nothing to do with the Great Society's social-action programs but with the introduction of "means-tested" welfare benefits.

One of the insights of game theory is the psychological importance of natural boundaries—those things that make it easier to quit smoking than to cut down and that lead bargainers to compromise on a round number or to "split the difference." With poor people, the boundary was accepting *no charity at all* from anyone outside the family. Many readers will be able to verify the power of this demarcation line from their earliest lessons about the family tradition: "We may not have had much money, but we never took a penny of charity," was one common formula; or "We have always paid our own way" or "We have always pulled our own weight." The idioms and the tradition were pervasive.

Means-tested programs effectively ended such useful boasts. One may approve or disapprove of Food Stamps and Medicaid and housing assistance, but one result was unavoidable. Virtually all low-income persons became welfare recipients (. . . by 1980 Food Stamps alone counted more than 21,000,000 recipients). Pride in independence was compromised, and with it a certain degree of pressure on the younger generation to make good on the family tradition.

More importantly, the working people who made little money lost the one thing that enabled them to claim social status. For the first time in American history, it became socially acceptable within poor communities to be unemployed, because working families too were receiving welfare. Over a period of years, such changes in the rules of the economic game caused status conventions to flip completely in some communities. Why, at bottom, should working confer social status? Originally, there were two reasons. One was that nonworking people were a threat to the wealth and well-being of the rest of the community. The second was that nonworking people were visibly outcasts; they lived worse than anyone else. Once these highly functional sources of the status are removed, the vaunted "work ethic" becomes highly vulnerable. The notion that there is an intrinsic good in working even if one does not have to may have impressive philosophical credentials, but, on its face, it is not very plausible—at least not to a young person whose values are still being formed. To someone who is not yet persuaded of the satisfactions of making one's own way, there is something laughable about a person who doggedly keeps working at a lousy job for no tangible reason at all. And when working no longer provides either income or status, the last reason for working has truly vanished. The man who keeps working is, in fact, a chump.

THE GREAT SOCIETY
WAS A SUCCESS

SAR A. LEVITAN AND ROBERT TAGGART

Many historians and political commentators believe Johnson's
Great Society legislation failed to deliver its promised benefits
and created long-term problems such as welfare dependency,
excessive government spending for social programs, and ineffi-
cient bureaucracy at the federal government level. Sar A. Levitan
and Robert Taggart offer a contrary view. They insist that the
Johnson years ushered in an era of progress in many areas, including civil rights and efforts to reduce poverty, and that critics have greatly exaggerated the negative consequences of Great
Society legislation. Levitan, who died in 1994, was a public policy commentator who specialized in employment, education,
and poverty issues. Taggart is coauthor (with Levitan and
William B. Johnson) of *Still a Dream: The Changing Status of
Blacks Since 1960* and *The Promise of Greatness*.

P RESIDENT LYNDON JOHNSON'S SOCIAL WELFARE PHILOSO-
phy captured the imagination of the country in the
mid-1960s and spurred it into action after a decade of
lethargy. In Johnson's words, "We have the opportunity to
move not only toward the rich society and the powerful
society, but upward to the Great Society. The Great Society
rests on abundance and liberty for all. It demands an end
to poverty and racial injustice." Under the banner of the
Great Society, there was a dramatic acceleration of govern-

Excerpted from "The Great Society Did Succeed," by Sar A. Levitan and Robert Taggart, *Political Science Quarterly*, vol. 91, no. 4 (Winter 1976–1977), pp. 601–18.
Reprinted by permission of *Political Science Quarterly*.

mental efforts to ensure the well-being of all citizens; to equalize opportunity for minorities and the disadvantaged; to eliminate, or at least mitigate, the social, economic, and legal foundations of inequality and deprivation. Congress moved ahead on a vast range of long-debated social welfare measures and pushed on into uncharted seas. In its 1,866 days the Johnson administration moved vigorously to implement these new laws and to fully utilize existing authority. The Warren Court aided this dynamism with sweeping, precedent-setting decisions on a number of critical issues. The public supported this activism, giving Lyndon Johnson in 1964 the largest plurality in history, his Democratic party an overwhelming majority in both Houses of Congress, and his administration high public approval ratings as action got underway.

Yet only eight years after the end of the Johnson administration, the view is widely held that the Great Society failed. The charge is that it exaggerated the capacity of government to change conditions and ineffectively "threw money at problems," overextending the heavy hand of government, pushing the nation too far, too fast, leaving a legacy of inflation, alienation, racial tension and other lingering ills. The repudiation of the Great Society in the late 1960s was based on a tide of analyses alleging to demonstrate the failures of the Johnson administration's domestic endeavors. There was extensive documentation of the "welfare mess." A crisis in medical care was declared and decried. Scandals and high costs in subsidizing housing were exposed, giving support to theoretical arguments about the inherent ineffectiveness of government intervention. Manpower programs, it was claimed, had little lasting impact on employment and earnings of participants. Doubts were cast on the outcomes of education investments. Urban and racial unrest were blamed on civil rights action and community organization. The economic problems of the 1970s were blamed on economic mismanagement during the 1960s.

A Positive Assessment

A careful reexamination of the evidence for the complete spectrum of the 1960s social welfare initiatives suggests that the conventional wisdom of the Great Society's failure is wrong. Our own assessments of the Great Society and its legacy, based on analysis of a vast array of program data, evaluations, and related statistics, challenge the widespread negativism toward governmental social welfare efforts. We contend that the findings provide grounds for a sense of accomplishment and hope.

1. *The goals of the Great Society were realistic, if steadily moving, targets for the improvement of the nation.* By concentrating on the small minority of welfare recipients who are cheaters or who shun work, critics have chipped away at the ambitions of the Great Society, and have suggested that those in need somehow deserve their fate. This view ignores the overwhelming majority of welfare recipients who have no other alternatives, workers who either cannot find employment or are locked into low-wage jobs, and the millions of disenfranchised who are seeking only their constitutionally guaranteed rights. Other less strident critics emphasize the difficulties in changing institutions and socioeconomic patterns. No matter how desirable a change may be, it is likely to have unwanted side effects, and the process itself can be an ordeal. Where opportunities and rewards are distributed unequally and unjustifiably, redistribution will obviously affect the previously chosen people. Improvements cannot be accomplished without effort and sacrifice, and the existence of impediments is not proof of unrealistic or unattainable goals.

2. *The social welfare efforts initiated and accelerated in the 1960s moved the nation toward a more just and equitable society.* The claims that these programs were uselessly "throwing dollars at problems," that government intervention cannot change institutions or individuals, or that problems remain intractable are glib rhetoric. The results

of government intervention varied, undesirable spillover effects occurred, and the adopted intervention strategies were sometimes ill designed; but progress was almost always made in the desired direction. The gains of blacks and the poor, the two primary target groups of federal efforts, offer the most striking evidence. Government programs significantly reduced poverty and alleviated its deprivations. Blacks made major advances in education, employment, income, and rights in the 1960s.

3. *The Great Society's social welfare programs were reasonably efficient, and there was frequently no alternative to active intervention.* The government operates in a fishbowl, so that all its mistakes and excesses are laid bare to the public; similar problems in the private sector are hidden away, leaving the impression of greater efficiency. Criticism of programs is part of the process by which needed or desired changes are engineered, and the discovery of failure is part of a continuing process of improvement.

4. *The negative spillovers of social welfare efforts were often overstated and were usually the unavoidable concomitants of the desired changes.* Examples are legion. Medical care programs were blamed for the inflation in medical costs. Busing was heatedly opposed as inconveniencing the many to help the few. In fact, however, medical costs rose largely because demand was increased suddenly while supply could respond only slowly. Inflation is unavoidable when reliance is placed on the price mechanism to expand and redistribute resources. Busing to achieve racial balance involves difficulties but critics have not offered alternatives to integrate the schools. Every program generates problems, but these have usually been manageable.

5. *The benefits of the Great Society programs were more than the sum of their parts, and more than the impact on immediate participants and beneficiaries.* In attacking a specific problem such as unemployment, for instance, there is a whole nexus of variables. On the supply side, considera-

tion must be given to the education and vocational training of the unemployed; their access to jobs, their knowledge of the labor market; and their work attitudes, impediments, and alternatives. On the demand side, the quality and location of jobs must be considered along with their number. Discrimination and hiring standards are also crucial factors. Unemployment might be combated by education and training, better transportation, improved placement services, sticks and carrots to force the unemployed to take jobs, provision of child care, economic development in depressed areas, equal opportunity enforcement, and a variety of other measures. None of these alone is likely to have much impact, but together they can contribute to change, not only in the labor market, but in all those dimensions of life so intimately related to work.

6. *There is no reason to fear that modest steps which are positive and constructive in alleviating age-old problems will in some way unleash uncontrollable forces or will undermine the broader welfare of the body politic.* Only dedicated pessimists and gainsayers can doubt our capacity to achieve substantial improvements. And there is no reason to abandon the aim of providing a minimal level of support for all who remain in need. Progress has been meaningful; it can and must continue. As we enter our third century as a nation, we must reevaluate the recent, as well as distant, past to get a realistic understanding of our limitations but also a greater confidence in our potential. We have the power, if we have the will, to forge a greater society and to promote the general welfare.

Evaluating the Record

Many critics of the Great Society have focused on the least successful attempts at social improvement with their attendant horror stories. There is an opposite temptation to concentrate on and generalize from the areas of accomplishment. The only valid approach is to consider the successes and failures over the entire range of social welfare activities.

The expansion of income transfers during the 1965–1975 decade has been criticized from many angles. Aid to Families with Dependent Children [AFDC]—usually called "welfare"—drew the brunt of criticism. Supplemental Security Income—the reformed system of aid for the aged, blind, and disabled—then came under fire, as did unemployment compensation. Even the previously sacrosanct social security program was questioned. In reality, the Great Society had less impact on the transfer system than on any other social welfare dimension. To blame it for the "welfare mess" or for the problems of the social security system is to ignore the complicated factors involved; to associate it with the vast expansion in unemployment compensation in the 1970s or with the difficulties of public assistance for the aged, blind, and disabled is an anachronism. Nonetheless, a major thrust of the Great Society was to provide for the needy. If the programs that attempt to do this are ineffective, then the Great Society's vision must be faulted. Is the transfer system indeed a mess?

Doubts about the soundness of the social security program are, if not groundless, certainly exaggerated. During the 1965–1975 decade benefits were raised substantially in real terms, and the system matured to the point where coverage of workers and benefits to the elderly became nearly universal. The redistributive features of the programs were expanded but social security remained a good insurance buy for most workers.

The system remains secure. Declining birth rates mean fewer workers per beneficiary in the future and may require increased revenues. But this problem is more than a quarter century away, during which time productivity gains should provide the wherewithal for the needed transfers. Government contributions from general revenues are a likely possibility to finance the redistributive aspects of the system. And as a result of past improvements, benefits now meet basic needs and will not have to be raised in real terms as rapidly as in the past. . . .

Controversy over Welfare

Aid to Families with Dependent Children has been the center of controversy. The tripling of caseloads and the quadrupling of costs between 1965 and 1972 was alarming to some, as was the subsequent failure to achieve welfare reform. In retrospect, however, the process was neither incomprehensible nor inimical. AFDC benefits were raised substantially to provide most recipients, in combination with in-kind aid, a standard of living approaching the poverty threshold. With liberalized eligibility rules and more attractive benefits, most low-income female-headed families were covered by the welfare umbrella in the early 1970s. Once this had occurred, the momentum of growth slowed.

The welfare explosion did have side effects. No doubt some recipients chose welfare over work as benefits rose above potential earnings. In part, welfare freed mothers from low-paid drudgery to take care of their families. Moreover, the difficulties of placing even the most employable and motivated recipients in jobs paying adequate wages suggested the limited options for the majority of clients. As benefits stabilized in the 1970s, the increase in real wages promised to reduce the attractiveness of welfare to unskilled workers.

The welfare system's bias against families with a male head offered some inducement for nonmarriage or desertion. In cases where AFDC provided a higher or steadier income than male family heads could earn, the costs of broken families had to be balanced against the benefits of improved living standards. The stabilization of real benefits and the rise in real wages should, over time, diminish the inducement to break up homes.

The income support system, including social security,

veterans' programs, unemployment insurance, workman's compensation, public assistance for the aged, blind, and disabled, AFDC, and near-cash programs such as food stamps, is incredibly complex. Yet "messiness" is inevitable where needs are multifaceted and where goals clash. Concentrating aid on female-headed families yields high target efficiency, since these families have the most severe needs and fewest options, but undesirable results are unavoidable. High marginal tax rates may discourage work, but they also tend to keep down costs and to help the most needy. Benefits may be too high in some areas and too low in others, but on the average they are close to poverty levels and geographic differentials are declining. Most families receiving multiple benefits have severe or special needs.

The income maintenance system is thus functioning reasonably well. The developments that seemed chaotic and dysfunctional have created a system within sight of assuring at least a poverty threshold standard of living for all citizens through a combination of cash and in-kind aid.

Health Care

The Great Society went far toward eliminating the main concern of the aged and a major problem of the poor—health care. Medicare and Medicaid have generally fulfilled President Johnson's promise of assuring the "availability of and accessibility to the best health care for all Americans regardless of age, geography or economic status."

Medicare experienced early difficulties in striving for a balance between assuring adequate services and avoiding overutilization. Problems were associated most frequently with innovations. For instance, extended care was initiated as an alternative to longer hospital stays but became a subsidy for nursing home care until corrective measures were taken. Overly long hospital stays were shortened through a variety of utilization review methods. Perhaps to quell fears that government intervention would mean government control, Medicare may have displayed excessive generosity in considering the desires of doctors and other vested interests. After problems emerged, however, steps were taken to cut the fat from the system.

Medicaid remains an object of much criticism because of its rapid and unexpected growth. The scapegoats were overutilization and inefficiency, but quite clearly the basic cause was the explosion of AFDC. By the early 1970s the momentum of growth had already subsided as the eligible universe was reached and measures were taken to discourage overutilization and waste. Being tied to AFDC, Medicaid shared the geographic inequalities of that system, with even greater disparities resulting from the extension of aid to the medically indigent not on welfare in only some of the states. Yet these inequities were reduced over the years as more open-handed states cut back on frills while the tight-fisted ones became more generous. . . .

Attempts to blame Medicare and Medicaid for the alleged (and very questionably documented) failure of our health care system are misplaced and even critics must admit these programs' effectiveness in performing their basic missions. . . .

Civil Rights

One of the primary aims of the Great Society was finally to secure the fundamental rights of blacks. Along with its impressive legislative record, the administration exerted its leverage in the marketplace and its power as a rule setter while the courts expanded the government's responsibilities and prerogatives. The Nixon and Ford administrations were less forceful, some critics argue. Nevertheless, the stalling points such as employment quotas or busing to end de facto segregation were far different from those of the early 1960s when the rights, rather than the corrective measures, were being debated.

The salutary effects of these civil rights advances were

not difficult to ascertain. Black registration and voting increased, with a visible payoff in office holding. Equal employment opportunity efforts had little direct effect in the 1960s, but the screws were tightened considerably in the 1970s. De jure school segregation was largely eliminated and busing to achieve racial balance became widespread despite fervent opposition in some cases and repeated efforts in Congress, with administration prodding, to proscribe busing as a weapon in combating segregation. Fair housing machinery provided legal backing for some victims of discrimination, but little leverage to overcome patterns and practices was included in housing acts or administrative decisions.

While attention was focused on racial issues, there were other areas of advancement. At the beginning of the 1960s, recipients or potential recipients of governmental aid were dependent on the whim and caprice of government bureaucracies. Antipoverty legal efforts established the principle of due process under social welfare programs and pressed the notions of equal protection and welfare as a right, chalking up some noteworthy victories in overturning the man-in-the-house and state residency restrictions.

The neighborhood legal services program was a vital tool in combating poverty, establishing new rights through law reform as well as providing traditional legal aid. Suits on behalf of clients against state and local governments got the program into political hot water. However, since the courts decided most cases in favor of the poor, the program was criticized for its effectiveness and not for its shortcomings.

Maximum feasible participation—an ill-defined and much maligned goal—was a basic approach of the Great Society. The aim was to give minorities and the poor a degree of organizational power in order to change institutions, to protect their interests, and to design innovative strategies to serve themselves. Community action agencies, model cities, concentrated employment projects, neighborhood health centers, and community development corporations, though no more participatory or democratic than other groups in our society, had the express purpose of representing the needs of the poor. In doing so, it was necessary to step on firmly entrenched toes, and this generated antagonism, as did efforts to bring about institutional change. Friction was an inevitable ingredient in the process, and though new community leaders sometimes made a virtue of antagonizing the establishment, conflict was mainly rhetorical. Community groups initiated a number of innovative approaches and were condemned for the waste and high failure rate implicit in experimentation. Yet many of the seeds bore fruit locally and nationally.

The community-based programs defy rigorous assessment because of their diversity, but the more narrowly focused efforts can be compared with alternative approaches. Neighborhood health centers, for instance, provided care at roughly the same cost as established institutions. The quality of care was equal, but accessibility and amenability were greater. Health centers used paraprofessionals and took other steps to reach out to those in need, increasing the level of usage. Community development corporations were no more successful in establishing viable businesses in poverty areas than other establishment-run efforts, but the CDC's helped organize the neighborhood and generated short-term employment and income for the poor.

Improving the Status of Blacks

As a result of Great Society civil rights and other initiatives, blacks made very substantial gains on a number of fronts during the 1960s. The purchasing power of the average black family rose by half. The ratio of black to white income increased noticeably. The Great Society's efforts were instrumental in generating advancement. But relative black income fell during the 1971 recession and did not recover subsequently.

Earnings were the primary factor in the income gains made by blacks, although income support and in-kind aid also rose. Blacks moved into more prestigious professional, technical, craft, and secretarial jobs previously closed to them. Earnings rose absolutely and relatively as discrimination declined. Sustained tight labor markets, improved education, manpower programs, and equal employment opportunity efforts all played a role.

The improvements in schooling were dramatic and consequential. Black preschoolers were more likely to enroll than whites, largely because of federally financed early education programs. High school completion increased significantly and compensatory programs provided vital resources to the schools where black youths were concentrated. At the college level, absolute and relative enrollment gains were dramatic, the direct result of government aid programs.

Economic and social progress was not without serious drawbacks. Dependency increased, the black family was buffeted, and already high crime rates accelerated. Without minimizing the negative spillover, there is clear proof that blacks were far better off before the advent of the economic slump than a decade earlier. There is a long way to go to equality and progress has been uneven, but advances have been made.

The War on Poverty

While the war on poverty was not unconditional, it was more than a mere skirmish. The Economic Opportunity Act programs were only one—and not the primary—front in this assault. The Great Society's economic policies, which combined tight labor markets with structural measures such as minimum wages and manpower programs, helped the employable poor. Welfare, social security, and in-kind aid focused on persons with limited labor market attachment.

The number of poor declined sharply in the 1960s then leveled off. The early declines were achieved by raising the income of the working poor, and their place was taken by female heads with little opportunity for self-support. The combination of deteriorating labor markets, declining numbers of working poor, and accelerating family breakups caused poverty to level off despite the fact that the government's antipoverty expenditures continued to rise in the 1970s.

The continuance of poverty does not mean government efforts have been ineffective. In 1971, 43 percent of the otherwise poor were lifted out of poverty by income transfers, compared with 30 percent in 1965. In-kind aid and services going to the poor are not included as income in the poverty measurements, yet they cost more than the cash poverty deficit. If victory in the war on poverty means providing the minimal standard of living, then the war has very nearly been won, though some battles remain to be fought.

JOHNSON AND
CIVIL RIGHTS

THE EVOLUTION OF
JOHNSON'S POSITION
ON CIVIL RIGHTS

MONROE BILLINGTON

Many commentators question the sincerity of Johnson's commitment to the cause of civil rights for blacks, pointing out that Johnson opposed civil rights legislation during his years in the House of Representatives and the Senate. In the following essay, Monroe Billington traces Johnson's evolving stance toward minorities throughout his political life. Johnson's strong opposition to civil rights legislation was politically appropriate when Johnson represented Texan constituencies, Billington writes, but eased as Johnson emerged as a national leader in the mid-1950s. In 1956, when Johnson finally believed the timing was right, he changed his stance to support federal civil rights legislation and remained firmly committed to this course for the rest of his life. Billington, formerly a professor of history at New Mexico State University, is the author of *The American South: A Brief History* and *The Political South in the Twentieth Century*.

H ISTORY WILL AWARD PRESIDENT LYNDON B. JOHNSON A prominent role in advancement of civil rights for blacks. Judicial decisions, presidential actions, and congressional legislation promoting those rights occurred during the presidencies of Roosevelt, Truman, Eisenhower, and Kennedy, but these were only a prelude to the Johnson administration. Even though much remained undone when

Excerpted from "Lyndon B. Johnson and Blacks: The Early Years," by Monroe Billington, *Journal of Negro History*, vol. 62, no. 1 (January 1977), pp. 26–42. Reprinted by permission of the Association for the Study of African-American Life and History, Inc.

Johnson left office, the years when he was President—1963–1968—constituted an important era in the progress of civil rights for blacks. Passed during the Eisenhower administration, the Civil Rights Acts of 1957 and 1960 inaugurated the post-Reconstruction legislation helpful to blacks. Considerably more significant was the Johnson administration's Civil Rights Act of 1964, an omnibus bill whose most far-reaching provisions related to nondiscrimination in public accommodations. Fast upon the heels of this measure came the Voting Rights Act of 1965, providing for elaborate and more effective federal machinery for registering voters and assuring the right to vote in certain areas of the nation. In early 1968 Congress passed another comprehensive civil rights bill, whose major provisions dealt with the reduction of discrimination in housing. While President, Johnson pressed for the passage of these three bills, and he willingly signed each of them into law.

In addition, Johnson took other public actions which helped identify his administration with black civil rights. In February 1965 he issued an Executive Order designed to coordinate the various agencies of the federal government involved in the elimination of discrimination and the promotion of equal opportunity. Also, Johnson appointed a number of blacks to high office.

Johnson spoke many times in behalf of the civil rights of black Americans. During the years he was President, on at least 232 occasions he made public references to the subject. The highpoint of the President's public remarks came on March 15, 1965, when he spoke on black civil rights before a joint session of Congress and a national television audience. Referring to black voting rights, equal economic opportunity, and adequate housing, Johnson issued an emotional appeal to the nation to put aside "the crippling legacy of bigotry and injustice." No President had ever publicly identified himself so closely with the problems of the nation's largest racial minority.

Was President Johnson sincere when he pressed for civil rights legislation, issued Executive Orders, and spoke out publicly for black rights? Did he always hold such expressed views? Was he consistent throughout his career regarding civil rights for blacks? Or was he an expedient politician who desired only to advance his own career by yielding to current pressures? This essay, focusing on Johnson's early relationships with and attitudes toward blacks and their civil rights, is addressed to these questions.

The Roots of Johnson's Racial Attitudes

Lyndon B. Johnson was born in 1908 on a farm in Blanco County in central Texas, and he grew up in the small town of Johnson City, Blanco's county seat. Of the county's 4,311 inhabitants in 1910, only 350 were black. By 1920 the population had declined to 4,063, with blacks totaling only 169; and in 1930 these two figures had further declined to 3,842 and 133. With so few blacks residing in the county during his childhood years, young Johnson had hardly any occasion to know or have dealings with blacks. Sometimes a black family passed through Johnson City on the way somewhere else; an occasional black migrant was hired to help the family harvest its crops; but that was about all. Young Johnson matured without strong color prejudice. He neither liked nor disliked blacks. Not being visible, blacks were not an issue in his life. Reflecting the southern attitudes of other whites in the county, Johnson assumed that blacks and whites should be separated; but Blanco County was not a part of the old Confederacy, and Johnson later confessed that he "never sat on my parents' or grandparents' knees listening to nostalgic tales of the antebellum South." Southern traditions and blacks were on the margin of young Johnson's frame of reference. The Mexican-American minority in Blanco County was no greater than was the black, although Johnson had a few Mexican-American playmates. The only minority of some significance was the German-Americans, and distinctions between them and the Anglo-Americans were virtually nonexistent. Under these circumstances, Johnson had no reason to be prejudiced toward any minority group—nor to feel any sympathy for such groups if they were downtrodden. Johnson did not seethe with indignation in regard to class or race struggles. In the cultural isolation of the Pedernales Valley, he took his own rights for granted and paid little attention to his fellow men who did not have the same rights.

This situation was altered when Johnson became a young adult. After attending Southwest Texas State Teachers College for a year and a half, Johnson took a job as an elementary school teacher in Cotulla, Texas, a small LaSalle County community in south Texas. Cotulla had a large Mexican-American population, and because of the tradition of segregation only Mexican-American pupils attended the small school to which he was assigned. During the 1928-29 school year at Cotulla, Johnson had intimate contact with Mexican-Americans. He came to love the children. He spent money from his own pockets so his poverty-stricken pupils could have play equipment at their impoverished school. He spent hours outside the classroom with his pupils in extracurricular activities such as softball, volleyball, debating, and a literary society. In his later years Johnson often made reference to his Cotulla experience and the deep impressions his young pupils made upon him. Also, for the first time in his life he became conscious of the white society's discrimination toward the Mexican-American minority, and in later years this consciousness was extended to include blacks. This consciousness evolved into a genuine caring for members of minority groups.

This concern became apparent when Johnson was director of Texas' National Youth Administration (NYA) from July 1935 to February 1937. The youngest state administrator in the nation, Lyndon Johnson was eager to succeed as he directed the activities of the largest NYA state agency. Johnson wrote thorough reports, unceasingly strove to acquire more money for Texas youth, instituted programs which were copied by other states (the most notable being the construction of "pocket-sized" highway parks), and garnered more than his share of newspaper publicity. His generally good job as state administrator greatly impressed the national office of the NYA.

Johnson's concern was to help the youth of Texas—regardless of color—during the gloomy days of the Great Depression, and his administration was generally nondiscriminatory. Soon after Johnson set up his statewide headquarters in Austin, he initiated a meeting with black leaders in the city. In the basement of a black Methodist Church, Johnson informed the blacks that he was eager to assist jobless black youths. Some blacks were surprised that he would make such an overture, and many were distrustful of his motives. One black contemporary has concluded that Johnson helped blacks not only because he desired to do a good job, but also because he "cared for people.". . .

Johnson did not consciously discriminate against black youths, but he did not appoint blacks to paid supervisory capacities, and he was interested only in helping black youths economically, not in altering traditional social patterns. In a special report to his superiors, Johnson wrote: "The racial question during the past one hundred years in Texas . . . has resolved itself to a definite system of customs which cannot be upset overnight. So long as these customs are observed, there is peace and harmony between the races in Texas, but it is exceedingly difficult to step over a line so long established, and to up-set a custom so deeply rooted, by any act which would be shockingly against precedence. . . ." Johnson's was a paternalistic administration committed to the status quo in regard to race relations.

A Traditional Southern Congressman

Johnson retained this general attitude toward Texas blacks throughout his nearly twelve-year stint as a national congressman. Having resigned from his NYA job in March 1937 to run for the position vacated by the death of the incumbent congressman of Texas' Tenth District, Johnson won the special election and took his seat in July 1937. The Tenth District is composed of ten counties in central Texas, including Travis, in which the state capital is located. On the western edge of the state's black belt, the district's counties varied greatly in the percentages of blacks in their populations. In 1940 the eastern-most Washington County was highest in black percentages with 38.1, while Burnet, the northwestern-most county, had only 1.7 percent of its population black. The average for all ten counties was 20.7 percent blacks. During an era when blacks were generally disfranchised, Johnson felt no compulsion to appeal to them. Even though he campaigned on the basis of being a representative for all the people, he omitted blacks when he listed the people in the district who had problems which he hoped to help solve. No evidence indicates that the subject of black rights or problems arose in Johnson's 1937 congressional campaign, nor that black rights were issues in the subsequent congressional elections. The same statement can be made for Johnson's successful attempt in 1941 to move up to the Senate.

Congressman Johnson concerned himself with constituent requests of both whites and blacks. He tried to answer every letter on the day it was received, and he earned the reputation of having never failed to answer a letter from a constituent. He was not embarrassed to be called "the bell boy" for his district. At the end of his congressional career he stated that he had been happy to run errands for "the farmer, the veteran, the little businessman, and all the people." While he did not specifically list blacks, he did not exclude them from his assistance. When federal slum clearance money was first made available, Johnson persuaded Congress to earmark $500,000 for a public housing project to alleviate somewhat the horrible conditions in an Austin slum inhabited by blacks and Mexican-Americans. In addition to looking after his black constituents specifically, Johnson worked and voted for legislation which would help both white and black Texans. He always favored more money for the Farm Security Administration, which provided relief for tenant farmers and sharecroppers, and in the late 1930's a bureaucrat in that agency observed that Johnson "was the first man in Congress from the South ever to go to bat for the Negro farmer." He favored increased appropriations for the National Youth Administration and the Civilian Conservation Corps, and he worked to insure that blacks were included within the provisions of the Agricultural Adjustment Act of 1938.

Throughout his congressional years, Johnson made few public statements revealing his attitudes toward blacks. While he did not join his southern colleagues in their anti-black remarks in Congress, neither did he protest their rantings; indeed, viewed from the perspective of his voting record alone, Johnson was a traditional southern congressman on the subject of civil rights for blacks. He voted against an anti-lynching bill in 1940, as well as anti-poll tax bills in 1942, 1943, 1945, and 1947. During the Second World War, when the Congress desired to provide more convenient absentee ballots for overseas soldiers, he voted with southerners who favored a state (as opposed to a federal) ballot, so that the states could control the voting process (i.e. regulate the black vote). In 1946 when Congress was considering a federal school-lunch program, he voted "No" on an antidiscrimination amendment offered by Adam Clayton Powell of Harlem, and in that same year he voted with those southerners who successfully employed parliamentary tactics to kill a bill to create a permanent Fair Employment Practices Commission (FEPC). Johnson justified these votes on the basis of states' rights. He believed that law enforcement, voting quali-

---

The Mock Champion of Civil Rights

Robert Sherrill is among those who believe that Johnson's conversion to the civil rights cause was motivated by political expediency.

The evolution of Johnson as the mock champion of civil rights began after the splintering of his [presidential] hopes in 1956. He got the message: victory lay in the cities, victory lay within the union blocs, the black blocs, the immigrant blocs, the big city bosses, with the independent voters, and if possible with the farm blocs, though that was the last to worry about. Johnson saw that he who gets the South gets naught. At no time in the last fifty years, with the exception of Truman's victory in 1948, was the Dixie electoral vote possibly responsible for the election of a president; except for 1948, the South could have stayed at home. LBJ saw that he had to get that magnolia blossom out of his lapel, and he coolly set about it. He would pass a civil rights act. If necessary he would pass two. Nothing to get the nation in a turmoil, just something nice and American like saying a citizen should be allowed to vote—without giving the Attorney General the right to enforce it. And furthermore he had to do it in such a subtle fashion that he could claim in Texas that he wasn't doing it at all. The 1957 bill that he created fitted that need perfectly, but when it failed to get him the nomination in 1960, he again lost interest in civil rights, and his interest was not revived until his own presidential race in 1964.

Robert Sherrill, *The Accidental President.* New York: Grossman, 1967.

---

fications, and economic opportunity were the proper do-
mains of the states, and he did not want the national government involved in these areas of American life. Whenever he made these statements, he sounded very much like
his southern colleagues. He protested that he was not
"against" blacks, but was rather "for" states' rights.

When Johnson spoke with black constituents in his
congressional district, he often tediously explained that he
did not actually vote against particular civil rights bills;
rather he voted to recommit them for revision or study. He
hoped these technical explanations would make blacks less
unhappy with his votes. At other times he frankly informed the blacks that he had to vote with the southern
leaders in Congress so that he could obtain their support
on other matters of importance. He reminded the blacks
that the civil rights bills against which he had voted would
not have passed anyway, and he preferred to wait and vote
"Yes" when his vote would make a difference. Johnson said,
"I must vote this way, but I'm for you and I will get what I
can for you in the future." In reference to civil rights, over
and over again Johnson said, "Timing is important." Black
supporters knew they were taking chances by backing
Johnson during those years, but they had faith that Johnson "would do something for them when he had a real opportunity." But many Texas blacks were suspicious of Johnson. They did not believe that he sincerely wanted to help
them, and they looked upon him as cynically opportunistic in regard to their civil rights. These blacks believed not
only that Johnson's public stands were conservative, but
also that his private views were conservative. Johnson left
no records revealing his private thoughts, but his public
stance tended to undermine his protestations that he was a
true friend of blacks.

Johnson continued to take anti-civil rights stands after
his career in the House of Representatives ended. When he
ran for the Senate in 1948, he opposed President Harry

Truman's announced civil rights program. Opening his senatorial bid on May 22 before a large crowd in Austin and over a twenty-station radio hookup, Johnson said: "The Civil Rights Program is a farce and a sham—an effort to set up a police state in the guise of liberty. I am opposed to that program. I have voted AGAINST the so-called poll tax repeal bill; the poll tax should be repealed by those states which enacted them. I have voted AGAINST the so-called anti-lynching bill; the state can, and DOES, enforce the law against murder. I have voted AGAINST the FEPC; if a man can tell you whom you must hire, he can tell you whom you can't hire."...

Throughout his first term in the Senate, Johnson continued to hold the same public stand in regard to civil rights for blacks which he had previously held. In May 1949 he voted "Yes" on a discriminatory public accommodations amendment proposed by Mississippi Senator James Eastland to the perennial District of Columbia home rule bill. In 1950 he voted to table an amendment to outlaw poll taxes; he voted down the line with his southern colleagues against an FEPC measure the Senate was considering; he voted to table an amendment to prohibit racial discrimination in unions; and he supported an unsuccessful amendment to a military draft law providing that a young man have the right to choose to serve in a unit composed only of members of his own race.

When the San Antonio branch of the NAACP [National Association for the Advancement of Colored People] approved a resolution demanding that Johnson support Civil Rights Legislation, since citizens were "being denied the rights of first-class citizenship," Johnson replied, "I cannot agree that the civil rights legislation as it is currently written would extend to any citizen 'the rights of first-class citizenship.' First-class citizenship begins at the meal table, in the schools, at the doctor's office, and many places other than in court. . . . In the future, as in the past, I shall work to equalize the opportunity and reward of all Americans through better housing, better schooling, better health, and all those things which are the true rights of first-class citizenship." To those who protested his stand, Johnson reminded them that he had supported public housing, federal aid to education, and many other measures "which have raised the living standards of all our people and expanded the economic opportunity for all." Even while opposing anti-lynching bills and the FEPC, he wrote, "I shall support those measures which will help make America a better place for men to live." To another he wrote, "I should not like to see the people of Texas and the South undergo the wave of riots and stress which I believe would follow if we tried to force people to do what they are not ready to do of their own free will and accord."

When the Supreme Court in 1954 handed down its famous decision requiring the desegregation of the nation's schools, southerners in Congress circulated a "Southern Manifesto" expressing their opposition. Every senator from the old Confederacy except Johnson signed the protest document. He was "firmly opposed to forced integration," and he believed that "the states should be allowed to work out their own solutions to problems coming within their proper jurisdiction," but he could not sign the document. To a constituent he wrote, "Now that the Supreme Court has ruled, . . . I can only hope that the problem will be worked out reasonably and with fairness to all concerned." In the wake of the Supreme Court decision blacks and others more strongly pressured the Congress to pass civil rights legislation, and a second "Southern Manifesto" was circulated in March 1956. Johnson did not sign this statement either. Having been elected Minority Leader in 1953 and elevated to Majority Leader in 1954, Johnson refrained from signing the documents because he did not want to endanger his position of leadership in the Senate. He told reporters, "I am not a civil rights advocate." A few months later when a well-known reporter entitled a column "Lyndon Pushes Civil Rights," Johnson protested that he was not involved in planning civil rights legislation. Johnson was upset that a nationally-circulated newspaper column so clearly identified him with efforts on Capitol Hill to legislate in this area.

Time for Decision

Despite these protests, for the first time in his life Johnson in 1956 began to give serious thought to the possibility of the passage of a civil rights bill and to his role in that action. In a three-page memorandum to the Senator, George Reedy addressed himself to the then current civil rights "uproar" in the Democratic party. Reedy relegated to failure any policy which would approach the civil rights issue from the standpoint of recovering lost votes for the Democratic party; "Nevertheless, some effort should be made to produce legislation along the civil rights lines—not to recover votes but simply because the issue has reached a point where some action is necessary." Johnson had always believed that "timing is important." With the Democratic party on the verge of splitting over the civil rights issue, with black pressures mounting, with Johnson's leadership under fire because of inaction, and with the Senator beginning to have more than vague aspirations to be President, Johnson decided that the time had come for Congress to pass a mild civil rights bill. The result was the Civil Rights Act of 1957. Whatever the weaknesses of that measure, it inaugurated an era of civil rights legislation unparalleled in the nation's history. Lyndon Johnson had taken a public stand for civil rights, and as Congress passed each succeeding law, he became more firmly committed to civil rights for all Americans. His later senatorial career, his vice-presidential years, and his presidency attest to his public posture. No evidence exists to indicate that his private thoughts in those years differed from his public statements and actions.

Cynics say that Johnson moved from anti-civil rights stands in the 1930's and 1940's to pro-civil rights stands in the late 1950's because he was ambitious, expedient, opportunistic, and politically motivated. Johnson saw himself as totally consistent, always the friend of blacks even when voting against civil rights bills. Johnson was too complex to be categorized simply as "consistent" or "expedient." The record shows that over three decades in public life Johnson was not consistent. But that record shows less expediency than the growth of an individual in public life. While he was a congressman from Texas' Tenth District, Johnson naturally reflected in his voting record the anti-civil rights views of the majority of his constituents, during an era when black pressures were not great and when publicity about the plight of minorities was limited. When he became a senator his early Senate voting record and speeches continued to reflect his now statewide constituency. Concurrent with his elevation to the leadership of the Democratic Party in the national Congress was an increased national consciousness of minority rights and Johnson's own thoughts about the presidency. The converging of these streams of consciousness pushed Johnson in the direction of public action for blacks and explains his dominant role in the passing of the first civil rights act since Reconstruction. As Vice-President and as President, Johnson had a nationwide constituency at a time when black frustrations often resulted in violence. His role as national leader compelled him to act for the interests not only of the oppressed minority but also for all the people of the country. The story of Johnson's public stance on civil rights is one of evolution, of maturation, of growth.

The same may be said of Johnson's attitudes toward blacks and their civil rights, although here the evolutionary process was less dramatic. Johnson's love for people, with him from his earliest years, compelled him to be concerned about minority groups—from the Mexican-American children in Cotulla in the 1920's to the bitter black rioters in the 1960's. Even though he did not support civil rights legislation in the 1930's and 1940's there is no reason to believe that he did not sincerely desire to help blacks. The practical situation tempered his private attitudes. He had often told blacks that he would help them when he had the power and when the timing was right; when those two conditions were met he carried out his promises.

Johnson Commits: The Civil Rights Act of 1964

Robert Dallek

One of Johnson's first actions as president was to commit himself absolutely to the passage of John Kennedy's civil rights bill, which was then stalled in Congress. Robert Dallek writes that Johnson had several reasons for deciding on this course of action: He believed it would help heal the nation in the wake of the Kennedy assassination; he was personally opposed to racial hatred and inequality; he saw it as a means to improve the image of the South; and he was aware that his political survival depended on it. Dallek describes Johnson's role in orchestrating the legislation's movement through the Senate, where it met with a Republican filibuster that was defeated by cloture, an unprecedented event in the Senate. Dallek is a professor of history at Boston University and the author of a two-volume biography of Johnson.

FROM THE MOMENT HE ASSUMED THE PRESIDENCY, [JOHNson] saw a compelling need to drive Kennedy's [civil rights] bill through Congress with no major compromises that would weaken the law.

As a southerner who had accommodated himself to segregation through most of his career, Johnson seemed like an unreliable advocate of a civil rights statute that would force an end to the system of racial separation in public facilities across the South. He could not fully divest himself of attitudes instilled by a southern upbringing. In January 1964, he told a Texas friend: "I'm gonna try to teach these nigras that don't know anything how to work for themselves instead of just breedin'; I'm gonna try to teach these Mexicans who can't talk English to learn it so they can work for themselves . . . and get off of our taxpayer's back." However patronizing to both minorities, Johnson was determined to rise above his own limitations on race and to bring the country with him. "I'm going to be the President who finishes what Lincoln began," he said to several people.

A few days after he became President, he asked Senator Richard Russell of Georgia, an unyielding segregationist, to come talk to him about the civil rights bill. "The President sat in a wing chair. The Senator sat at one end of a small couch. Their knees almost touched." As [special assistant] Jack Valenti remembered it, Johnson said: "'Dick, you've got to get out of my way. I'm going to run over you. I don't intend to cavil or compromise.' 'You may do that,' he replied. 'But by God, it's going to cost you the South and cost you the election.' 'If that's the price I've got to pay,' said the President, 'I'll pay it gladly.'"

The following week Johnson told labor leaders that "the endless abrasions of delay, neglect, and indifference have rubbed raw the national conscience. We have talked too long. We have done too little. And all of it has come too late. You must help me make civil rights in America a reality." Two days later, in a well-publicized meeting at the White House, he gave the same message to the country's principal black leaders. "This bill is going to pass if it takes all summer," he told them. "This bill is going to be enacted because justice and morality demand it."

His initial impulse had been to meet with the black leaders at his ranch. But Lee White, JFK's special assistant on civil rights, urged Johnson not to do something that would be seen as "so damned phoney." Though

Johnson followed White's advice, he told him on the phone from Texas: "I live down here. This is my home, and I ought to be able to invite people to my home." He was determined to show that black leaders would be treated the same as whites.

Why Johnson Committed to the Bill

He had several reasons for wanting to make good on civil rights. First, he felt that passing Kennedy's bill would help heal the wound opened by his assassination. To Johnson's thinking, the President's murder resulted from the violence and hatred dividing America and tearing at its social fabric. Roy Wilkins [head of the National Association for the Advancement of Colored People], one of the civil rights leaders who had met with LBJ in December, remembered that the tragedy of Kennedy's death hung over the civil rights bill and influenced Johnson's view of it. "And it was on this note that he [Johnson] felt the federal government had to take a stand to halt this schism between people—violence, bloodshed and that sort of thing."

As important, there was the moral issue or the matter of fairness that Johnson, the great political operator, felt with a keenness few could fully understand. Johnson—the prominent politician, the great Majority Leader, the Vice President, the all-powerful President—was at the same time Johnson the underdog, the poor boy from Texas struggling to emerge from the shadows and win universal approval. Johnson identified with and viscerally experienced the suffering of the disadvantaged.

He repeatedly told the story of Zephyr Wright, his cook, "a college graduate," who, when driving the Vice President's official car with her husband from Washington to Texas, couldn't use the facilities in a gas station to relieve herself. "When they had to go to the bathroom," Johnson told Mississippi Senator John Stennis, "they would . . . pull off on a side road, and Zephyr Wright, the cook of the Vice

President of the United States, would squat in the road to pee." He told Stennis: "That's wrong. And there ought to be something to change that. And it seems to me that if people in Mississippi don't change it voluntarily, that it's just going to be necessary to change it by law."

His sense of outrage was even more pronounced toward Alabama Klansmen who had killed four black youngsters by setting off a bomb at a Birmingham church in September 1963. He urged FBI Director J. Edgar Hoover to leave no stone unturned in finding the perpetrators. He also asked Hoover to step up his investigations of several other Birmingham bombings tied to racial intolerance. Hoover, a political chameleon with a keen feel for what served his interests, gave Johnson a detailed accounting of expanded bureau efforts to solve the crimes.

"Free at Last"

Yet all Johnson's rhetoric could not entirely disarm the suspicions of civil rights advocates. If he had felt so strongly about the issue, why had it taken him so long to act on it? Why was he going to make an all-out fight for the civil rights bill now? Roy Wilkins asked him at their December meeting. Johnson thought a minute, wrinkled his brow and said: "You will recognize the words I'm about to repeat. Free at last, free at last. Thank God almighty, I'm free at last." Borrowing from Martin Luther King's speech to the civil rights advocates who had marched on Washington in the summer of 1963, Johnson was describing himself as liberated from his southern political bonds or as a man who could now fully put the national interest and moral concerns above political constraints imposed on a Texas senator.

At the same time, Johnson saw civil rights reform as essential to the well-being of his native region. He had known for a long time that segregation not only separated blacks and whites in the South but also separated the

South from the rest of the nation, making it a kind of moral, economic, and political outsider, a reprobate cousin or embarrassing relative the nation could neither disown nor accept as a respectable family member. An end to southern segregation would mean the full integration of the South into the Union, bringing with it economic progress and political influence comparable to that of other regions. And though many in the South would abandon their roots in the Democratic party in response, Johnson was determined to administer the unpleasant medicine that would cure the region's social disease. The election of Presidents from Georgia, Texas, and Arkansas during the next thirty years testifies to the region's renewed influence in the nation anticipated by LBJ.

Johnson also saw personal political gain from pressing ahead with civil rights legislation. In the fall of 1963, 50 percent of the country had felt that Kennedy was pushing too hard for integration. Only 11 percent wanted him to go faster, while 27 percent were content with his pace. By February 1964 the number opposing more vigorous civil rights efforts had dropped to 30 percent, and the percentages favoring more aggressive action and what Johnson was doing had increased to 15 percent and 39 percent, respectively. By the last week of April, 57 percent of the public said they approved of the way Johnson was handling the civil rights problem, and just 21 percent disapproved.

It was welcome news to LBJ, who believed his election to the presidency depended in significant part on his firm advocacy of a civil rights law. "I knew that if I didn't get out in front on this issue [the liberals] would get me," he later told Doris Kearns. "I had to produce a civil rights bill that was even stronger than the one they'd have gotten if Kennedy had lived. Without this, I'd be dead before I could even begin." Richard Russell understood Johnson's dilemma: "If Johnson compromises," Russell told a reporter, "he will be called a slicker from Texas."

Risk of Defeat

Yet Johnson also had reason to think that a forceful stand on civil rights might ruin him politically, as Richard Russell had warned. Black civil rights leader Andrew Young said that, while Johnson knew that support of the civil rights bill was the way to assure his place in history and "the way to really save the nation, he knew it was not politically expedient."

Johnson also worried that an all-out push for a bill that didn't pass could be a serious blow to his political standing. And he saw defeat as a distinct possibility. When he asked [Senator] Hubert Humphrey to lead the civil rights act through the Senate, Johnson said: "This is your test. But I predict it will not go through." Partly because he believed it and partly to light a fire under Humphrey, Johnson launched into a diatribe about the ineffectiveness of Senate liberals. "You bomb-throwers make good speeches, you have big hearts, you believe in what you say you stand for, but you're never on the job when you need to be there. You spread yourselves too thin making speeches to the faithful."

Because they would be up against Richard Russell, who knew all the Senate rules better than the liberals, Johnson expected Humphrey to lose the battle. It was a "speech" Humphrey had heard repeatedly from Johnson, but it was less a cry of despair than a summons to do better. He firmly promised to back Humphrey to the hilt. "As I left, he stood and moved toward me with his towering intensity: 'Call me whenever there's trouble or anything you want me to do,'" Johnson said.

To guard against some of the political fallout from a possible congressional defeat, Johnson told Robert Kennedy: "I'll do ... just what you think is best to do on the bill. We'll follow what you say. . . . I'll do everything that you want me to do in order to obtain passage of the legislation." Johnson sent word to Senate Democratic leaders to get Bob

Kennedy's approval on everything. Why did he do that? an interviewer asked Kennedy. "He didn't think . . . we'd get the bill," Bobby answered. And if that were the case, "he didn't want . . . to have the sole responsibility. If I worked out the strategy, if he did what the Department of Justice recommended . . .—and particularly me—then . . . he could always say that he did what we suggested and didn't go off on his own." Kennedy believed that "for political reasons it made a great deal of sense." Johnson couldn't lose this way, because if the bill passed, he would still get "ample credit."

With this safeguard in place, Johnson made every effort to get congressional action. He "wanted to make it very clear—and did—right at the outset of his administration that this was something he was going to move forward in every possible way and with much more than deliberate speed," Deputy Attorney General Nick Katzenbach recalled. "There was nobody more ardent in his espousal of civil rights legislation than Lyndon B. Johnson," Larry O'Brien [head of Congressional relations and adviser to Johnson] says.

Through the House and to the Senate

At the outset, his legislative strategy was the same as Kennedy's: first, get a bill through the House. In the five months before his death, JFK had convinced House leaders from both parties to agree on a compromise law that concentrated its fire on giving southern blacks access to public accommodations and public schools and all citizens equal employment opportunities. This bill had received the approval of the House Judiciary Committee in October and was before the Rules Committee in November when Johnson became President.

On November 25, Johnson told the nation's governors that he expected bipartisan approval of the bill in the House. "The real problem will be in the Senate," he advised congressional leaders. But he took nothing for granted in the House, where Howard Smith of Virginia, Chairman of the Rules Committee, seemed determined to delay matters as long as possible. To put some heat on Smith, Johnson launched a campaign for a discharge petition that would bypass his committee. Republican supporters, seeing this as a liberal Democratic bid to take exclusive credit for the bill, resisted Johnson's pressure. Moderate Democrats, eager not to jeopardize bipartisan support, did the same. "I have talked to them all and don't get that do-or-die attitude out of them," Johnson told Senate Democrats. On January 30, after he had agreed to drop the petition, the Rules Committee approved the bill by an 11-to-4 vote.

Although Johnson and Larry O'Brien were fairly confident that the bill would pass the House, they worried that some of the Republicans might not stay committed and that various amendments, which could dilute the bill, might pass. Consequently, during the next eleven days, Johnson was constantly on the phone, bargaining with Democrats and Republicans alike. "We let them [the Congressmen] know that for every negative vote there was a price to pay," Jack Valenti recalls. "There were many times on that floor when even [Republican leader Charlie] Halleck, in spite of his commitment, would vote for crippling amendments, which we had to beat down," civil rights leader Clarence Mitchell remembers. "And there were many times when if it had not been for the Johnson intercession, we wouldn't have had enough votes on the floor to hold things."

On February 10, within minutes after the bill passed the House 290 to 110, Johnson was on the phone to congressmen praising their action. "We're rollin' now with tax and civil rights if we can just get this through the Senate," he told one of them. "I don't know how we'll ever do it, but we sure gonna try.". . .

Johnson's Role

Johnson carefully considered his role in trying to win Senate approval of the bill. "A President cannot ask the Congress to take a risk he will not take himself. He must be the combat general in the front lines. . . . I gave to this fight everything I had in prestige, power, and commitment." But he understood that it would be a poor idea to become too involved in the day-to-day tactics on the Hill. It was unbecoming to a President, and senators would resent it as an inappropriate Executive intrusion on their legislative function. Also, "I deliberately tried to tone down my personal involvement in the daily struggle so that my colleagues on the Hill could take tactical responsibility—and credit." Nevertheless, he had no intention of leaving anything to chance or letting Senate allies design a strategy. The evening of February 10 he told Robert Kennedy and Nicholas Katzenbach how Senate Majority Leader Mike Mansfield should proceed in leading the bill through the Upper House. The following afternoon he gave Mansfield marching orders on the telephone and kept in close touch with him on evolving strategy.

Johnson believed that he could best help advance the bill by repeated public appeals. At a February press conference he made clear that he expected a filibuster in the Senate, but that he would oppose any attempt substantially to change the House bill. During the next five months, while the Senate debated civil rights, hardly a week went by without a restatement of Johnson's conviction that a law should be passed just like the one approved in the House. We are "committed" to the bill with "no wheels and no deals," he said. He also made clear that, having won most of his legislative agenda for the session, he was ready for a long filibuster. "They can filibuster until hell freezes over," he declared. "I'm not going to put anything on that floor until this is done."

Johnson used the prestige of his office in other ways to

advance the cause of civil rights. In June of 1964, after three young men, two northern whites and a southern black, disappeared in Mississippi, Lee White pressed Johnson to accept a request from the parents for a meeting. The President was reluctant to set a precedent, which might force him to see other parents in the future. When White, however, pointed out that the newspapers might make much of his refusal to meet, he gave in. And once committed, he turned the occasion to effective account, using the meeting to suggest that the full majesty of the government was behind the search for these young men and equal treatment under the law a civil rights bill would assure.

Getting Ev Dirksen

Yet Johnson did not confine his efforts to public statements and symbolic gestures. Behind the scenes he continually gave direction and energy to the Senate battle for a bill. In January, he told Roy Wilkins "to get on this bill" and get twenty-five Republican votes for cloture. "You're gonna have to persuade [Senate Republican Minority Leader Everett] Dirksen why this is in the interest of the Republican party," LBJ said.

He believed that the key to overcoming a filibuster and winning approval for the principal features of the House measure was to weaken resistance among southern senators and to enlist Dirksen in the fight. Kenny O'Donnell [a consultant to John F. Kennedy who stayed on at the White House during the transition period] remembers Johnson telling the southerners, "You've got a southern president and if you want to blow him out of the water, go right ahead and do it, but you boys will never see another one again. We're friends on the q.t. Would you rather have me administering the civil rights bill, or do you want to have Nixon or [Republican Bill] Scranton? You have to make up your minds."

Johnson's appeal was effective. . . .

Whatever gains he made with the southerners, Johnson saw Dirksen as the lynchpin in the fight. "They say I'm an arm-twister," Johnson told Roy Wilkins, "but I can't make a southerner change his spots any more than I can make a leopard change 'em. . . . I'm no magician. I'm gonna be with ya, and I'm gonna help everywhere I can." But others need-ed to join in, especially Dirksen, whom he told could estab-lish a special place for himself in history by recognizing that civil rights reform was inevitable. He used the example of Senator Arthur Vandenberg of Michigan, whose shift from isolationism to internationalism during World War II won him a historical reputation as a statesman. At the same time, Johnson told Humphrey: "Now you know that this bill can't pass unless you get Ev Dirksen. You and I are going to get him. You make up your mind now that you've got to spend time with Ev Dirksen. You've got to let him have a piece of the action. He's got to look good all the time."

Humphrey, having arrived at the same conclusion, flat-tered and courted Dirksen at every turn. "I began a public massage of his ego," Humphrey writes, "and appealed to his vanity. I said he should look upon this issue as 'a moral, not a partisan one.' The gentle pressure left room for *him* to be the historically important figure in our struggle, the statesman above partisanship, . . . the master builder of a legislative edifice that would last forever. He liked it." Humphrey, as he said later, was ready to kiss "Dirksen's ass on the Capitol steps." Yet Humphrey also felt that as much as Dirksen liked the stroking, his "sense of history and his place in it" would ultimately be the difference in winning his support. Johnson agreed and egged Humphrey on.

Humphrey, in fact, had a better sense of how to man-age Dirksen and other senators than Johnson. When Dirk-sen wanted to schedule a cloture vote at the end of April, after a month's debate, Humphrey, with Johnson's help, convinced him to wait. No Senate filibuster had ever been ended before by cloture, and Humphrey foresaw that additional weeks of debate would be needed before such a groundbreaking development could occur. . . .

On June 10, after seventy-five days of debate, the Senate took a cloture vote. The night before, Johnson called Humphrey to ask whether he had the sixty-seven votes, or two-thirds needed to end the debate. "I think we have enough," Humphrey replied. Johnson wasn't satisfied. "I don't want to know what you think. What's the vote going to be? How many do you have?" Confident of only sixty-six supporters, Humphrey spent the evening working on three southwestern Democrats whose votes were not certain. Though Johnson largely left the lobbying and head counting to Humphrey, he had promised a Central Arizona water project to Carl Hayden for his backing—a vote which seemed likely to tip several other senators to the administration's side, including the two from Nevada. . . .

Predicting that they would get sixty-nine votes, Humphrey followed the proceedings with keen anticipation. Senator Clair Engle of California, who was dying of a brain tumor and could not speak, arrived in a wheelchair and pointed to his eye when called to vote. The final tally of 71 to 29 exceeded Humphrey's expectations. He "involuntarily" raised his arms over his head at what he saw as the culmination of a lifetime in politics fighting for equal rights.

Johnson took great satisfaction from this historic gain. Should we have a major signing ceremony or should we do it quietly? Johnson asked legislative aide Lee White. "It's so monumental," White answered. "It's equivalent to signing an Emancipation Proclamation, and ought to have all the possible attention you can focus on it." In a simple, dignified ceremony in the East Room of the White House attended by government officials, foreign diplomats, and black and white civil rights advocates, Johnson signed the bill before a national television audience on the evening of July 2. One panoramic photograph of Johnson at a small table before the more than 100 dignitaries seated in long rows conveys the sense of importance Johnson and his audience attached to the occasion.

"We believe all men are entitled to the blessings of liberty," Johnson said. "Yet millions are being deprived of those blessings—not because of their own failures, but because of the color of their skin. The reasons are deeply imbedded in history and tradition and the nature of man. We can understand—without rancor or hatred—how this happened, but it cannot continue. . . . Our Constitution, the foundation of our Republic, forbids it. The principles of our freedom forbid it. Morality forbids it. And the law I will sign tonight forbids it."

Yet Johnson also had his doubts and anxieties about an act of law that was about to change the social structure of the South. . . .

Johnson remained concerned that the South might resist the law. He feared it would lead to violence, bloodshed, public anarchy, economic dislocation, and defeat for his administration and the Democratic party in the 1964 campaign. In fact, nothing of the kind occurred, as Richard Russell predicted to Clarence Mitchell after his defeat on cloture. Because the civil rights bill was an act of Congress rather than "judge or court made law," Russell expected the South to accept the outcome with little trouble. It did. By the 1980s access to public facilities across the South for blacks was so commonly accepted that youngsters born in the 1970s could not imagine the segregated society of pre-1964.

Johnson Greatly Furthered the Cause of Civil Rights

Steven F. Lawson

Steven F. Lawson examines Johnson's decisions on civil rights and concludes that Johnson did more for the cause of black civil rights than any previous president. Johnson's choice, early in his presidency, to commit himself to the cause of racial equality resulted in the passage of three landmark laws: the Civil Rights Act of 1964, the Voting Rights Act of 1965, and the Civil Rights Act of 1968. While these legal remedies were insufficient to lift all blacks from poverty and powerlessness, Lawson concedes, they removed many of the legal barriers to first-class citizenship for African Americans. Lawson is a history professor at the University of Carolina at Greensboro and the author of *Black Ballots: Voting Rights in the South, 1944–1969*; *In Pursuit of Power: Southern Blacks and Electoral Politics, 1965–1982*; and *Running for Freedom: Civil Rights and Black Politics in America Since 1941.*

L YNDON JOHNSON SPENT THE FINAL MONTHS OF HIS LIFE filled with memories of the civil rights struggle that had greatly influenced his political career. In December 1972, at a symposium held at the Johnson Library, the former President heard an array of notable civil rights leaders commemorate his achievements in promoting racial justice. Several weeks later, during his last televised interview, Johnson spoke about civil rights. With the sound of explo-

Excerpted from "Civil Rights," by Steven F. Lawson, in *Exploring the Johnson Years*, edited by Robert A. Divine. Copyright ©1981. Reprinted by permission of the University of Texas Press.

sions in Southeast Asia fading and in the relaxed one-to-one format in which he clearly excelled, the retired chief executive passionately recalled for Walter Cronkite the way it was in demolishing Jim Crow. These farewell appearances, unlike so many other presentations during his presidential years, did not generate charges of a credibility gap. Indeed, Johnson's remarkable performance in the area of civil rights commanded overwhelming praise during his lifetime, and the accolades have continued seven years after his death. The Texas politician who so zealously courted consensus would be pleased with the widespread acclaim for his civil rights record. . . .

Opportunity from Tragedy

An accurate assessment of President Johnson's role in civil rights must take into account the distance traveled by the Texan since the beginning of his political career. Johnson developed gradually into a forceful advocate of racial emancipation. He was not a Negrophobe, but until 1957 he faithfully followed the southern congressional coalition in opposition to civil rights legislation. In 1957 and 1960, however, he used his position as Senate majority leader to maneuver passage of the first civil rights bills enacted since Reconstruction. At the time, commentators speculated that Johnson had changed his mind, hoping to enlarge his appeal nationally and to increase his availability as a Democratic presidential candidate. . . .

Several months after a long, hot season of demonstrations culminating in a mammoth march on Washington, D.C., tragedy presented Lyndon Johnson with the opportunity and power to prove how deep his concern for racial equality had grown. The murder of President Kennedy gave Johnson a chance to fulfill what he had come to recognize as his "moral obligation to every person of every skin color" and also to help his native South cast aside the oppressive race issue. The extension of freedom to blacks carried the potential of liberating white southerners from a caste system which economically and socially impoverished both races in the region. Tom Wicker, a native-born North Carolinian and an astute columnist for the *New York Times,* observes that Johnson "*as a Southerner* . . . was better placed than any man to recognize that full national unity and sweeping national progress . . . was not possible until the South had somehow been brought back into the Union." Building on this journalistic analysis, Professor T. Harry Williams remarks, "It has been insufficiently appreciated that Johnson believed the elimination of segregation would lift an onus from his section, would enable southern whites to stand as equals with that majority that had looked down on them for their racial practices."

Over the next five years, President Johnson signed into law three civil rights measures aimed at crushing the barriers of racial separation in public accommodations, education, and housing; extending equal employment opportunities; and expanding the right to vote. Their passage tested the President's ability to construct a consensus around controversial proposals and to patch up the coalition when it showed signs of cracking. President by virtue of assassination, Johnson had much to prove. Doris Kearns recalls his saying, "I knew that if I didn't get out in front on this issue, [the liberals] would get me. . . . I had to produce a civil rights bill that was even stronger than the one they'd have gotten if Kennedy had lived. Without this, I'd be dead before I could even begin." At the outset, the martyrdom of John Kennedy and vivid memories of southern blacks suffering [police commissioner] "Bull" Connor's racist brutality in Birmingham [in April 1963] created the right political atmosphere for Johnson to work his miracles in Congress. However, the chief executive had to exercise his formidable skills in a hostile climate once the feeling of national bereavement wore off and liberals attacked the administration's escalation of the war in Vietnam. Thus, passage of a series of monumental civil rights bills occurred under varying circumstances within a short span of years.

When Johnson took office on November 22, 1963, his predecessor's civil rights bill lay stalled in the Rules Committee of the House of Representatives. The Kennedy administration had conducted intensive negotiations with members of Congress in order to write legislation with sufficient clout and favorable chances for enactment. Such a proposal had emerged from the House Judiciary Committee, which was dominated by civil rights proponents. Committed to its passage as a memorial to the slain Kennedy, on November 27 President Johnson delivered a stirring civil-rights-as-redemption message to a grieving Congress. However, neither the preliminary work done in the preceding months nor the sorrow gripping the nation ensured swift approval of the administration-backed judiciary Committee bill. Before Johnson signed the measure into law on July 2, 1964, civil rights advocates had painstakingly broken fifty-seven days of filibustering in the Senate. At the same time, they had kept momentum for the bill rolling over the presidential primary bandwagon of George Wallace, the Alabama governor whose bigoted appeals found increasing acceptance in the North. . . .

Election and Beyond

Passage of the 1964 act came at a crucial juncture in the administration's involvement with the civil rights movement. Preparing to campaign for the presidency, Johnson did not want chaotic scenes of black agitation to frighten white voters into the camp of Barry Goldwater, the conservative Republican candidate who had voted against the civil rights bill. After the ceremony signing the measure into law, the President spoke privately with a group of civil rights leaders and admonished "that there be an understanding of the fact that the rights Negroes possessed could now be secured by law, making demonstrations unnecessary and possibly even self-defeating." Agreeing with the chief executive, each of his listeners except representatives from the Congress of Racial Equality (CORE) and the Student Nonviolent Coordinating Committee (SNCC), the most militant of the groups, urged blacks to suspend large-scale protests until after the November election. Although sporadic violence flared both in the South and the North, Johnson easily won the contest. However, brutal assaults on civil rights workers spending a summer in Mississippi and riots by blacks in urban ghettos of the North flashed ominous warnings that racial strife would bring new problems for the administration.

Elected President in his own right, Johnson preferred to postpone further legislative action on civil rights, but the resumption of mass protests in Selma, Alabama, in 1965 forced him to change his mind. The struggle for passage of the 1965 Voting Rights Act has received the fullest treatment of any aspect of Johnson's civil rights policies. Using documents in the Johnson Library, David Garrow's *Protest at Selma* and Steven Lawson's *Black Ballots* conclude that before Martin Luther King launched his demonstrations in Alabama, Johnson had authorized the Justice Department to sketch possible legislation removing obstacles that impeded black voter registration in the South. Lawyers at the Justice Department were roughing out their drafts when state troopers viciously assaulted a parade of protesters attempting to walk from Selma to Montgomery on Sunday, March 7, 1965. Both authors conclude the bloody attack ensured that the eventual bill "would be enacted into law, and with only minimal delay and no weakening amendments."

In a most interesting departure for others to follow, Garrow compares the unusually prompt passage of the Voting Rights Act with the prolonged deliberations that had preceded approval of the civil rights law a year earlier. He suggests that Congress reacted with greater speed to the Selma demonstrators than those in Birmingham because the former remained nonviolent and stuck to a single issue. This analysis emphasizes the impact of media coverage in shaping congressional responses to racial confrontations. Consideration should also be given to Johnson's augmented influence with the eighty-ninth Congress, which seated far more liberal members than those who had watched events unfold in Birmingham. Furthermore, a bill devoted to voting rights, long considered the foundation of representative government, had political advantages over a measure addressing the more controversial issues of education and employment. A comparison of mail received by the White House during the course of debates on the two civil rights bills might reveal the differences in public perception of the need for each piece of legislation. Nevertheless, in both instances, the violence inflicted upon peaceful civil rights activists in due course swung sentiment behind reform measures.

In contrast, the moral indignation that fostered enactment of these two powerful measures had subsided by the time a third proposal became law in 1968. The final legislative component in Johnson's civil rights trilogy, it combatted racial discrimination in housing and jury selection and punished those who interfered with civil rights workers encouraging the exercise of constitutionally guaranteed rights. Reflecting changing times, the act also included penalties for individuals who traveled across state lines to foment or participate in a riot. The consensus that sustained earlier legislative victories had fractured under the stress of the Vietnam War and ghetto riots, thus making passage of this omnibus bill a significant feat. . . .

Johnson's Response to Black Militancy

The most important issues arising from a study of the Civil Rights Act of 1968 concern Lyndon Johnson's responses to the changing configuration of the racial struggle. As the civil rights coalition diminished in size and white reactionary forces grew, Johnson refused to order a major retreat on the legislative front. However, in honoring his moral commitment to extend first-class citizenship, the President had to take into account the political considerations upsetting his legislative consensus. Critics have accused him of backing away from his firm support of civil rights after northern white voters exhibited their hostility not only to riots but to black militancy in general. James Harvey speculates that Johnson did not push the civil rights bill in 1966 because "he was thinking about the growing white backlash." However, such a conclusion, besides requiring verification, ignores the possibility that black agitation may have stiffened Johnson's resolve to persist in prying loose the civil rights bill from Congress.

The effects of rising black aggressiveness on White House policy offer exciting avenues for research. As SNCC and CORE abandoned white liberals and blacks in the ghettos spontaneously released their rage against symbols of white authority, the Johnson administration rushed to reinforce advocates of peaceful change. The prospects of racial violence in the cities, beginning with the summer of 1964, prompted Johnson advisers to find ways, as Eric Goldman notes, "to help the established Negro leaders, who may well be losing control of the civil rights movement, to reestablish control and keep the movement going in its legitimate direction." To accomplish this aim demanded sensitivity and finesse. Harry McPherson, who succeeded Lee White as Johnson's principal counselor on race, recalls the problem facing his boss: "Johnson . . . understood that while he needed [Whitney] Young and [Roy] Wilkins and [A. Philip] Randolph and [Bayard] Rustin, that his embrace of them would endanger them after a short time with the Negro community. And yet he needed them and did use them in urgent situations." An exchange of memoranda in September 1966 between McPherson and Attorney General Katzenbach delineates this thorny dilemma. The White House aide pointed out that "our lines of communication to the movement run generally . . . to the older Negro establishment. We have very few contacts with younger Negro leaders. We *must* develop these contacts." Katzenbach responded on a note of pessimism, contending that the "younger leaders who now exist are precisely those who . . . have consistently chosen an 'outside course': that is, Stokely Carmichael." Nevertheless, he did recommend that the National Association for the Advancement of Colored People (NAACP), the Urban League, and the Southern Christian Leadership Conference (SCLC) consider "establishing a militant but peaceful organization of young people who could successfully compete with SNCC." Nothing specific came of the idea, but the administration's attempts to develop alternatives to black violence and to bolster the position of conventional civil rights leaders merit a full investigation.

The annual outbreak of summer riots made matters worse for the White House. In contrast to the brutality suffered by peaceful protesters, the violence perpetrated by black mobs preaching physical retaliation hurt the administration politically. Recognizing that "every night of rioting costs us the support of thousands," one Johnson lieutenant suggested that the chief executive "appeal to the good sense and conscience of the country both white and Negro. Denounce violence, but recognize frustration. Be firm in the insistence on obedience to law." Plagued by urban upheavals that increased in intensity each year during his second term, Johnson adopted a moderate course of action. Aimed at extending victories won by his loyal civil rights allies, the President's program also acknowledged the fears for personal safety voiced by Americans, white and black. McPherson echoes the difficulty liberals experienced in striking a delicately balanced response: "'By God, there's law and order here. You can't get away with this,' followed by 'Of course we understand why you rioted. We know you could hardly do anything else.'" How to respond to social and economic maladies infecting the ghettos without "rewarding the rioters" continuously perplexed the President and his advisers. . . .

Achievement and Limitations

The Johnson years were a watershed in the struggle for racial equality in the United States. More than any president before him, Lyndon Johnson helped blacks discard the legal barriers blocking the attainment of first-class citizenship. Most of the uncompleted civil rights items on the legislative agenda he had inherited upon taking office in 1963 were enacted by the time he retired to his Texas ranch in 1969. The kind of president capable of ordering the public execution of Jim Crow, Johnson was not Eric Goldman's "wrong man from the wrong place at the wrong time under the wrong circumstances." Combining moral fervor and a finely honed sense of political timing, Johnson translated the ideals of civil rights protesters into practical statutory language.

However, as the goals of the racial struggle leaped beyond integration and strict equality under law, the President displayed the limitations of modern liberal reformers. By philosophy and style, he was suited for achieving legislative breakthroughs within the traditional boundaries of the constitutional system. But, when administration achievements boosted black expectations of immediate economic and political power, the conventional remedies of color-blind treatment decreed by law were inadequate. The Civil Rights Act of 1964 opened up public accommodations to black patrons, but it did not enable them to acquire the funds to afford admission. The 1965 Voting Rights Act removed discriminatory suffrage requirements in the South, but it stopped short of eliminating methods of diluting the franchise, and it did not supply the resources for mobilizing the potency of black ballots. The

Civil Rights Act of 1968 outlawed racial bias in the sale of houses and the rental of apartments, but it did not address

---

Keeping a Lid on Demonstrations

Bruce Miroff describes one of Johnson's methods for attempting to control civil rights demonstrations.

One of the Johnson Administration's principal worries was the potential escalation of civil rights demonstrations. As Eric Goldman has observed, Lyndon Johnson "was no enthusiast of mass demonstrations." His enthusiasm grew even fainter during the election year of 1964, when demonstrations threatened to turn white voters against a President identified with the black cause. Despite these feelings, Johnson did not take a public stand against demonstrations, as had President Kennedy in the summer of 1963. As Lee White, a presidential assistant whose chief responsibility was the field of civil rights, observed in a memo to Johnson on August 19, 1964, "The Administration has never publicly urged discontinuance of demonstrations or intimated that there was anything improper [about them]. . . ."

In private conferences, however, President Johnson made clear his desire to see demonstrations held to a minimum. After signing the 1964 Civil Rights Act on July 2, for example, he met with civil rights leaders and told them that the rights of blacks were now secured by law, ". . . making demonstrations unnecessary and possibly even self-defeating." Johnson avoided such expressions in public, where they might alienate or even activate black militants; privately he urged the established black leadership to keep matters under control.

Bruce Miroff, "Presidential Leverage over Social Movements: The Johnson White House and Civil Rights," *Journal of Politics*, vol. 43, no. 1, February 1981.

the problem of furnishing adequate incomes so that blacks could escape the slums. In this second Reconstruction as in the first, the unconquered frontier bordering full emancipation was economic.

The Johnson administration's approach to solving racial problems by a redistribution of economic and political power should be examined. In his Howard University address [in June 1965], the President passionately asserted the need to transcend ordinary solutions. He pointed the way toward affirmative action to compensate for past abuses, and investigators should search for documentary clues to measure how much success his regime had in reversing the effects of previous discrimination in education, politics, and employment. How did the chief executive view busing? What did he do to foster realignment of the Democratic party in fulfillment of its 1964 convention pledge to encourage increased representation by minorities? How did the administration view quotas for hiring? These questions and others must be asked to determine how far Johnson was willing to move in challenging the vestiges of racial inequality.

By liberal standards, Lyndon Johnson was the foremost practitioner of civil rights ever to occupy the White House. His greatest successes, T. Harry Williams notes, emerged from "measured manipulated change within the system and a consensus built on compromise." However, in staking out a middle ground of reform between white conservatives and black militants, he had trouble holding the center together. The challenge for future historians of the Johnson administration is to improve upon these extemporaneous comments of Harry McPherson:

> Johnson and I and Bill Moyers and many of us around the White House were Southern liberals. We believe in integration, we believe in reason, we believe that things are going to be fine if men of good will get together and if we put down the racists. We thought that if we could

be a sort of super YMCA saying "You can go to school with us, we'll educate you, train you, will get better housing" and all that sort of stuff. But we haven't really fixed it at the base which is money, security, families holding together, some power that is given to them by money.

. . . To date, the initial judgment that Lyndon Johnson played a striking role in promoting racial equality remains intact. The 1972 symposium that unveiled the civil rights papers brought to the speaker's rostrum Julian Bond, a former SNCC member, a caustic critic of Johnson's Vietnam policy, and one of the first blacks elected to the Georgia legislature after the Voting Rights Act of 1965. Addressing an audience gathered at the Johnson Library, the young lawmaker remarked about the library's namesake that "when the forces demanded and the mood permitted, for once an activist, human-hearted man had his hands on the levers of power and a vision beyond the next election. He was there when we and the Nation needed him, and, oh my God, do I wish he was there now." After inspecting the library's holdings it may be asked, are these words any less timely three presidential regimes later?

Johnson's Civil Rights Efforts Did Not Benefit Most Blacks

James C. Harvey

James C. Harvey argues that the three major bills passed during the Johnson presidency primarily benefited the black middle class and had virtually no impact on the masses of poor blacks in city ghettos or in rural areas. Removing legal barriers to public accommodations, the polls, and housing meant little to those who had no jobs or income, according to the author. Harvey maintains that the failure of Johnson's civil rights efforts stemmed from Johnson's weak enforcement of the new laws, his decision to eliminate a system for coordinating civil rights efforts, and his failure to adequately fund civil rights and poverty programs. Harvey is the author of *Civil Rights During the Kennedy Administration* and *Black Civil Rights During the Johnson Administration*, from which the following essay was excerpted.

OVERALL, MORE GAINS WERE MADE IN DESEGREGATING some of America's major institutions during the Johnson administration than in any previous ones of the modern presidency. Furthermore, the three major civil rights bills enacted during his five years of office were more far-reaching than the ones passed in 1957 and 1960 which were confined to weak efforts in the area of voting. The Civil Rights Act of 1964 was truly an omnibus bill covering many different areas. The Voting Rights Act of 1965 dealt

Excerpted from *Black Civil Rights During the Johnson Administration*, by James C. Harvey (Jackson: University and College Press of Mississippi, 1973). Reprinted by permission of the publisher.

with voting, and it was a comparatively strong bill. The Civil Rights Act of 1968 was concerned with several policy areas, but the housing section was the most important covering in theory around 80 percent of the nation's housing after it went through the three stages of implementation.

President Johnson was aware that there was still much left to be done to bring black people into the mainstream as he was about to leave office. On December 6, 1968, he received the first achievement award of the United Negro College Fund for "distinguished leadership and significant achievements in the field of education and civil rights." In accepting the award, the president stated that he intended to encourage future presidents to continue "the very long march" for civil rights. He also declared that he hoped that his administration's efforts in civil rights might represent a small step or two forward in that long march in the years ahead.

On December 17, 1968, several hundred black federal government officials held a farewell reception for the president at the Federal City Club in Washington, D.C. He again referred, in language that must have sounded patronizing to some blacks, to the long march ahead when he declared: "What we've got to learn is that we've got a long way to walk, and there are going to be a lot of bruised and bloody feet. You're just like a grandson. You've just learned to walk." He claimed that the civil rights legislation passed during his administration had opened the chance of a "marvelous future." However, he said:

> We waste our time, and we defraud ourselves if we look back on what we've accomplished. Those accomplishments were infinitesimal in the face of the tasks still to be completed and good just to pep us up for the work ahead.
>
> You are the vanguard. Behind you there are millions of others who are proud that a Negro is a Justice of the

Supreme Court . . . yet these millions of Americans cannot get a decent job. These are the Negroes who are locked in poverty, locked in ill paying jobs, locked out of American promise.

Some of these millions, especially the young, want a place in the prosperous democracy that they cannot find. Some of them feel that their only course is to attack the institutions of this society and all who made it.

The quality of life in America five years from now or 10 years from now will depend on how the nation responds to the needs and desires of these millions of impoverished Negroes.

If we turn a deaf ear to them, or if we try to patronize them, or if we simply try to suppress their impatience and deny its causes then we are not going to solve anything. All we are going to do is just compound our troubles.

Just before leaving office, President Johnson made the following remarks in his last State of the Union address on January 14, 1969:

The Nation's commitments in the field of civil rights began with the Declaration of Independence. They were extended by the 13th, 14th, and 15th amendments. They have been powerfully strengthened by the enactment of three far-reaching civil rights laws within the past five years, that this Congress, in its wisdom, passed. On January 1 of this year, the Fair Housing Act of 1968 covered over 20 million American houses and apartments. The prohibition against racial discrimination in that Act should be remembered and it should be vigorously enforced throughout the land.

I believe we should also extend the vital provisions of the Voting Rights Act for another 5 years.

The three major civil rights bills that passed during Johnson's term of office, though important, chiefly benefited the black middle class. They had little or no effect on the black masses located in the ghettos or in rural poverty areas. What good was it to be able to eat or sleep at the Holiday Inn if one could not afford it? Of what importance was it to the black man without a job to find out that if he could afford it he might possibly be able to purchase a home in the plush suburbs? As one writer, Donald H. Smith, pointed out, none of the legislation had "begun to show any appreciable difference in the ghettos of our huge urban complexes. A man who lives in a slum tenement, who has no job, and who has lost his self-respect because he must accept charity, finds little comfort in the knowledge his Southern brother can now vote and sleep in white hotels. In fact, the more he hears on television how much better off he is, and how much conditions have changed, the more bitter he becomes."

Yet, in spite of these serious deficiencies, in a certain sense many blacks would be concerned about civil rights for a long time to come, though the civil rights movement, coinciding with the push for major legislation, seemed to many people by the late 1960s to be dead. As Alice Walker, a brilliant young black writer, noted, many of the white liberals and civil rights sponsors were disenchanted in seeing that relatively little if anything had been accomplished. Moreover, she wrote:

> The movement is dead to the white man because it no longer interests him. And it no longer interests him because he can afford to be uninterested; he does not have to live by it, with it, or for it as Negroes must. He can take a rest from the news of the beatings, killings and arrests that reach him from the North and South—if his skin is white. Negroes cannot now and will never be able to take a rest from the injustices that plague them for they—not the white man—are the target.

What good was the civil rights movement? If it had just given this country Dr. King, a leader of conscience once in our lifetime, it would have been enough. If it had just taken black eyes off white television stories, it would have been enough.

If the civil rights movement is "dead," and if it gave us nothing else, it gave us each other forever. It gave us some bread, some of us shelter, some of us knowledge and pride, all of us comfort. It gave us our children, our husbands, our brothers, our fathers, as men reborn and with purpose for living. It broke the pattern of black servitude in this country. It shattered "the phony promise" of white soap operas that sucked away so many pitiful lives. It gave us history and men better than Presidents. It gave us houses, unselfish men of courage and strength, for our little boys to follow. It gave us hope for tomorrow. It called us to life.

Because we live, it can never die.

In summary, it is difficult to evaluate the accomplishments of the Johnson administration in any absolute sense. True, the statistics showed more black employment, more school desegregation in the South; more blacks could vote in the South; they had gained more access to public accommodations such as restaurants and motels. Moreover, more major civil rights bills (three) had been pushed through than during any of the previous modern administrations.

However, the groundwork for the act of 1964 was laid by the Kennedy administration, and in a sense its passage was a tribute to Kennedy's memory more than anything accomplished by Johnson. The Voting Rights Act of 1965 came largely as a reaction to the events in Alabama. In the case of the Civil Rights Act of 1968 with its housing section, Clarence Mitchell deserves more credit for its passage than Johnson himself. However, the president did utilize a number of levers at his disposal to assist in the passage of these laws, including the following: public addresses, messages to Congress, meetings with interested groups, private communications with key congressmen, and the like.

Johnson's Poor Administration

Nevertheless, if President Johnson is to be faulted it is not so much in his role as a legislator but in that of administration. No president can ever merely issue an order and assume that it will be carried out. However, if he is persistent in his demands on the bureaucracy he will be heard. It seems as though once a bill had been passed into law, he gave its enforcement relatively little attention. Needless to say, without his pressure and support the bureaucracy was often unable or unwilling to cope with the counter-pressures of strategically placed southern congressmen and the recalcitrance of their white constituents in opposition to the implementation of civil rights laws. Moreover, many members of the vast bureaucracy were at best indifferent, if not hostile, to the cause of civil rights for black people. This problem merely compounded some of the weaknesses in the bills, such as the inadequate authority given to the Economic Employment Opportunity Commission in the Act of 1964.

Southern political leaders, with the backing of their white constituents, often used the language of federalism and states' rights to buttress white supremacy in their states. As one black political scientist, Hanes Walton, Jr., pointed out:

> For the most part, the problems of federalism for blacks started through reluctance of the federal government to move in and vigorously defend the rights of blacks because of the possibility of interfering with the doctrine of states' rights. Whether the problem is simply the national government's deference to the rights of states, or whether it is the ability of states to use the least invasion

of their sovereignty to embarrass the federal government by crying authoritarianism and forcing the federal government to move slowly, cautiously, or not at all is irrelevant. Moreover, whether or not southerners have more power in Congress and more influence with presidential candidates, though significant in the final analysis, is not sufficient. The fact remains that the major problem of American federalism is neither the system itself, not its inbred weaknesses, but its unwillingness, because of entrenched racism, to effectively establish and protect black rights. . . . The cry of states losing their rights to the federal government has become in many instances only a smoke screen to deny blacks their full civil rights.

To overcome the tendency of states' rights to hurt the cause of civil rights for black people, strong presidential leadership was needed. It never was forthcoming.

President Johnson missed a golden opportunity when he dismantled the vehicle he had established early in 1965 for a centralized coordination of civil rights efforts under the chairmanship of Vice-President Humphrey. If he had retained that instrumentality and given it his full support there would have been much greater progress than there was in implementing civil rights. However, Johnson decided for unknown reasons not to maintain this coordinated effort. One can only speculate that he gave in to southern pressures in return for support of an increasingly unpopular war. Moreover, he may not have wished to magnify the image of the vice-president as a champion of civil rights. In any case, the major responsibilities for coordination were turned over to the attorney general—for the all-important Title VI enforcement; but there was never the emphasis needed in the Justice Department to make the programs work. The same general statement can be made about the other agencies dealing with civil rights enforcement other than under Title VI. Diffusion of authority meant civil rights would suffer.

One can agree with Dick Gregory who often said that he did not want his civil rights "on an installment plan." After all, why should black people have to struggle so hard for rights as American citizens which should be automatically theirs? They have the responsibilities, e.g., paying taxes and serving in the armed forces. Blacks should, therefore, also have the rights of citizenship. However, there is another dimension of the problem. No matter what civil rights laws were passed and implemented by the Johnson administration, these measures did not deal adequately with the cold hard facts of being poor and black. Civil rights, to be fully fruitful, have to be supplemented with adequate jobs and incomes. They are so intertwined that adequate jobs and income should be regarded as civil rights. The efforts made to deal with the war on poverty were pitifully inadequate in the Johnson administration, Much as the president discussed the possibility of having both "guns and butter" and being able to wage a battle against poverty as well as fight in Vietnam, the domestic front always took the back seat. Congress never funded the civil rights and poverty programs adequately. Top priority went to the war abroad, and despite some splendid rhetoric at times on the part of the president, the war to eliminate poverty and racism at home never seriously got off the ground. The black middle class fared somewhat better, but at the end of the Johnson administration the black masses were if anything in some respects worse off than before. This is not to say, however, that all blacks did not still suffer from discrimination.

PRESIDENTS
and their
DECISIONS

CHAPTER
3

ESCALATING THE VIETNAM WAR

The Summer of 1965: Johnson Americanizes the War

Larry Berman

Johnson began to order bombing raids and send relatively small numbers of combat troops to Vietnam in August 1964. He made perhaps the most fateful decision of his presidency in July 1965, when he authorized sending 175,000 to 200,000 troops to Vietnam and promised to send more if needed. Larry Berman writes that while deliberating this decision, Johnson sought the opinions of numerous top-level advisers, one of whom advised him to pull out while most advocated large increases of troops and combat activities against North Vietnam. Berman explains that Johnson was fully aware that the war would cost billions of dollars, last up to five years, and require up to 600,000 soldiers without guaranteeing victory. Johnson decided to pursue escalation while misleading the public about the size of his commitment and its costs. Berman is a professor and acting director of the University of California, Davis, Washington Center and the author of *Lyndon Johnson's War: The Road to Stalemate in Vietnam* and *Planning a Tragedy: The Americanization of the War in Vietnam*.

T HROUGHOUT JUNE AND JULY 1965 THE QUESTION OF Americanizing the war was at the center of all foreign policy discussion. Undersecretary of State George Ball first attempted to influence President Johnson's future ability to control events. In an 18 June memorandum entitled

Excerpted from "Coming to Grips with Lyndon Johnson's War," by Larry Berman, *Diplomatic History*, vol. 17, no. 4 (1993), pp. 523–31. Reprinted by permission of Blackwell Publishers.

"Keeping the Power of Decision in the South Vietnam Crisis," Ball argued that the United States was on the threshold of a new war. "In raising our commitment from 50,000 to 100,000 or more men and deploying most of the increment in combat roles we were beginning a new war—the United States directly against the Viet Cong. The President's most difficult continuing problem in South Vietnam is to prevent 'things' from getting into the saddle—or, in other words, to keep control of policy and prevent the momentum of events from taking command."

The president needed to understand the effect of losing control: "Perhaps the large-scale introduction of American forces with their concentrated fire power will force Hanoi and the Viet Cong to the decision we are seeking. On the other hand, we may not be able to fight the war successfully enough—even with 500,000 Americans in South Vietnam we must have more evidence than we now have that our troops will not bog down in the jungles and rice paddies—while we slowly blow the country to pieces." Ball tried to review the French experience for Johnson, reminding the president that "the French fought a war in Vietnam, and were finally defeated—after seven years of bloody struggle and when they still had 250,000 combat-hardened veterans in the field, supported by an army of 205,000 South Vietnamese. To be sure, the French were fighting a colonial war while we are fighting to stop aggression. But when we have put enough Americans on the ground in South Vietnam to give the appearance of a white man's war, the distinction as to our ultimate purpose will have less and less practical effect."

Ball urged the president to act cautiously—make a commitment to the one hundred thousand level, but no more. The summer would then be used as a test of U.S. military performance and South Vietnam's resolve. Ball focused on the political context in South Vietnam. "We cannot be sure how far the cancer has infected the whole body politic of South Vietnam and whether we can do more than administer a cobalt treatment to a terminal case." (In a later memorandum Ball wrote "politically, South Vietnam is a lost cause. The country is bled white from twenty years of war and the people are sick of it. . . . Hanoi has a government and a purpose and a discipline. The 'government' in Saigon is a travesty. In a very real sense, South Vietnam is a country with an army and no government. In my view, a deep commitment of United States forces in a land war in South Vietnam would be a catastrophic error. If ever there was an occasion for a tactical withdrawal, this is it.") Ball recommended that the president direct his top advisers to prepare a plan for accelerating the land war, a plan for a vigorous diplomatic offensive designed to bring about a political settlement; and, perhaps most difficult, plans for bringing about a military or political solution—"short of the ultimate U.S. objectives—that can be attained without the substantial further commitment of U.S. forces." Ball recognized that his last proposal should "be regarded as plans for cutting losses and eventually disengaging from an untenable situation."

Robert McNamara's Recommendations

Ball's arguments would have little influence on policymakers. In retrospect there was a remarkable cogency to his position that fell on deaf ears. Ball was isolated from the majority opinion among policymakers, an undersecretary of state taking on the highest ranking officials in government—beginning with the Secretary of Defense, Robert McNamara, and with Ball's own superior, Secretary of State Dean Rusk. On 26 June McNamara circulated his "Program of Expanded Military and Political Moves with Respect to Vietnam." McNamara admitted that the Vietcong were clearly winning the war and that "the tide almost certainly cannot begin to turn in less than a few months and may not for a year or more; the war is one of attrition and will be a long one." McNamara defined winning as the creation of "conditions for a favorable settlement by demonstrating to the VC/DRV [Vietcong/Democratic Republic of (North) Vietnam] that the odds are against their winning. Under present conditions, however, the chances of achieving this objective are small—and the VC are winning now—largely because the ratio of guerrilla to anti-guerrilla forces is unfavorable to the government." Secretary McNamara developed three options for the president: (1) cut U.S. losses and withdraw with the best conditions that could be arranged; (2) continue at about the present level, with U.S. forces limited to about seventy-five thousand, holding on and playing for the breaks while recognizing that the U.S. position would probably grow weaker; (3) expand substantially the U.S. military pressure against the Vietcong in the South and the North Vietnamese in the North. At the same time launch a vigorous effort on the political side to get negotiations started.

McNamara unequivocally supported the third option— a series of expanded military moves as prerequisites for a negotiated settlement on U.S. terms. The secretary recommended that US/GVN [Republic of (South) Vietnam] ground strength be increased to whatever force levels were necessary to show the VC that they "cannot win." The increases would bring U.S. and third-country troop levels to forty-four battalions and be accomplished by a call-up of one hundred thousand reserves. McNamara's military recommendations included a quarantine on the movement of all war supplies into North Vietnam, the mining of North Vietnam's (DRV) harbors, the destruction of all rail and highway bridges from China to Hanoi, armed reconnaissance of communication lines from China, destruction of all war-making supplies inside of North Vietnam, and destruction of all airfields and SAM [surface to air missile] sites.

Conflicting Views

Writing directly to McNamara on 30 June, National Security Adviser McGeorge Bundy criticized the secretary's position, deriding it as "rash to the point of folly." Bundy was critical of tripling the U.S. air effort "when the value of the air action we have taken is sharply disputed." It was also preposterous to consider mining "at a time when nearly everyone agrees the real question is not in Hanoi, but in South Vietnam." Bundy was extremely critical of McNamara's proposed deployment figure, arguing that a 200,000-man level was based "simply on the increasing weakness of Vietnamese forces. But this is a slippery slope toward the U.S. responsibility and corresponding fecklessness on the Vietnamese side." Bundy noted that McNamara's paper "omits examination of the upper limit of U.S. liability." Bundy asked, "If we need 200 thousand men now for these quite limited missions, may we not need 400 thousand later? Is this a rational course of action? Is there any real prospect that U.S. regular forces can conduct the antiguerrilla operations which would probably remain the central problem in South Vietnam?" Bundy concluded with a question: "What is the real object of the exercise? If it is to get to the conference table, what results do we seek there? Still more brutally, do we want to invest 200,000 men to cover an eventual retreat? Can we not do that just as well where we are?"

Assistant Secretary of State William Bundy joined the battle with a memorandum and position paper entitled "A Middle Way Course of Action in South Vietnam." The plan involved moving ahead slowly and testing military capabilities and limits. Bundy believed that his plan avoided the pitfalls of either Ball's or McNamara's alternatives. "It may not give us quite as much chance of a successful outcome as the major military actions proposed in the McNamara memo, but it avoids to a major extent the very serious risks involved in this program in any case, and the far more disastrous outcome that would eventuate if we acted along the lines of the McNamara memo and still lost South Vietnam." William Bundy's program rejected withdrawal or negotiated concessions and equally rejected a decision to raise U.S. force levels above eighty-five thousand. In Bundy's carefully selected words the program provided "a fair test" because "we simply do not know, and probably cannot know, whether raising the U.S. force level and combat involvement would (1) cause the Vietnamese government and especially the army to let up (2) create adverse public reactions to our whole presence on 'white men' and 'like the French' grounds."

Johnson next heard from Secretary of State Dean Rusk. In a rare personal memorandum to the president on 1 July that had not been circulated to the other principals, Rusk argued that "the central objective of the United States in South Vietnam must be to insure that North Vietnam not succeed in taking over or determining the future of South

President Johnson's decision to escalate the war in Vietnam resulted in the deployment of an additional 175,000 to 200,000 troops in July 1965.

Vietnam by force, i.e. again defined as denial. We must accomplish this objective without a general war if possible." The war aim of the United States was not and could not be concerned with hypothetical issues such as what the South Vietnamese people would do if left alone: "The sole basis for employing U.S. forces is the aggression from the North." If this aggression were removed, the U.S. forces would also leave. Rusk rejected Ball's position by casting the issue within a much broader context with significant consequences. "There can be no serious debate about the fact that we have a commitment to assist the South Vietnamese to resist aggression from the North. . . . The integrity of the U.S. commitment is the principal pillar of peace throughout the world. If that commitment becomes unreliable, the communist world would draw conclusions that would lead to our ruin and almost certainly to a catastrophic war.". . .

President Johnson now decided to send Secretary McNamara to Vietnam, ostensibly to meet with General Westmoreland and ascertain force requirements. McNamara's trip received much public attention, and the president's public statement hinted at the possibility of major escalation. On the second day of McNamara's visit to Saigon, he received a back channel cable of the utmost importance from his deputy, Cyrus Vance. "Yesterday I met three times with highest authority [President Johnson] on actions associated with 34 battalion plan," the cable read. (The remaining ten battalions of the forty-four-battalion request were to come from Korea and Australia.) Vance went on to summarize what Johnson had told him. (This is perhaps the most significant declassification available to scholars):

1. It is his current intention to proceed with 34 battalion plan.

2. It is impossible for him to submit supplementary budget request of more than $300–$400 million to Congress before next January.

3. If larger request is made to Congress, he believes this will kill domestic legislative program.

4. We should be prepared to explain to the Congress that we have adequate authority and funds, by use of deficit financing, $700 million supplemental [appropriation] and possible small current supplemental to finance recommended operations until next January, when we will be able to come up with clear and precise figures as to what is required.

I asked highest authority whether request for legislation authorizing call-up of reserves and extension of tours of duty would be acceptable in the light of his comments concerning domestic program, and he said that it would.

I pointed out that we would have great difficulties with Senator [John] Stennis concerning this course of action. He said that he recognized that but we would just have to bull it through. He requested that I talk to Senator [Richard] Russell Monday and I will.

Johnson had clearly made his decision to Americanize the war by changing the entire context of commitment. When McNamara returned to Washington on 20 July he presented the president with a report warning of the incipient collapse of South Vietnam. McNamara elaborated and defended an option of "expand[ing] promptly and substantially the US military pressure . . . while launching a vigorous effort on the political side." McNamara called for approval of Westmoreland's request for 100,000 more American troops, which would bring the American troop level up to thirty-four battalions (175,000 troops), or forty-four battalions (200,000) if third-country troops (principally Korean) proved available. He indicated that a twenty-seven-battalion second-phase increase of another 100,000 men might be needed by early 1966, with further increments thereafter. McNamara also urged the president to ask Congress to permit calling up 235,000 reservists to active service and to provide a supplemental appropriation to cover the increased costs of the war.

The McNamara proposal became the focal point of extensive White House deliberations over the next few days. At both the NSC [National Security Council] meeting of 21 July and the Joint Chiefs meeting the following day, Johnson provides ample evidence of his awareness that an upper limit deployment might very well be in the range of six hundred thousand men. At one meeting he asked the Joint Chiefs "do all of you think the Congress and the people will go along with 600,000 people and billions of dollars being spent 10,000 miles away?" The declassified minutes from the meetings of 21 July show that Johnson challenged Ball to prove a case that could not be proven— that the consequences of non-engagement (really disengagement via neutralization) would be better than military engagement. "You have pointed out the danger," President Johnson told Ball, "but you haven't really proposed an alternative course." To illustrate just how intent policymakers had become in molding their local ally during the meeting, Henry Cabot Lodge noted that "there is not a tradition of a national government in Saigon. There are no roots in the country. Not until there is tranquility can you have any stability. I don't think we ought to take this government seriously. There is simply no one who can do anything. We have to do what we think we ought to do regardless of what the Saigon government does. As we move ahead on a new phase, we have the right and the duty to do certain things with or without the government's approval."

Ball's Final Day in Court

Ball's final day in court came that afternoon when he faced the president and his peers. Ball told the group that

we cannot win. . . . The war will be long and protracted.

The most we can hope for is a messy conclusion. There remains a great danger of intrusion by the Chinese. But the biggest problem is the problem of the long war. The Korean experience was a galling one. The correlation between Korean casualties and public opinion showed support stabilized at 50 percent. As casualties increase, the pressure to strike at the very jugular of North Vietnam will become very great. I am concerned about world opinion. If we could win in a year's time, and win decisively, world opinion would be alright. However, if the war is long and protracted, as I believe it will be, then we will suffer because the world's greatest power cannot defeat guerrillas.

Reprinted below is part of the dialogue that followed Ball's recommendation:

The President: But George, wouldn't all these countries say that Uncle Sam was a paper tiger, wouldn't we lose credibility breaking the word of three presidents, if we did as you have proposed? It would seem to be an irresponsible blow. But I gather you don't think so?

Ball: No sir. The worse blow would be that the mightiest power on earth is unable to defeat a handful of guerrillas.

The President: Then you are not basically troubled by what the world would say about our pulling out?

Ball: If we were actively helping a country with a stable government, it would be a vastly different story. Western Europeans look upon us as if we got ourselves into an imprudent situation.

McNamara: Ky will fall soon. He is weak. We can't have elections there until there is physical security, and even then there will be no elections because as Cabot said, there is no democratic tradition.

McGeorge Bundy: To accept Ball's argument would be a radical switch in policy without visible evidence that it should be done. George's analysis gives no weight to losses suffered by the other side. The world, the country, and the Vietnamese people would have alarming reactions if we got out.

Rusk: If the communist world found out that the United States would not pursue its commitment to the end, there was no telling where they would stop their expansionism.

Lodge: I feel there is greater threat to start World War III if we don't go in. Can't we see the similarity to our indolence at Munich? I simply can't be as pessimistic as Ball. We have great seaports in Vietnam. We don't need to fight on roads. We have the sea. Let us visualize meeting the VC on our own terms. We don't have to spend all our time in the jungles. If we can secure our bases, the Vietnamese can secure, in time, a political movement to, one, apprehend the terrorists, and two, give intelligence to the government. The procedures for this are known. . . . The Vietnamese have been dealt more casualties than, per capita, we suffered in the Civil War. The Vietnamese soldier is an uncomplaining soldier. He has ideas he will die for.

Meeting with the Joint Chiefs

The following day President Johnson met with the Joint Chiefs to hear their responses to McNamara's program. The chiefs were in a position similar to Ball, in the sense of advocating a policy extreme. The president began the meeting by identifying the three options: "The options open to us are: one, leave the country, with as little loss as possible; two, maintain present force and lose slowly; three, add 100,000 men, recognizing that may not be enough and adding more next year. The disadvantages of number three option are the risk of escalation, casualties high, and the prospect of a long war without victory. I would like you to start out by stating our present position as you see it, and where we can go."

The chiefs warned Johnson that the time had arrived to up the ante, "If we continue the way we are now," warned Admiral D.L. McDonald, "it will be a slow, sure victory for the other side. But putting more men in it will turn the tide and let us know what further we need to do. I wish we had done this long before." When Johnson asked if one hundred thousand men would be enough, McDonald responded that "sooner or later we will force them to the conference table." When Johnson then asked about the chances for success, Paul Nitze answered "if we want to turn the tide, by putting in more men, it would be about sixty-forty." Nitze concluded that another one hundred thousand would be needed by January 1966. When Johnson asked what type of reaction this would produce, General Wheeler noted "since we are not proposing an invasion of the North, the Soviets will step up material and propaganda, and the same with the Chicoms. The North Vietnamese might introduce more regular troops. . . . The one thing all North Vietnam fears is the Chinese. For them to invite Chinese volunteers is to invite China taking over North Vietnam. The weight of judgment is that North Vietnam may reinforce their troops, but they can't match us on a buildup."

The discussion soon turned to the real crux of the matter for LBJ—the costs of escalation and the change in mission. When Admiral McDonald recommended giving Westmoreland all he needed as well as mobilizing the reserves and increasing draft calls, President Johnson asked "do you have any ideas of what this will cost? Do you have any idea what effect this will have on our economy?" Secretary McNamara responded "twelve billion dollars in 1966. It would not require wage and price controls in my judgment. The price index ought not go up more than one point or two." The president asked "doesn't it really mean that if we follow Westmoreland's requests we are in a new war? Isn't this going off the diving board?" Secretary McNamara answered, "if we carry forward all these recommendations, it would be a change in our policy. We have relied on the South to carry the brunt. Now we would be responsible for [a] satisfactory military outcome." President Johnson next heard General Wallace M. Greene report that to accomplish the U.S. objectives it would take "five years, plus 500,000 troops. I think the American people would back you." Johnson asked, "how would you tell the American people what the stakes are." "The place where they will stick by you is the national security stake," responded Greene.

The dialogue was without optimism or short-run terms of reference. President Johnson clearly knew where he was headed when he asked, "do all of you think the Congress and the people will go along with 600,000 people and billions of dollars being spent 10,000 miles away. . . . If you make a commitment to jump off a building and you find out how high it is, you may want to withdraw that commitment." The president's military advisers emphasized that it would take hundreds of thousands of men and several years to achieve military goals. The Joint Chiefs urged Johnson to call up the reserves and the National Guard and to seek public support on national security grounds.

The Announcement

But President Johnson decided that there would be no public announcement of a change in policy. Johnson also rejected McGeorge Bundy's proposal that he go before a joint session of Congress or make his statement in a fireside address. Instead, he simply called a midday press conference. The content as well as the forum of Johnson's message downplayed its significance. The expected call up of the reserves and the request for new funds were absent. Moreover, Johnson also used the afternoon news conference to announce John Chancellor's nomination as head of the United States Information Agency and Abe Fortas's as associate justice of the Supreme Court. JCS [Joint Chiefs of Staff] Chairman Wheeler cabled General Westmoreland and informed him that McNamara's recommendation for troop increases had been approved and would be announced the next day. "Do not be surprised or disappointed if the public announcement does not set forth the full details of the program, but instead reflects an incremental approach," Wheeler advised. "This tactic will probably be adopted in order to hold down [the] international noise level."

In announcing the troop increase, Johnson did not fully reveal the levels he had now authorized—175,000 to 200,000. Instead, he noted only the immediate force increment—fighting strength would grow from 75,000 to 125,000. Nor did he tell the American people that just a few days earlier Clark Clifford had warned against any substantial buildup of U.S. ground troops. "This could be a quagmire," warned the president's trusted friend. "It could turn into an open-ended commitment on our part that would take more and more ground troops, without a realistic hope of ultimate victory."

Instead, Johnson chose to deceive the American people with respect to the goals of military involvement and their anticipated costs. "Additional forces will be needed later, and they will be sent as requested," LBJ observed at his afternoon press conference. He made a seemingly passing remark that correctly indicated that the American commitment had become open ended: "I have asked the Commanding General, General Westmoreland, what more he needs to meet this mounting aggression. He has told me. We will meet his needs."

JOHNSON ESCALATED THE WAR TO ENSURE NATIONAL SECURITY

JACK VALENTI

Jack Valenti was a special assistant to Johnson during Johnson's presidency. He is the president of the Motion Picture Association of America and the author of *A Very Human President*, a memoir of his experience working in the Johnson administration. Valenti writes that Johnson's decision to escalate U.S. involvement in Vietnam was supported by nearly all of the president's advisers as the only reasonable alternative. Three presidents prior to Johnson had committed the United States to the support of South Vietnam, he points out; America's credibility would have been compromised had Johnson withdrawn. Johnson and his aides were also influenced by the "domino theory"—the belief that a Communist victory in South Vietnam would lead to the spread of communism throughout the region. Valenti concludes that regardless of the lessons of hindsight, at the time of the decision Johnson, along with most of the experts around him, was sincerely convinced that escalation was necessary to ensure U.S. security.

I N THE SUMMER OF 1965, THE THIRTY-SIXTH PRESIDENT WAS faced with more than the fearsome question of whether or not to commit even larger bodies of American troops than were then positioned in South Vietnam. It was a total decision to determine whether to pull out completely from Vietnam or to stay. The slow accumulation of public state-

Excerpted from *A Very Human President*, by Jack Valenti. Copyright ©1975 by Jack Valenti. Used by permission of W.W. Norton and Company, Inc.

ments, presidential policies, and national intent were now weighing down on the available alternatives.

This is crucial. Lyndon Johnson was the only one of four presidents to be confronted with the leprous alternative: *get out* or *get in with more, much more.* All the previous presidents escaped, through circumstance or chance, an ugly confrontation with this decision.

Each previous president—Truman, Eisenhower, and Kennedy—had examined the situation and each had done what he thought to be right in the long-range best interests of the country whose future he swore by solemn oath to protect and defend. Each decision by each president narrowed the alternatives of his successor. It is difficult for critics to be dispassionate, that is, to set the scene exactly as it happened. The critic is fortified by hindsight, that which give him gifts of knowledge that at the time of the crucial decision were nowhere to be found.

In the hot summer of 1965, the curtain went up on the bullet-biting crisis of the Johnson administration.

Essentially, the military high command had examined the nature of the war at that moment in time and found that the entire bastion was crumbling. In their judgment the South Vietnamese armed forces were not capable of stemming the tide of reinforcements from the North; the war was going so badly, worsening so swiftly, that the Joint chiefs had concluded everything was going down the tubes, and fast, unless the United Sates was prepared to commit large bodies of troops, *now.* The alternative was disaster for the Vietnamese and the prospect of evacuation of American forces immediately.

The unaskable question had now been asked.

It had to be answered. . . .

Those who sat in on all the meetings over the week-long torment [July 21–28, 1965] know that Lyndon Johnson had listened carefully to every viewpoint; he never hurried or seemed frustrated by the need for meetings and more meetings. It was as if he were determined to dredge up every piece of information that might have even the barest relevancy to the decision.

The men around the president's table [in the Cabinet Room of the White House] who advised him in the decision were men of honor and decency. There was no meanness in their thoughts or decisions. They cared very much about their nation, and had spent, most of them, a good portion of their working lives serving their countrymen, at modest or great sacrifice. They had applied to this problem all the rigor their minds and consciences could bring to bear and they knew the enormity of the counsel and advice they had offered to the president, for they understood the dimensions of the decision that had been taken.

Every one of the advisers concurred in the final decision. (I have recorded the reservations made during the discussions, notably those of Mike Mansfield and George Ball.) Opinions may have changed later but at the time of decision in 1965, there were no staff dissents. . . .

Hoops of Commitments

From the first decision to give aid to Indochina in April 1950, to the summer of 1965 decisions, the hoops of commitments bound the U.S. tighter and tighter. Every president, as the record so clearly shows, found it a fact of life to regard Southeast Asia as essential to the security of the free world. Once you let Southeast Asia fall to Communist domination, went the prevailing official opinion, the unravelling of that part of the world, insofar as it concerned our own security, would begin.

This view was staunchly held by every American administration since 1950. It was reinforced by President Kennedy when on September 9, 1963, two and a half months before his death, he was interviewed on NBC by David Brinkley, and the following exchange occurred:

Brinkley: Mr. President, have you had any reason to doubt this so-called "domino theory" that if South Vietnam falls, the rest of Southeast Asia will go behind it?

The President: No, I believe it. I believe it. I think that the struggle is close enough. China is so large, looms so high just beyond the frontiers, that if South Vietnam went, it would not only give them an improved geographic position for a guerrilla assault on Malaya, but would also give the impression that the wave of the future in Southeast Asia was China and the Communists. So I believe it.

Thus, the domino theory riding high in the water. It would be some years later before its edges became frayed. But in mid-1965, the moorings of the domino theory were still tautly held and LBJ felt its pull.

Of course, there was risk in going in further in Vietnam, but, reasoned the president and his advisers, what of the larger and even more crippling risk of total U.S. incredibility in Asia? How do we justify all that was said and done, not by one president, but by three and counting Johnson, four presidents, if we suddenly shifted gears and left the South Vietnamese alone to fend for themselves? Moreover, could an American president have withstood the fury of criticism beating in on him the day that Southeast Asia was indeed Communist encircled? No matter if the interment of democratic government there was either good or bad; no matter, for the critics would have justly argued that we fled when we didn't have to. What would have happened if there were thousands of Vietnamese massacred by a vengeful Ho Chi Minh? (That Ho would be capable of this was aptly proved by the murders he committed in his own domain as well as the Hue massacre [of 1968].) Is it possible for an administration in the face of this bitter indictment, this careless neglect of a word firmly given, of a pledge solemnly offered, is it possible for such an administration to find afterward any promise or purpose it pursues worthy of belief?

Every public man knows he cannot take refuge in what might have been. He has to stand or fall on what happens. President Kennedy's bleak assessment of the Bay of Pigs—"Success has a thousand fathers, but failure is an orphan"—is a very accurate accounting.

All this weighed heavily on the group around the table in the Cabinet Room. Each man at the meetings probably toyed with the thought of defeat in South Vietnam. Imagine a president saying to the people of the nation, after massacres in South Vietnam, after the toppling of every government in Southeast Asia and the installation of a Communist apparatus, imagine an American president saying: "If we had not allowed this to happen, we would have suffered a terrible defeat in a war in South Vietnam." There would have been no proof of this. How would a president explain the desertion of friends, the loss of allies, the fall of governments, and the murder of innocents when his own act of abandonment was the cause.

What really happened around the cabinet table in the summer of 1965 was a commitment without the remedial benefits of hindsight. The clearest, most unobstructed view a human can have is the one which allows him to see what *has already happened.* It is what Edmund Burke called "retrospective wisdom." It does make wise men of us all.

Inescapable Decision

Every piece of evidence placed before the participants in all the meetings on Vietnam made it inescapable that no decision other than the one taken would be approved. I believe it is a fair and just statement that to every man in the meetings, with the exception of Senator Mansfield and Under Secretary of State George Ball, the final decisions taken in 1965 on Vietnam were right and sensible, and worthy of the risk involved, and, indeed, the only course

Johnson Considered the Alternatives

David M. Barrett examines the prevailing myths regarding Johnson's deliberations on escalating the Vietnam War.

A mythology has been prevalent for some years regarding Lyndon Johnson, his willingness to listen to varied advice on handling the Vietnam situation in 1965, and the scope of the advice he in fact received before deciding on escalation. The most important myth is that Johnson was a "victim of groupthink," that is, that he did not receive wide ranging opinions from significant advisers about whether or not to intensify America's military role in Vietnam. This myth suggests that with one principle exception no important advisers urged Johnson to keep combat troops out of Vietnam. A secondary and related myth claims that Johnson's personality and ego were such that he would not countenance the expression of conflicting advice that might raise the possibility that the United States would be wrong to increase its military presence in Vietnam.

Documentation declassified in recent years and di-

possible under the circumstances. Once that initial, crunching decision had been ordered, then a number of subsequent decisions, obviously, flowed automatically. Once the commitment was weighed and studied, and commanded to be kept on course, our choices in Vietnam narrowed so sharply that ultimately we had no choices.

To the counsel of those who urged the president to go all out in bombing the North, mining the harbors of Haiphong, invading Cambodia and even the North, the president always listened but never followed. He was haunted by the ceaseless fear of Russian or Chinese entry into the war. He agonized over "the start of World War III." He knew

verse secondary sources, some of which have been available for many years, [demonstrate] that Johnson was not a victim of groupthink and that he received and listened to significant advice warning him against sending troops to Vietnam. . . . It is certainly true that the distinct majority of Johnson's advisers told him that the United States had no choice but to send in the troops in order to save South Vietnam. However, the myths that a pathological advisory process or a tremendously egotistical personality prevented Johnson from considering alternatives to (and the drawbacks of) escalation in Vietnam should be laid to rest. In retrospect, it is clear that Lyndon Johnson made a tragically bad decision when he committed ground troops to a land war in Southeast Asia. But unlike the picture drawn in many accounts, the President certainly heard and seems to have agonized over the different options facing him before making the decision.

David M. Barrett, "The Mythology Surrounding Lyndon Johnson, His Advisers, and the 1965 Decision to Escalate the Vietnam War," *Political Science Quarterly*, vol. 103, no. 4, 1988.

his course was a cautious one, at variance with the stern importunings of the generals, admirals, and hawks in the Congress, and he knew too that he risked the frustration of the American public (which when it came, came in avalanches), but the vision of a "wider war" was more powerful than the dazzle of military victory prophecies. He hung back from the brink. "Some damn fool will drop some TNT down the smokestack of a Russian freighter in Haiphong, or some plane will get lost and dump its bombs over China, and we're in World War III. I just can't risk it," was his response to the urgings of those who said seductive things to him about getting it over quick.

What went wrong?

In the more than a decade that has gone by, the readiest narrative and the most accessible prose have testified to the bitter tragedy of Vietnam. But it may be that de Tocqueville had the answer when he wrote (about the French Revolution), "the people grow tired of a confusion whose end is not in sight."

If one believes it was wrong, clearly wrong, for any American president to commit forces to a distant part of the world for any reason, then even the proffering of economic or other aid was a mistake, because that was the beginning.

But if you believe that the U.S.A. was right in trying to help a small country defend itself against aggression, then de Tocqueville's sour commentary has a special warrant. The struggle was too long, the drain on our resources endless, the enemy too diffused, the objectives too obscure. Under those conditions it is difficult to ask any people, particularly those with no stomach for dreary victory-less conflicts, to fasten their resolve to the sticking place. If World War II had gone on for four more years, or five more years, would we have been ready to seek a negotiated peace in Europe and Asia? Who really knows?

In the long, lamentable catalogue of Vietnam, of only one fact can I be certain. It is this: What Lyndon Johnson did, he did because he believed the long-range security of the nation he had sworn to protect and defend was best served by his actions. That was the only reason for his decisions. If he was terribly wrong, then history will have to make that accounting. He always believed that history would prove him right.

JOHNSON ESCALATED THE WAR TO PRESERVE HIS PERSONAL CREDIBILITY

FREDRIK LOGEVALL

Fredrik Logevall rejects the arguments that Johnson escalated the war in Vietnam to protect South Vietnam from northern aggression, to protect his Great Society legislation from political defeat, or because he was manipulated into escalation by his advisers. Instead, Logevall insists that the decision to escalate was primarily Johnson's and was mostly motivated by a need to secure his personal credibility. Withdrawal from Vietnam would have been a personal humiliation and a threat to Johnson's sense of his own manhood, according to Logevall. Logevall is associate professor of history at the University of California, Santa Barbara, and the author of *Choosing War: The Lost Chance for Peace in the Escalation of War in Vietnam,* from which the following essay is excerpted.

━━━━━━

FOR THE LEADING CAUSES OF THE 1965 ESCALATION WE must look to the short term, and especially to the year 1964 and to the interaction in that period of Lyndon Baines Johnson and his most senior advisers, [Secretary of Defense] Robert McNamara, [National Security Adviser] McGeorge Bundy, and [Secretary of State] Dean Rusk. . . . To a large extent these four men made the Vietnam policy, made it with input from various assistant secretaries, to be sure, and from the Joint Chiefs of Staff and the various

---

members of the National Security Council, and, especially, from ambassador to Saigon General Maxwell Taylor, but with decisive power preserved for themselves.

Why did they choose war? Publicly they insisted they did it principally to defend a free people from external aggression, but this was false. Though policymakers constantly proclaimed that all they wanted for the South Vietnamese was the right of self-determination, they worked to thwart that right whenever it appeared that southern leaders might seek to broaden their base of support by shifting the emphasis of the struggle from the military to the political plane. . . . No doubt they believed that what they were doing served the Vietnamese people's ultimate interests, and that the inhabitants of the South would be grateful in the end. No doubt this assumption made them sleep better at night. But it had little to do with why they acted.

For the key consideration behind the decision for war we must look to the other rationale articulated by policymakers: *credibility* and the need to preserve it by avoiding defeat in Vietnam. This was the explanation typically advanced by officials when they addressed knowledgeable audiences in off-the-record meetings—one finds scant references to "moral obligations" or "defending world freedom" in the records of their interaction with congressional committees, with foreign government leaders, with journalists in private sessions. In these settings, the emphasis was almost always on abstract (and closely related) notions of prestige, reputation, and credibility and how these were on the line in Vietnam. Even here, however, the picture that emerges is incomplete, inasmuch as the "credibility" referred to was always a purely national concept, having to do with the position of the United States on the world stage. That is, it was *American* credibility that was at stake in Southeast Asia, *American* prestige that needed to be upheld there. Though it can be right and proper to de-

President Lyndon B. Johnson (at far left) meets with U.S. troops at the height of the Vietnam War.

fine the credibility imperative in exclusively national terms, it will not suffice as an explanation for policy making in Vietnam. For Vietnam a broader definition is essential, one that also includes domestic political credibility and even personal credibility. For it was not merely the United States that had a stake in the outcome in Vietnam; so did the Democratic Party (or at least so Kennedy and Johnson believed), and so did the individuals who had helped shape the earlier commitment and who were now charged with deciding the next move.

We may go further and argue that, within this three-part conception of the credibility imperative, the national part was the least important. Geostrategic considerations were not the driving force in American Vietnam policy in The Long 1964, either before the election or after; partisan political considerations were; individual careerist considerations were. True, some officials did see Vietnam as a vital theater in the larger Cold War struggle against world communism, did see American credibility as very much on the line—Dean Rusk was one, [security adviser] Walt Rostow another. Most, however, were more dubious. [Assistant Secretary of State] William Bundy and [assistant secretary of defense for international security affairs] John McNaughton, two of the key players in the policy deliberations in late 1964, not only shared much of [Undersecretary of State] George Ball's pessimism about the long-term prospects in the war but on several occasions endorsed his relatively benign view of the likely consequences of defeat in South Vietnam. (Ball's views were at once more widely shared in the government and less influential in decision making than is often assumed.) Robert McNamara and McGeorge Bundy worried about the implications for America's world position of a defeat in Vietnam and were highly effective exponents of a staunch U.S. commitment to the war—never more forthrightly than in their "Fork in the Y" memo of 27 January 1965. But they cannot be considered true believers on Vietnam, at least not after the latter part of 1964, in the sense of truly believing that the United States had a moral obligation to help the South Vietnamese or that American national interests were seriously threatened by events in Indochina. So why did they favor Americanization? Less out of concern for America's credibility, I believe, than out of fears for their own personal credibility. For more than three years, McNamara and Bundy had counseled the need to stand firm in the war (a relatively easy thing to do in, say, 1962, when the commitment was small and the Cold War situation considerably more tense), and to go against that now would be to expose themselves to potential humiliation and to threaten their careers. It is not difficult to imagine both men, and especially McNamara, arguing with equal effectiveness for the need to cut losses and get out of the conflict, had they served a president who sought such a result.

Presidential Primacy

Even if we draw back from this conclusion, even if we assume that all of the principal advisers meant it when they said that America's global credibility was on the line in Vietnam, it would still not necessarily mean that we had arrived at the main motivation behind the decision for war. For it would not tell us anything about the position and role of the central figure in the policy making, the president of the United States. And on this there can be no doubt: Kennedy and Johnson were the key players in this policy process, not merely in the obvious sense that they had to give final approval to any and all policy decisions but in the sense of actively shaping the outcome of the deliberations. Because Johnson was fated to be president when the critical choices came, it is his imprint on the policy that is our central concern. It is commonplace to emphasize Johnson's dominance in the policy making in the later years of his tenure (1966–1968), when his obsession with the war became nearly total; the argument here is that his imprint was deeper than anyone else's in the early period as well. During the conflict itself and to some degree in the years after, much noise was made about Vietnam being "McNamara's War," but it was never the defense secretary's war. From 23 November 1963 it was "Lyndon Johnson's War."

This is not to deny that Johnson relied in important ways on the triumvirate of McNamara, Bundy, and Rusk. He obviously did. . . . But Johnson was always first among equals, as the internal record makes clear. If his top Vietnam aides intimidated him with their accomplishments and academic pedigrees, he also intimidated them with his forceful presence and his frequent resort to bullying tactics, and he established firm control of his administration from the start. Furthermore, no president is a prisoner to his advisers—Eisenhower and Kennedy had rejected policy recommendations on Vietnam, and Johnson might have done the same had he so desired. (He showed a capacity to do so on non-Vietnam issues.) He did not. What, then, drove Johnson's approach to the Vietnam issue? Chiefly its potential to do harm to his domestic political objectives and to his personal historical reputation. Both concerns were there from the start—he determined already in late 1963 that Vietnam would be kept on the back burner in 1964, so as to avoid giving Republicans an issue with which to beat up on Democrats in an election year, and he vowed only hours after the Dallas assassination that he would not be the president who lost Vietnam.

Understanding this duality in Johnson's thinking about the war, in which partisan calculations competed for supremacy with concerns for his personal reputation, is essential to understanding the outcome of the policy process in Washington in the fifteen months that followed his taking office as president. The former explains his determination to keep Vietnam from being lost in an election year, a year in which he also sought to pass major pieces of the Democratic Party's legislative agenda. But it cannot by itself explain his willingness to proceed with a major military intervention—whose importance and viability he himself doubted—after the glorious election results, which brought not only a smashing victory over Barry Goldwater but also huge Democratic majorities in both houses of Congress. It cannot explain Johnson's refusal to even consider possible alternatives to a military solution, never more resolutely than in those important weeks after the election.

For this reason it would be wrong to overemphasize the importance of the Great Society in the decision to escalate the conflict—that is, to give too much weight to the idea that LBJ took the nation to war because of fears that if he did not, Republicans and conservative Democrats would oppose and possibly scuttle his beloved domestic agenda. Concerns along these lines certainly existed within Johnson, and they directly influenced the *way* in which he expanded the war—in particular, they dictated that the escalation be as quiet as possible so as to avoid the need for choosing between the war and the programs, between guns and butter. But strategizing of this sort cannot be considered the primary *cause* of the decision for escalation. McGeorge Bundy spoke well to this point years later; "I think if [Johnson] had decided that the right thing to do was to cut our losses, he was quite sufficiently inventive to do that in a way that would not have destroyed the Great Society. It's not a dependent variable. It's an independent variable." In Bundy's view, Johnson saw achieving victory in Vietnam as important for its own sake, not merely as something necessary to ensure the survival of some domestic agenda. LBJ had vowed steadfastness in Vietnam in his very first foreign-policy meeting in November 1963 and had adhered to that line at all points thereafter.

A Personal Issue

A healthy dose of skepticism is always warranted when considering the recollections of former policymakers, especially when the subject is responsibility for policy mistakes. But here Bundy had it right. Lyndon Johnson was a hawk on Vietnam, and he was so for reasons that went beyond immediate domestic political or geostrategic advantage. For it was not merely his country's and his party's reputation that Johnson took to be on the line, but also his own. His tendency to personalize all issues relating to the war, so evident in the later years, in 1966 and 1967 and 1968, was there from the start, from the time he vowed to not be the first American president to lose a war. From the beginning, he viewed attacks on the policy as attacks on himself, saw American credibility and his own credibility as essentially synonymous. In so doing he diminished his capacity to render objective judgment, to retain the necessary level of detachment. He failed to see that the international and domestic political context gave him considerable freedom of maneuver, if not in the period before the November 1964 election then certainly in the weeks thereafter.

It would be difficult to exaggerate the importance of this conflation of the national interest and his own personal interest in Johnson's approach to Vietnam. Skeptical readers may nevertheless think I have done so, that I have overestimated LBJ's commitment to standing firm in Vietnam, especially in the early months of his presidency, and underestimated the influence of his top advisers on shap-

Johnson once exposed his surgery scar to a group of reporters. David Levine seized on this incident to comment on Johnson and Vietnam.

David Levine. *The New York Review of Books*, 1966. Used with permission.

ing that approach. It is true that Johnson did not come into office looking for a fight in Vietnam. He was no war-monger. There is no reason to doubt his frequent asser-tions that he hated the war, hated what it was doing to his country and his dreams for creating a Great Society that would eliminate poverty, illiteracy, and homelessness among his people (and they were always *his* people). It is also clear that he always possessed considerable skepticism about the prospects in Vietnam—not infrequently his doubts on that score surpassed those of his closest aides. But warriors need not be enthusiastic or optimistic to be committed. From the start of his tenure, perhaps even from the time he visited South Vietnam on Kennedy's be-half in mid 1961, Lyndon Johnson's position on the Viet-nam issue did not deviate from the fundamental position that defeat there had to be avoided.

This included defeat disguised by some kind of negoti-ated settlement, one providing a "decent interval" before the reunification of the country under communist control. Had Johnson been concerned only with, or even primarily with, preserving *American* credibility and/or *Democratic* credibility, he surely would have ordered extensive contin-gency planning for some kind of fig leaf for withdrawal in the months leading up to escalation, when the outlook looked grimmer than ever. He would have actively sought, rather than actively avoided, the advice of allied leaders like Harold Wilson and Lester Pearson and given much deeper reflection to the urgings of anti-Americanization voices on Capitol Hill and in the press community. His dislike of the war was hardly less intense than theirs, after all, his evaluation of the Saigon government's potential not significantly more rosy. But the end result of the sce-nario these critics espoused—American withdrawal with-out victory—was one Johnson could not contemplate, largely because of the damage such an outcome could do to his own personal reputation.

Johnson's Insecurity

The concern here went deeper than merely saving his political skin. In private LBJ would sometimes say that he could not withdraw from Vietnam because it would lead to his impeachment, but he was too smart a politician to really believe such a thing. What he really feared was the personal humiliation that he believed would come with failure in Vietnam. He saw the war as a test of his own manliness. Many have commented on the powerful element of *machismo* in Johnson's world view, rooted in his upbringing and fueled by his haunting fear that he would be judged insufficiently manly for the job, that he would lack courage when the chips were down. In his world there were weak and strong men; the weak men were the skeptics, who sat around contemplating, talking, criticizing; the strong men were the doers, the activists, the ones who were always tough and always refused to back down. Thus [Senator Mike] Mansfield could be dismissed as spineless, as "milquetoast"; thus [Senator J. William] Fulbright could be castigated as a "crybaby." Though Johnson on occasion showed himself quite capable of asking probing questions in policy meetings, he had little patience with those who tried to supply probing answers. His macho ethos extended to relations among states. "If you let a bully come into your front yard one day," he liked to say, in reference to the lesson of Munich, "the next day he will be up on your porch and the day after that he will rape your wife in your own bed." In such a situation, retreat was impossible, retreat was cowardly. Johnson's approach did not make him reckless on Vietnam—he was, in fact, exceedingly cautious—but it made him quite unable to contemplate extrication as anything but the equivalent of, as he might put it, "tucking tail and running."

This personal insecurity in Johnson, so much a feature of the recollections of those who knew him and worked with him, might have been less important in Vietnam policy if not for the way it reinforced his equally well documented intolerance of dissent. Even in the early months of his presidency he was incredulous to learn that some Americans might be opposed to his policy of fully supporting South Vietnam; it was un-American, he believed, to make an issue during the Cold War of national security matters. Throughout his career Johnson had made his way in politics by intimidation, by dominating those around him, and he did not change this modus operandi once he got into the White House. "I'm the only president you have," he told those who opposed his policies. His demand for consensus and loyalty extended to his inner circle of advisers, a reality that, when combined with his powerful personality, must have had a chilling effect on anyone inclined to try to build support for a contrary view. Recall the point made later by McGeorge Bundy, certainly no contrarian voice: "You can't organize against Lyndon Johnson without getting bombed before breakfast, because in his view that's the final and ultimate conspiracy." When Vice President Hubert H. Humphrey (one of the "weak" men in Johnson's lexicon) in early 1965 gingerly began advocating a de-escalated American involvement and made the crucial mistake of voicing his concerns not merely in a private memo to LBJ but also in a meeting of the National Security Council, Johnson banned him from Vietnam policy discussions for a year. Canadian prime minister Lester Pearson suffered the same fate in April 1965 after suggesting a pause in the bombing of the DRV [Democratic Republic of (North) Vietnam]; for the remainder of the Johnson presidency, Canada would be in the dark about U.S. policy in the war.

Access thus did not equal influence. A large number of individuals had the former; only a few also had the latter. Johnson would hear the critics out—he frequently talked to them privately, often professed sympathy with their views, and accepted their private memos—but there is no evidence that he ever really considered their arguments. The implications for our analysis are enormous. Johnson's aversion to dissent and his obsessive fear of leaks created a cloistered decision-making system that effectively excluded contrarian voices from the deliberations and discouraged in-depth reexamination of the fundamental issues among those who remained. A conformist atmosphere reigned. (George Ball, the one high-level official to question the move to a larger war, was himself a conformist, willingly accepting the assignment of in-house "devil's advocate" and always making clear that he would remain the loyal insider regardless of what policy decision emerged.)

In this way, while responsibility for the outcome of the policy process rested with all of those who participated in it, it rested chiefly with the president. Johnson, no one else, ensured that the critical decisions on Vietnam were made by a small and insular group of individuals who by the latter part of 1964 had been involved in policy making for several years in most cases, who had overseen the steady expansion in the U.S. commitment to the war, and who had a large personal stake in seeing that commitment succeed. He more than anyone determined that there would be not a single NSC [National Security Council] meeting from October 1964 to the eve of the Pleiku incident in February 1965, and that those that occurred after that date were mostly about rubber-stamping decisions already reached. (After February 16 there would be only four more until July.) Bundy and others may have encouraged him in this schedule, but it also corresponded with the way he liked to do business. Johnson was poorly served by his advisory system, but it was a system he in large measure created.

Johnson's Middle-of-the-Road War Strategy

H.W. Brands

H.W. Brands writes that in managing the Vietnam War, Johnson sought to balance competing domestic and international interests. In an attempt to support South Vietnam without provoking a response from China or the Soviet Union, he rejected the most aggressive tactics suggested by his hard-line advisers. On the other hand, he sought to appease antiwar protestors by periodically halting his bombing campaign while attempting a diplomatic solution to the war. Johnson's middle-of-the-road tactics proved unsuccessful. In the wake of the Tet offensive of February 1968, Johnson had little choice but to begin the process of American disengagement from the war. Johnson's decision to withdraw from the 1968 presidential race opened the door for a significant shift in U.S. policy in Vietnam. Brands is a professor of history at Texas A&M University and the author of *The Wages of Globalism: Lyndon Johnson and the Limits of American Power*, from which the following essay was excerpted.

JOHNSON'S JULY DECISION TO AMERICANIZE THE WAR WAS the most important action he took regarding Vietnam. What came afterward followed naturally, almost inevitably, from this decision. In defending his decision to his closest advisers, the president encapsulated his entire approach to the conflict in Southeast Asia: "We have chosen to do what is necessary to meet the present situation,

Excerpted from *The Wages of Globalism: Lyndon Johnson and the Limits of American Power*, by H.W. Brands. Copyright ©1995 by H.W. Brands. Used by permission of Oxford University Press, Inc.

but not to be unnecessarily provocative to either the Russians or the Communist Chinese."

In the summer of 1965 this strategy appeared reasonable. None could fault Johnson's caution in trying to forestall direct Soviet or Chinese involvement in the fighting, and South Vietnam's position did not seem irretrievable. "The present military situation is serious but not desperate," [General] Maxwell Taylor [former chairman of the Joint Chiefs of Staff] asserted at the beginning of August.

Yet Taylor at the same time sounded a warning and underscored the weakness of Johnson's gradualist approach. "No one knows how much Viet Cong resilience is still left," Taylor said. The troops Johnson was dispatching to South Vietnam would prevent the communists from winning—at the communists' current level of fighting. "By the end of 1965, the North Vietnamese offensive will be bloodied and defeated without having achieved major gains," Taylor predicted. But once the communists adjusted to the American escalation, they might well up the stakes themselves. "Hanoi may then decide to change its policy."

While waiting for the communists to react to his troop decision, Johnson had to deal with responses at home. The Americanization of the war sparked the first sustained antiwar protests in the United States. Shortly after Johnson's troop announcement, some one thousand demonstrators took a page from the manual of the civil rights movement and held a sit-in outside the White House. The protests mounted during the succeeding weeks, reaching a crescendo, for the moment, in a November 1965 march of twenty thousand in Washington. William Fulbright ... added his voice to the protest. The Arkansas senator denounced the escalation of the war and called on the president to stop the bombing.

The criticism had an effect on Johnson, though he didn't like to admit it. Robert McNamara [secretary of defense], after August visits to the foreign affairs committees of the Senate and House, described the sentiment there regarding the administration's war policies. "In both the Senate and the House Committees," McNamara told Johnson, "there is broad support, but it is thin. There is a feeling of uneasiness and frustration." McNamara noted that the indications of uneasiness and frustration came from the right as well as from the left. Suggestions that the president was going too far in Vietnam were countered by complaints that he was not doing enough.

Middle-of-the-Road Strategy

Johnson, as earlier, sought the middle of the road. At the end of September the administration announced the second installment of the July escalation package. This move further evidenced the president's resolve and presumably pleased the right. Two months later Johnson followed up the dispatch of new troops with a halt to the bombing, a move calculated to placate the left. In addition, the bombing halt would remind the world that what the United States wanted in Vietnam was not war but peace. . . .

To further demonstrate his pacific intentions, the president accompanied the bombing halt with a well-publicized diplomatic offensive. He sent envoys to European, Asian, African, and Latin American capitals carrying a message of America's desire for peace. He specially contacted Soviet chairman [Aleksei] Kosygin to convey the same message. He emphasized his great desire for peace in his January 1966 State of the Union address.

Neither the pause nor the professions moved Hanoi, which refused to retreat from its demand that the American imperialists exit Vietnam at once, and by the fourth week of January the president was thinking seriously about resuming the bombing. Objections from American generals were increasing. With every day that North Vietnam resupplied the communists in South Vietnam unhindered, the generals argued, American soldiers came under more serious danger. The bombing must recommence forthwith. Johnson felt the force of this argument, but he wanted to check congressional opinion before making a decision.

On January 25 he invited the congressional leaders to the White House. . . .

For all the encouragement at this meeting, Johnson recognized that support for the war was not what it had been. On January 28 the president predicted to his advisers that resumption of the bombing might lead to "deep divisions in our government." Opponents remained far from a majority, but he guessed that if something like the Gulf of Tonkin resolution were placed before the legislature now, some forty senators and representatives would vote against it. Although this was not a great many out of 535 legislators, it was still considerably more than the two naysayers of August 1964.

If any single sentiment captured American feelings about the war early in 1966, it was frustration. As the remarks of Richard Russell and others at the January 25 meeting indicated, Americans felt frustrated over the inconclusive character of the fighting. At this same session representative Mendel Rivers put the mood best. "Win or get out," the South Carolina Democrat said.

Eventually Johnson would admit that the issue came down to this stark choice, but for the time being he still thought he could finesse things. He refused to court the dangers associated with an unrestrained effort to win the war. For fear of provoking the Chinese or the Soviets or both, he rejected all ideas of invading North Vietnam. For fear of killing his domestic reforms, he rejected proposals to place the country on a war footing. Yet though he wouldn't win, neither would he get out. Getting out would demoralize America's allies and hearten America's enemies, and it would subject his administration to devastating criticism at home.

At the end of January 1966 Johnson judged the costs of getting out higher than the costs of staying in. And he judged that staying in required resumption of the bombing. His decision to resume reflected a felt obligation to American soldiers in the field. "I don't want to fail the men out there," he said. It also reflected fear of a conservative backlash against his fruitless peace efforts. Such a backlash could easily make the antiwar movement seem a minor annoyance. "I certify that the Fulbrights and the [Wayne] Morses will be under the table and the hardliners will take over, unless we take initiatives," Johnson asserted. The initiative he selected on January 31 was renewed bombing.

As long as he possibly could, Johnson continued to avoid making the choice Mendel Rivers described. As before, he sought the middle course between the opponents of the war, who advocated withdrawal, and his military advisers, who recommended, if not all-out war, at least considerably more war than they were fighting. "What do you want most?" the president had asked General [Harold] Johnson during discussions of bombing resumption. "A surge of additional troops," the army chief of staff had replied. "We need to double the number now and then triple the number later. We should call up the reserves and go to mobilization to get the needed U.S. manpower. This involves declaring a national emergency." During the spring of 1966 the generals agitated for permission to bomb petroleum facilities in the Hanoi-Haiphong area, previously off limits for fear of forcing the hand of China or the Soviet Union, the latter perhaps by accidentally hitting a Soviet ship. In June 1966 General [Earle] Wheeler suggested going still further and mining Haiphong harbor. . . .

Johnson gave the military part of what it wanted, but not all. He authorized additional increases in American troop levels, to almost 400,000 by the end of 1966, and to nearly half a million during the following year. He let the bombers hit the petroleum facilities and much else besides. But he refused to declare a national emergency and to go to full mobilization, and he rejected the mining of Haiphong.

The actions the president did allow more than sufficed to spur the growing antiwar movement to unexampled efforts of opposition. . . .

By the end of 1967 American public support for the war had dropped drastically. In March 1965 Gallup had reported 66 percent approval for the president's handling of the war. An August 1967 poll showed only 39 percent of the American public approving of the president's performance.

The Tet Offensive

The criticism of the war crescendoed in February 1968, in the wake of the most extensive Vietcong-North Vietnamese offensive of the war. During the Tet holiday, the communists launched attacks on most of South Vietnam's provincial capitals, nearly all its major cities, and over one hundred smaller villages and hamlets. They assaulted the presidential palace and the airport in Saigon, and for several hours occupied the American embassy compound in the heart of that city.

After initial setbacks, American and South Vietnamese forces dug in, then successfully counterattacked. Fierce fighting consumed most of February, producing hundreds of deaths among American and South Vietnamese troops, thousands among communist forces, and thousands among noncombatants—with some four thousand persons executed by communist units in Hue—and throwing tens of thousands of new refugees into the maelstrom of wartime homelessness.

Tactically, the Tet offensive proved a severe defeat for the communists, but strategically it marked the turning point of the war. Johnson caught a glimpse of the transformation on the eleventh day of the offensive. After a meeting with his top military advisers, the president remarked, "The chiefs see a basic change in the strategy of the war. They say the enemy has escalated from guerrilla tactics to more conventional warfare." This first glimpse was correct but also misleading, for it suggested that the communists were now playing to America's strength. America's advantages in firepower and maneuverability would soon begin to tell, and, indeed, it was exactly this telling that allowed the American and South Vietnamese troops to beat back and then punish the Tet attackers.

But more important, even in defeat the breadth and strength of the communist assault knocked the political wind out of the American effort in Vietnam. (It also threatened to knock out the economic wind, straining the dollar internationally and provoking a run on gold.) Johnson did not have to read the polls to know the American popular mood. "There has been a dramatic shift in public opinion on the war," the president said. Clark Clifford explained the administration's public-opinion problem succinctly: "The major concern of the people is that they do not see victory ahead." Dean Rusk [secretary of state] put the matter more strongly: "The element of hope has been taken away by the Tet offensive. People don't think there is likely to be an end."

Johnson's generals, however, did not appear discouraged. William Westmoreland advocated more of the same: two hundred thousand troops more. With the enemy shifting to conventional warfare, Westmoreland argued, now was the time to press hard for victory. Earle Wheeler forwarded Westmoreland's request to Johnson with recommendation for approval.

The last thing Johnson desired to hear at this stage was a request for more of the same. At a meeting of the Tuesday lunch [a weekly meeting of Johnson and his top advisers] some months before the Tet offensive, the president had directed General Johnson to "search for some imaginative ideas to put pressure to bring this war to a conclusion." He told the army chief of staff not merely to recommend nuclear weapons or more men. The president said he could think of those ideas himself. The demand was a measure of Johnson's frustration, for on sober reconsideration he must have realized he was asking the impossible. He had ruled out an invasion of North Vietnam to prevent provoking the Chinese and the Russians. For the same reason he refused to widen the war into Laos and Cambodia to interdict the Ho Chi Minh trail or to destroy communist sanctuaries there. The one genuinely original idea the Pentagon proposed—an electronic fence along the 17th parallel—proved even more unworkable than most of America's hightech approaches to the conflict, and was abandoned. . . .

The Aftermath of Tet

In any event, the Tet offensive threw thoughts of expanded operations out nearly all administration windows. The Joint Chiefs wanted to escalate further, but they could not even convince their boss at the Pentagon. Robert McNamara, increasingly discouraged at the failure of the policies he had championed, had drifted gradually in the direction of [Undersecretary of State] George Ball. In the autumn of 1967 McNamara wrote Johnson that continuation on the present path would be "dangerous, costly in lives, and unsatisfactory to the American people." Johnson, at this pre-Tet point, was not ready for such dismal realism, and when the World Bank, with White House encouragement, offered McNamara its directorship, Johnson gladly accepted the offer.

Johnson replaced McNamara with Clark Clifford. A thoroughgoing realist in political matters, Clifford had stuck by Johnson after the president had overruled his opposition to the Americanization of the war. Clifford had tried to moderate the more extravagant recommendations of administration hawks, but by no means was he a dove. While he lacked the organizational flair and experience McNamara had brought to the Defense Department, he possessed political sensitivities second only to Johnson's.

At the beginning of 1968, in fact, Clifford's senses were sharper than Johnson's, since the president's had been numbed by four difficult years of responsibility. To some degree Johnson's appointment of Clifford to replace McNamara indicated an understanding on the president's part that the war had become more a domestic political problem than a foreign military one.

Clifford lost no time after the Tet offensive in telling Johnson that the political problem of the war had grown insoluble. At a White House meeting early in March, Clifford said the Tet offensive had come as "a shock." No one had thought the communists could mount such an operation. No one expected them to be able to repeat the performance soon, but obviously they had a lot more fight left in them than American analysts had recognized. The American public wondered whether the administration knew where it was going. Clifford urged Johnson to reject Westmoreland's request for additional troops. If the general got these two hundred thousand, he would soon be back asking for another two hundred thousand. Americans would not stand for a war of attrition. Vietnam was a "sinkhole," Clifford said. "We put in more—they match it. We put in more—they match it." Absent a major change in policy, only grief lay ahead. "I see more and more fighting with more and more casualties on the U.S. side, and no end in sight to the action."

When the Wise Men [Johnson's foreign-policy advisers] met a short while later, they agreed with Clifford. McGeorge Bundy [national security adviser] spoke for the majority of the group when he told the president that there had been "a very significant shift in our position" since the previous autumn. "When we last met we saw reasons for hope. We hoped then that there would be slow but steady progress." The Tet offensive had shaken these hopes, if not shattered them entirely. "A great many people—even very determined and loyal people—have begun to think that

Guns *and* Butter?

Irving Bernstein describes the origins of the "guns-or-but-ter" metaphor, which is frequently invoked in discussions of Johnson's presidency.

The choice between peace and war goes back to an early stage in human history, but the guns-or-butter metaphor did not emerge until the twentieth century. It was invented, according to William Safire, by Joseph Goebbels, Hitler's propaganda minister, who said, "We can do without butter, but, despite all our love of peace, not without arms. One cannot shoot with butter but with arms." Shortly, Hermann Goering, the head of the German Air Force, said in a radio speech: "Guns will make us powerful; butter will only make us fat." Goering must have spoken from the heart because he was very fat.

In the first phase of the Americanization of the Vietnam War President Johnson insisted that the U.S. could have both guns *and* butter:

Vietnam really is a bottomless pit. We have had no solid and visible successes there." Nor did any seem likely soon.

Dean Acheson put the matter more directly. "We can no longer do the job we set out to do in the time we have left," the former secretary of state said. Acheson did not go so far as to say the war was unwinnable, but he was certain the American public, after the blow of Tet, would not allow the administration the time victory required. From the moment in 1947 when Acheson had helped persuade Truman to give a fighting speech in support of aid to Greece and Turkey, Acheson had understood the necessity of public backing for foreign policy. That backing was evaporating rapidly. "We must begin to disengage," he concluded.

Most but not all of those at this meeting agreed with

I believe we can do both. We are a country which was built by pioneers who had a rifle in one hand and an ax in the other. We are a nation with the highest GNP, the highest wages, and the most people at work. We can do both. And as long as I am president we will do both.

He repeated this empty promise in his 1966 State of the Union message and the press immediately called it guns and butter. Chairman Wilbur Mills of the House Ways and Means Committee said, "The Administration simply must choose between guns and butter."

This dilemma was the key to the tragedy of Lyndon Johnson's presidency, perhaps the most tragic in the history of that great office. He acted as though he could have both, while everyone, himself included, knew that he could not.

Irving Bernstein, *Guns or Butter: The Presidency of Lyndon Johnson*. New York: Oxford University Press, 1966.

the Bundy-Acheson view. George Ball, Arthur Dean [chief Korean War negotiator], Cyrus Vance [deputy secretary of defense under McNamara], and Douglas Dillon [former ambassador to France] assented, for reasons similar to those cited by Bundy and Acheson. Robert Murphy [a former career ambassador], Maxwell Taylor [former chairman of the Joint Chiefs of Staff], and Omar Bradley [former chairman of the Joint Chiefs of Staff] thought the disengagers were allowing themselves to be stampeded by the unwarranted pessimism that had seized the American political system. Events had proven the early reports of military disaster wrong. To grant the communists politically what they had failed to achieve militarily would be disastrous. Now was the time to move forward to victory.

Johnson Cuts Back

Johnson, after considerable ego-wrestling, accepted the essence of the disengagers' case. He rejected Westmoreland's troop request and decided, on Rusk's recommendation, to cut back significantly on the bombing of North Vietnam. In a March 31 televised address he explained that only enemy staging areas just north of the 17th parallel would remain subject to American attack. In the same speech he reiterated his desire to commence negotiations to stop the fighting. To this end he appointed Averell Harriman his personal negotiator. Most significantly, he declared that he would not be a candidate for the presidency in the 1968 election.

The special significance of the final announcement consisted in the fact that it took Johnson out of the war. Nixing more troops was no great new departure, since the president consistently had given the generals less than they had wanted. Besides, the situation in South Vietnam had continued to stabilize in the month since Wheeler had endorsed Westmoreland's request, making additional American soldiers less necessary than they had seemed at the time. Further, with American prodding, the South Vietnamese government of President Nguyen Van Thieu had unveiled plans to substantially enlarge the South Vietnamese army, thus laying the basis for what would be called "Vietnamization."

Neither was the bombing halt revolutionary. Since February 1965 Johnson had grounded the bombers or reduced their range of targets more than a dozen times. The longest complete halt was the one running from December 1965 through January 1966. Other groundings lasted from twenty-four hours to several days. Four times the president had declared Hanoi off-limits to American attacks. In any event, the bombing halt was revocable at presidential discretion.

Johnson's announcement of his desire to negotiate an

end to the war was equally unnovel. Repeatedly the president had asserted his administration's willingness to engage in unconditional discussions with the communists. Although the diplomatic grapevine had recently carried hints that Hanoi might be more interested than previously in talking, none of the hints conveyed any intimation Hanoi was modifying its demand that the United States get out of Vietnam and leave the country to the Vietnamese. Put otherwise, the communists might talk, but they would not deal.

By contrast, Johnson's declaration of lame-duckhood was both novel and for all practical purposes irrevocable, and it opened the door to substantial change in American policy. While the basic American objective in Vietnam remained as before—an independent, noncommunist South Vietnam—Johnson's departure hinted that Washington might be adjusting its sights downward. Johnson constantly compared Vietnam to Korea, and he couldn't have helped remembering how in the Korean case a new chief executive—Eisenhower—had been able to accept a settlement that would have elicited calls for Truman's impeachment. In 1969 a new president, Democrat or Republican, would enter the White House unburdened by much of the political baggage of Johnson's policies.

This is not to say Johnson was jettisoning his policies. He may even have felt his withdrawal would give those policies the greatest chance of success. Vain as he was, he understood that much of the animus against the war focused on him personally. At the least, protesters who chanted, "Hey, hey, LBJ, how many kids did you kill today?" would have to rewrite their rhymes after January 1969.

Yet whether or not he judged his policies still feasible, Johnson appreciated that a change was necessary. His withdrawal from the political arena would facilitate that change.

PRESIDENTS
and their
DECISIONS

CHAPTER

4

DE-ESCALATING THE WAR AND WITHDRAWING FROM THE PRESIDENTIAL RACE

JOHNSON'S DECISION TO DE-ESCALATE THE WAR

HERBERT Y. SCHANDLER

Herbert Y. Schandler is a retired army colonel who served as an infantry commander in Vietnam. He is the author of *The Unmaking of a President: Lyndon Johnson and Vietnam*, from which the following essay was excerpted, and coauthor (with Robert McNamara and others) of *Argument Without End: In Search of Answers to the Vietnam Tragedy*. Schandler describes the deliberative process that led to Johnson's March 31, 1968, decision to halt the bombing of North Vietnam, set limits on troop deployments, and call for negotiations with the North Vietnamese. This decision was made following the Tet offensive, a massive, coordinated attack on numerous targets in South Vietnam, which took place on the Vietnamese New Year (Tet) of 1968. According to Schandler, it became clear, in the wake of Tet, that the political and economic costs of the previous Vietnam policy were too high.

WHATEVER THE INTENTIONS OF THE PRESIDENT AND HIS advisors, the decisions of March 31, 1968, led the Americans and the North Vietnamese to the conference table in Paris to begin the journey on what was to be a long road to peace. A limit to the United States commitment of ground forces was established, and the South Vietnamese were put on notice that they would be expected to do more in their own defense. The limited United States political

---

objectives in South Vietnam were, for the first time, affirmed. The new American military commander's ground strategy was based on these limited objectives: a ceiling on an eventual reduction of American forces and increased participation of South Vietnamese forces.

It is not difficult to force the rich, chaotic, and confused flow of events and particular conjunction of circumstances of the early months of 1968 into a scheme of decision making that may have significance for many other aspects of the Vietnamese war and of the decision-making process in general. The picture that emerges is of a president dedicated personally and politically to an objective and a course of action, surrounded by advisors who generally had fashioned and continued to support that objective and course of action, but now challenged not only by the press of events but by an advisor who had begun to question both the objectives and the course being pursued.

The Tet offensive showed that the attainment of American objectives in Vietnam, if possible at all, was to be far in the future. The political reality was that more of the same in South Vietnam, with an increased commitment of American lives and money, accompanied by an immense effect on the domestic life of the United States, and with no guarantee of military victory in the near future, had become unacceptable to large elements of the American public. Another alternative had to be found.

Only then were our ultimate national objectives toward Vietnam brought out and reexamined. The Clifford Task Force [a group formed in February 1968 to consider the military's request for troop increases], while pointing out that new guidance was needed and that new and modified objectives had to be formulated and approved, could not itself clearly develop those objectives. This was a task that required presidential attention. Disagreement over national objectives became critical, and only the president could establish new national objectives. . . .

United States Objectives in Vietnam

Before the bureaucracy can function, it is necessary to know what objectives are being sought. Objectives, in both domestic and foreign policy, ultimately determine the values and beliefs of a society. But once the objectives are determined, the bureaucracy also has an obligation to the president to apprise him of the costs, both political and economic, of attaining those objectives. This function of the bureaucracy is routinely performed in government.... But when the objectives of the United States were established by the president in Vietnam, the decision-making process failed to address the problem of determining cost, both in resources and time, of attaining the objectives.

United States goals in South Vietnam were clear and remained constant. The major concern remained that of preventing the loss of South Vietnam to communism by force. This goal was primary in Johnson's thinking because of the perceived international and domestic repercussions of such a loss. Internationally, Vietnam was seen as a test of the United States military commitments to its allies around the world. Vietnam was also seen as a vital clash of wills between communism and the system of alliances established by the United States after World War II. Vietnam was the testing ground where the challenge of Communist wars of national liberation would be met by counterinsurgency warfare. The cost of aggression would be shown to be too high for the Communists to pay, and the principle that armed aggression would not be allowed to succeed would be validated.

Domestically, the successful defense of South Vietnam was seen to be essential to the political well-being of the United States. In his memoirs, President Johnson justified American policy in Vietnam in the following manner: "I knew our people well enough to realize that if we walked away from Vietnam and let Southeast Asia fall, there would follow a divisive and destructive debate in our country...."

A divisive debate about 'who lost Vietnam' would be, in my judgment, even more destructive to our national life than the argument over China had been. . . . Our allies . . . throughout the world would conclude that our word was worth little or nothing. . . . Moscow and Peking could not

Johnson's Withdrawal Speech

The following passages were excerpted from Johnson's March 31, 1968, announcement of his decision to deescalate the war and withdraw from the presidential race.

Tonight, I renew the offer I made last August—to stop the bombardment of North Vietnam. We ask that talks begin promptly, that they be serious talks on the substance of peace. We assume that during those talks Hanoi will not take advantage of our restraint.

We are prepared to move immediately toward peace through negotiations.

So, tonight, in the hope that this action will lead to early talks, I am taking the first step to deescalate the conflict. We are reducing—substantially reducing—the present level of hostilities.

And we are doing so unilaterally, and at once.

Tonight, I have ordered our aircraft and our naval vessels to make no attacks on North Vietnam, except in the area north of the demilitarized zone where the continuing enemy buildup directly threatens allied forward positions and where the movement of their troops and supplies are clearly related to that threat.

The area in which we are stopping our attacks includes almost 90 percent of North Vietnam's population, and most of its territory. Thus there will be no attacks around the principal populated areas, or in the food-producing areas of North Vietnam. . . .

I believe that a peaceful Asia is far nearer to reality

resist the opportunity to expand their control into the vacuum of power we would leave behind us."

Thus, Johnson felt that the alternative to defending South Vietnam would not be peace but an expanded area of conflict. With the fall of Vietnam, according to the

---

because of what America has done in Vietnam. I believe that the men who endure the dangers of battle—fighting there for us tonight—are helping the entire world avoid far greater conflicts, far wider wars, far more destruction, than this one. . . .

Through all time to come, I think America will be a stronger nation, a more just society, and a land of greater opportunity and fulfillment because of what we have all done together in these years of unparalleled achievement.

Our reward will come in the life of freedom, peace, and hope that our children will enjoy through ages ahead.

What we won when all of our people united must not now be lost in suspicion, distrust, selfishness, and politics among any of our people.

Believing this as I do, I have concluded that I should not permit the Presidency to become involved in the partisan divisions that are developing in this political year.

With America's sons in the fields far away, with America's future under challenge right here at home, with our hopes and the world's hopes for peace in the balance every day, I do not believe that I should devote an hour or a day of my time to any personal partisan causes or to any duties other than the awesome duties of this office—the Presidency of your country.

Accordingly, I shall not seek, and I will not accept the nomination of my party for another term as your president.

Lyndon B. Johnson, Address to the Nation, March 31, 1968.

domino concept, communism would spread throughout Southeast Asia, other United States commitments would be called into question, and the nation would be split by a vicious internal debate as to the wisdom of the policy adopted. President Johnson has been quoted as saying as early as 1963, "I am not going to be the President who saw Southeast Asia go the way China went."

In pursuing this objective, President Johnson was not prepared to run the risk of a direct military confrontation with the Soviet Union or China, perhaps with the ultimate possibility of a nuclear war. The avoidance of such a confrontation became, in effect, an equally important objective.

Thus, Johnson's policy objectives translated into doing the minimum amount militarily to prevent a South Vietnamese defeat while convincing Hanoi that it could not succeed in its aggression. The long-term goal was a political settlement that would "allow the South Vietnamese to determine their own future without outside interference." In a speech at Johns Hopkins University in April 1965, the president laid out for the American people what would be done in Vietnam: "We will do everything necessary to reach that objective [that the people of South Vietnam be allowed to guide their own country in their own way]. And we will do only what is absolutely necessary."

These policy objectives were implemented by a gradual step-by-step American military involvement in Vietnam. Johnson had to resist pressures from the military for victory, for doing more, on the one side, and pressures for disengagement or for deescalation and negotiation from those who opposed our military intervention, on the other. These pressures were accommodated by a decision-making process that shied away from decisive action, that failed to develop a cohesive and realistic strategy for attaining these objectives, that failed to examine the ultimate costs, and that attempted to compromise the various pressures for winning and for disengaging by a gradual military escalation that would satisfy the hawks by appearing to be doing more while satisfying the doves by calling for negotiations.

In seeking this middle-of-the-road consensus, the price, as one commentator [Leslie H. Gelb] has stated, was "a middle road of contradictions and no priorities for action." Guided by judgments of domestic reaction, careful not to take actions that would lead to Chinese or Russian intervention, the president made at least eight separate decisions on United States force levels in Vietnam over a four-year period. But as late as May of 1967, the secretary of defense could be told by one of his principal civilian advisors that the "'philosophy' of the war should be fought out so that everyone would not be proceeding on their own major premises and getting us in deeper and deeper."

Thus, the issues that were addressed and the decisions that were made were always tactical in nature. The only alternative policies examined were alternative force levels or alternative bombing campaigns. Since the cost of not intervening in Vietnam was deemed to be greater than the cost of intervening, the ultimate military cost of that intervention was not measured. The only cost that had to be considered was continued public support, and, consequently, decisions about additional military resources for Vietnam had to be measured against public support for such actions.

Gradual escalation was therefore the strategy chosen for achieving United States objectives. Domestic politics dictated the minimum necessary disruption in American life. But with each passing year of war, the domestic political position of the president grew weaker. Optimism without results produced, in time, a credibility gap.

A Limitless but Restricted Effort

To insist that the cost of not intervening to save Vietnam would be far greater than any cost that could be incurred in defending American interests in Southeast Asia was to place an unlimited commitment on American resources and was also to have a stultifying effect upon any serious examination of alternatives. Indeed, the strategy adopted assigned more rationality to the North Vietnamese decision-making process than it did to our own. By the gradual application of power, the United States would find that elusive point at which the war would become too costly to the old revolutionaries in North Vietnam, causing them to abandon their goals in the South. But there would be no limit on the effort we would expend in driving them to that point. In the application of this strategy, the nation's leaders repeatedly misjudged the enemy's ability to frustrate American aims and to counterescalate at every stage.

At some point, it should have been clear that the costs, both political and economic, incurred by the United States in defending Vietnam could indeed exceed the costs of disengagement, or, conversely, that the costs we were willing to pay could not guarantee victory. But to state this, or seriously to question Vietnam's place in our international and domestic priorities, was not encouraged in the Johnson administration and was seen as indicating an unacceptable lack of resolve in meeting the Communist challenge. Some few officials foresaw the eventual cost or, at some point, indicated that they felt the cost had become too high, but they either had little influence or were shuffled off the scene.

On the other hand, those who advocated a stronger United States effort in and around Vietnam, especially the Joint Chiefs of Staff, were disarmed in a different fashion. Denied a strategic concept and the military freedom they felt was needed to win the war, the military chiefs were pacified by gradual increases in force levels and in bombing targets and, eventually, by the replacement of a secretary of defense who had become anathema to them. But these increases in military authority were always within the president's guidelines. And so the military chiefs, while each sought a larger role for his own service, in effect became sophisticated yes men for the president's policies, assuring the public, as did General [William] Westmoreland, that every request from the field commander had been met, and seldom raising in public their view of the eventual military consequences in Vietnam of the president's restrictions. . . .

Thus, fundamental assumptions concerning objectives were never questioned. The decision-making process was never engaged to determine ultimate costs and to draw up a balance sheet as to when these costs would become excessive. Alternatives were not examined, and decisions concerning the allocation of American resources to Vietnam were made on the basis of what was the minimum additional that could be done while maintaining public support for the war. There was no coherent strategy to win American objectives. The strategy was to persevere so as not to pay the domestic political price of failure and to convince the Communists, with the minimum force necessary, that our will was firm and that they could not win. The consequences of this failure to develop a precise clear aim with necessary limitations, consequences certainly unintended by civilian leaders, at least, were a large-scale bombing campaign against North Vietnam and a commitment of half a million American troops to a ground war in Asia.

Only when the price of attaining United States objectives became so dear in lives, dollars, and public confidence and the benefits became so intangible, remote, and even implausible did our national leadership match the objectives that were being pursued with the resources and time needed to attain them. Only when the cost had *already* become too high were the objectives that were being pursued and the strategy being followed to attain them matched to see if they were in accord. This was the failure of the decision-making process as it operated at the highest levels of the government.

After Tet 1968 the decision-making process functioned properly for the first time. Objectives were matched to the resources required to achieve those objectives, and the strategy being followed was modified when it was seen that the costs, political and material, of attaining those results within a reasonable period of time would be more than the nation was willing to pay. Afterward the debate became an issue of policy—how to attain national objectives with limited resources, how to modify the objectives without abandoning them completely, how to regain public acceptance for subsequent American actions in South Vietnam.

The existing policy, which had enjoyed public support for several years, was shown not to be producing the results expected in a reasonable time or at an acceptable cost. The public could not see an end to the war. In order to produce quicker or more decisive results, the commitment of resources would have to be increased vastly, and the whole nature of the war and its relationship to the United States would be changed. There was strong indication that large and growing elements of the American public had begun to believe that the cost had already reached unacceptable levels and that the objective was no longer worth the price. It was brought home to Johnson finally that the policy being pursued in Vietnam would no longer be supported by the American electorate. The political reality—one recognized by the president—was that, without renouncing the former policy, a new direction, a new and less costly strategy, had to be found.

Thus, the president's decisions of March 1968 were based upon two major considerations:

1. The conviction of his advisors, particularly Secretary of Defense [Clark] Clifford, that an increased American effort would not make the achievement of American objectives more likely or more rapid; and

2. His own deeply felt conviction that unity must be restored to the American nation. . . .

Tet 1968, then, represented a turning point in American policy toward Vietnam. American objectives in Vietnam remained the same. But, after years of military effort and political anguish, the American government finally, in March of 1968, developed a strategy for attaining those objectives that it hoped would not place an unlimited burden upon national economic and military resources, and that could, over time, hold public acceptance. As Kissinger later pointed out: "The Tet offensive marked the watershed of the American effort. Henceforth, no matter how effective our actions, the prevalent strategy could no longer achieve its objectives within a period or with force levels politically acceptable to the American people. . . . This made inevitable an eventual commitment to a political solution and marked the beginning of the quest for a negotiated settlement."

Johnson's Decision Not to Run for Reelection

Joseph A. Califano Jr.

Joseph A. Califano Jr. was Johnson's special assistant for domestic affairs from 1965 until the end of the Johnson administration. The following essay is excerpted from his memoir *The Triumph & Tragedy of Lyndon Johnson: The White House Years.* Califano describes the events of early 1968 leading up to Johnson's March 31 announcement of his decision to withdraw from the presidential race. During those months, Johnson frantically pressed for the passage of his domestic agenda as his administration came increasingly under siege over issues including the Vietnam War and racial strife. According to Califano, Johnson believed that removing himself from the presidential race would facilitate the passage of his domestic programs, help resolve the Vietnam War, and "heal the wounds now separating the country." Califano is currently chairman of the National Center on Addiction and Substance Abuse at Columbia University.

T HE PREPARATION OF THE PRESIDENT'S JANUARY 1968 STATE of the Union message and legislative program became a battleground for the President's mind. [Henry (Joe)] Fowler pressed hard for major cuts in domestic programs, urging what I viewed as abandonment of the Great Society. Johnson's inability to get a tax bill out of Congress strengthened Fowler's hand. In his own soundings on the Hill, the President heard several variations of the Treasury

Secretary's theme. In late November 1967, he was talking about trimming social programs in order to reach an accommodation with House Ways and Means Committee Chairman Wilbur Mills. . . .

In the end, the message not only defended the Great Society programs Congress had enacted, but urged passage of those still pending and proposed major new ones. Johnson may have been wavering in December, but in January he was still willing to spend whatever capital he had left—and it was dwindling fast—to get his work done without waiting for the war to be over.

LBJ laid another heavy workload on Congress—not only the unfinished agenda of numerous bills and the massive new job and housing programs, but new consumer bills, a major expansion of child-health programs, tougher drug laws, farm programs, medical-cost-control proposals, antipollution efforts, even some increases in domestic spending—and a big push for his tax surcharge. Four years into his presidency, he was still striving to do more. . . .

The White House Under Siege

Six days after the address, North Korea seized the USS *Pueblo*, a spy ship stationed off its coast, and took the crew as prisoners. The next week, on January 30, the North Vietnamese mounted the Tet offensive, a full-scale assault on South Vietnam's cities, stretching over more than three weeks. The press reported it as a setback for U.S. and South Vietnamese forces, and the psychological blow reverberated through the Congress, the public, and the administration. The military was claiming victory because they had repelled the enemy and inflicted enormous losses on the Vietcong and North Vietnamese, but even in the White House many of us had our doubts.

The administration had declared that the Communists were losing the war. Victory or not, the sheer ability of the North Vietnamese and Vietcong to mount such a large-scale offensive had shattered the American people's confidence in the President's word. For the first time, large numbers of Americans thought their country might lose the war.

There was a sense of siege in the White House. It was increasingly difficult to find public forums for the President that avoided disruption from demonstrators opposing the war or demanding more money and programs for blacks and poor people. On January 3, Senator Eugene McCarthy, the Minnesota Democrat whose campaign for the presidential nomination had not been taken seriously when he announced it in November 1967, had expressed his intention to mount a "vigorous" effort in the New Hampshire primary on an antiwar platform. That same day, former Alabama Governor George Wallace congratulated cheering supporters in California for qualifying his new American Independent Party on the California ballot in his unannounced third-party bid to unseat Johnson and roll back his civil rights policies. . . .

Knowing now that his time was running out, Johnson almost frenetically continued to press the contentious 90th Congress for domestic reforms. On February 5, right in the middle of the Tet fighting, he sent a special message asking Congress for increased funds for elementary and secondary education, a new vocational education program, an Educational Opportunity Act for college students, and increased support for universities. . . .

The President could not hurl programs at Congress and the public fast enough. He was irritable and impatient when I did not have a draft special message in his night reading to go to Congress the next day. In our haste, we sometimes slipped up on notifying a key committee member, an unspeakable offense in prior years. Often we put so many complex proposals out in a day that reporters were unable to write clearly about them, as our own stories vied with each other for front-page coverage. During these hectic weeks, McCarthy and his student supporters in New

Hampshire worked the President over on the war, Wallace announced his third-party candidacy and stirred up the white backlash against Johnson, and an increasingly critical Robert Kennedy found fault with something in almost every proposal LBJ put forward.

There was a whirl of desperate haste about the President. I suggested more than once that he was sending messages too fast. He would say, "I want to get them up there so I can get my program passed. Time is important, especially if I don't run for reelection." But I never doubted that he would run. After all, he had talked about not running in 1964. . . .

Time to Wind Down in Vietnam

On February 27, [White House counsel Harry] McPherson and I went to luncheon in the Secretary of State's private dining room with [Secretary of State Dean] Rusk, [Robert] McNamara, Clark Clifford (who would replace McNamara as Defense Secretary), [National Security Adviser] Walt Rostow, Undersecretary of State [Nicholas] Katzenbach, and Assistant Secretary of State William Bundy. We were to discuss a speech that the President planned to give on Vietnam at the end of March. He would also try again to convince Congress and the public that we needed a tax surcharge. That's what accounted for my presence at the lunch.

It was the most depressing three hours in my years of public service. My job left me on the periphery of the war. This was the first time since early in 1966 that I had heard the President's advisers in an intimate discussion of Vietnam. McNamara, Katzenbach, and Assistant Secretary of State William Bundy were beyond pessimism. They sounded a chorus of despair. Rusk appeared exhausted and worn down.

The President had asked us to talk about the military's request for 205,000 troops on top of the half million already there. McNamara, his face lined and eyelids darkened, was tense. He called the request "madness . . . I've re-peatedly honored requests from the [General Earle] Wheelers of the world but we have no assurance that an additional 205,000 men will make any difference in the conduct of the war." Katzenbach and Bundy nodded in agreement, and McNamara added, "Nobody knows whether it will make any difference. It still may not be enough to win the war. There is no [military] plan to win the war." McNamara attacked the bombing of North and South Vietnam and Laos. We were "dropping ordnance at a higher rate than during the last year of World War II in Europe," the bombing was not stopping war supplies from getting to the Vietcong, and "[the destruction] is making us lasting enemies in Southeast Asia." Katzenbach said that it was clear the request for 205,000 men could not be honored; the only question was how to handle Wheeler.

Stating emphatically, "I am not pushing it," Clifford mentioned another possibility. They should consider putting in "500,000 to a million men." McNamara was sarcastic, "That has the virtue of clarity"; an increase of that proportion would at least indicate we were seeking "to accomplish the job." But he expressed grave doubts about the military, economic, political, diplomatic, and moral consequences.

Bundy said that South Vietnam was "very weak" and "our position may be truly untenable." He suggested that plans be made for withdrawal "with the best possible face" and a credible indication that we would defend the "rest of Asia."

Rusk and Rostow seemed more optimistic. They pointed out that the enemy had suffered heavy losses and gained little ground during the Tet offensive. Rusk shared McNamara's misgivings and proposed a bombing halt over North Vietnam, although the Secretary of State wasn't certain what, if any, conditions should be attached, and he admitted a halt might accomplish little or nothing.

Clifford said that despite optimistic reports about enemy casualties during Tet, "our people and world opinion believe we have suffered a setback." He asked, "How do we avoid creating the feeling that we are pouring troops down a rathole?" Before any decision is made, Clifford thought, "we must re-evaluate our entire posture in South Vietnam."

With the exception of Rostow, there was no certainty around the table that any number of additional troops could bring victory. Rostow believed that the bombing should continue and opposed any unconditional pause. He did not express a clear opinion about Wheeler's request for more troops, but he left me with the impression that he would have honored a good part of that request. As lunch ended, I thought that he was alone among the President's men in the belief that we could succeed in Vietnam.

McPherson and I drove back to the White House together in a state of depression. I was physically shaken. Both of us were completely drained.

"This is crazy," I said.

McPherson nodded.

"It really is all over, isn't it?" I said.

"You bet it is," McPherson responded.

It was at this moment, riding in the car, that I knew the President had somehow to wind the war down and get out of Vietnam. . . .

Johnson Ponders Stepping Down

Events were closing in. On March 7, during Senate debate on the administration's fair-housing bill, liberals and moderates suddenly demanded that the Senate be consulted before Johnson sent any more troops to Vietnam. On March 10, news of Wheeler's request leaked into *The New York Times*, and over the next two days the Senate Foreign Relations Committee grilled Rusk at length during televised hearings. On March 12, Senator Eugene McCarthy got a startling 42 percent of the New Hampshire primary vote.

Wheeler's request fell victim to the President's concern that more troops would not accomplish much. The battle raging in the government was now whether LBJ should announce a new bombing pause, and if so, how extensive. Having tried and failed with eight previous bombing pauses, the President remained undecided.

On March 16, Robert Kennedy entered the presidential race because, he said, "it is now unmistakably clear that we can change [the country's] disastrous divisive policies [in Vietnam and at home] only by changing the men who are now making them." Kennedy's announcement four days after McCarthy's unexpected show of strength in New Hampshire confirmed Johnson's belief, expressed privately as soon as the New Hampshire primary results became known, that the New York Senator was now sure to enter the race. While Kennedy claimed publicly that he intended to run in harmony with McCarthy, the Minnesota Senator scorned his rival as late to the fray, adding, "An Irishman who announces the day before St. Patrick's Day that he's going to run against another Irishman shouldn't say it's going to be a peaceful relationship." . . .

Bombing-halt proposals were still under debate when LBJ asked Harry McPherson and me to lunch on March 28. We sat down shortly before three in the Flower Garden and worked for an hour in the unseasonably warm sun. The first part of the discussion was on the speech to be delivered on March 31, particularly the bombing pause and tax surcharge. . . .

Then the President looked long at both of us and asked, "What do you think about my not running for reelection?" We both said he had to run, though McPherson added, "I wouldn't run if I were you." Johnson asked why we thought he had to run.

"Because you're the only guy who can get anything done."

Johnson gazed at us and said pensively, "Others can get

things done. The Congress and I are like an old married couple. We've lived together so long and we've been rubbing against each other night after night so often and we've asked so much of each other over the years we're tired of each other. They'd have a honeymoon. Any one of them. I wouldn't have one." Still, that afternoon neither McPherson nor I imagined Johnson would walk away.

We went back to the Oval Office, and LBJ sent McPherson off to produce a revised draft of the speech and asked me to stay behind. He sat down at his desk and turned his chair around to the signing table behind it, as I stood to his right. . . .

LBJ asked me again what I thought about his not running for reelection. I said I thought he should run, but running with the problems he now had—the war, racial tension, the poverty program, and civil disturbances—would subject him to a lot of abuse. I was afraid if he announced he was not running for reelection the legislative program would go down the tubes in Congress.

Johnson responded that if he pulled out of the race he might have even more leverage with the Congress and the North Vietnamese. He would be above politics. He could ask the people and the Congress for what he thought was right—bolstered by the sacrifice of his own political career for the good of the country. "That's far more than I ask any congressman to do when I ask him to vote for the tax bill" or a Great Society program. . . .

"Mr. President, if you run, I think you'll win."

"Win what? The way it is now we can't get the tax surcharge passed and Ho Chi Minh and Fulbright don't believe anything I say about ending the war."

The President spoke to me at some length about the divisions in the country. He felt he would only aggravate them if he ran for reelection. I said, "I'm afraid that if Nixon wins he would dismantle our programs. And Kennedy would be stymied on the Hill if he won."

"Whether Kennedy or Nixon won, at least the leadership would support them in the first year or so," Johnson said, adding after a thoughtful pause, "And that might provide the necessary time to heal the wounds now separating the country." . . .

The President sighed and talked again about the "divisions in the country" and his hope for "peace in Vietnam." He looked more exhausted than I'd ever seen him. "Only Bob McNamara and George Christian know how close I've come to announcing that I would not run. Now again," he sighed, "it is very much on my mind."

I later learned that LBJ had come very close to withdrawing when he presented his State of the Union message in January, but had drawn back because he didn't want to hurt his legislative program. He had told George Christian, one of the few individuals who knew he had actually prepared the announcement, "It just didn't fit. I couldn't go in there and lay out a big program and then say, 'Okay, here's all this work to do, and by the way, so long. I'm leaving.'"

Now, in my gut, standing there watching him exhausted, I began to realize that he was leaning against running. I wanted him to run; but he wasn't going to do it. . . .

The address on March 31 stunned the nation. Its ending caught most of the White House staff and cabinet by surprise. The President had already approved distribution of speech cards on his domestic achievements to his political supporters and an aggressive program to gather campaign data on a variety of topics, including McCarthy and Kennedy. White House aides Jim Gaither and John Robson were in my office preparing materials for the campaign when Johnson made his announcement.

And he left no doubt. On the last draft, he made a final edit, changing the sentence "Accordingly, I shall not seek—and *would* not accept—the nomination of my party for another term as your President" to "Accordingly, I shall not seek—and *will* not accept . . ."

As it turned out, Johnson had withdrawn barely in time to gather the strength he would need for the awful days ahead.

Praise and Popularity

Moments after the speech, the White House switchboard sparkled with calls. No one has done more to unify the nation . . . The most moving speech a President has ever made . . . A great President, willing to sacrifice his personal ambition for the people . . . Editorial pages and television commentators quickly took the chorus of praise to even higher octaves. *The Washington Post* rhapsodized that LBJ "has made a personal sacrifice in the name of national unity that entitles him to a very special place in the annals of American history. . . . The President last night put unity ahead of his own advancement and his own pride." When Johnson flew to Chicago the next day, crowds whose abuse the Secret Service had feared on Sunday were cheering and friendly on Monday, with people toting homemade signs, such as the one saying, "LBJ IS A GREAT AMERICAN."

Tuesday, at their weekly breakfast with the President, Democratic congressional leaders wanted to discuss the political implications of the President's withdrawal. He turned their questions aside. He said he was "tired of begging anyone for anything. I had a partnership with Jack Kennedy and when he died I felt it was my duty to look after the family and stockholders and employees of my partner. I did not fire anyone. The divisions are so deep within the Party that I could not reconcile them. I'm not going to influence the Convention . . . probably won't even go. Much to everyone's disbelief, I never wanted to be President to begin with. I'm leaving without any bitterness."

Our soundings already indicated that Congress was likely to be much more amenable to his programs than we had judged. The administration's housing and truth-in-lending proposals, in mortal danger the week before, had new life, and full funding for poverty programs now seemed possible. The President pressed the leadership to act on his request for increased taxes. That afternoon the Senate passed the President's tax-surcharge bill by a wider than expected margin. For the first time any of us dared remember, even North Vietnam was on the defensive. On April 3, Hanoi expressed a readiness to talk and LBJ quickly took them up on it. In an instant, the President regained a credibility he hadn't possessed in years.

And his popularity soared. On April 4, when he traveled to New York for the installation of Terence Cooke as Archbishop, bystanders cheered him as he walked up the steps to St. Patrick's Cathedral. Even New York's paparazzi were smiling and waving to him. As the President walked down the center aisle, the overflowing congregation rose as one and clapped and cheered him; only Pope Paul VI had ever received a standing ovation in the cathedral.

After the service, the President spoke briefly to Jacqueline Kennedy and then stopped by Archbishop Cooke's residence directly behind the cathedral on Madison Avenue. The President asked to see Nelson and Happy Rockefeller, gave Happy a picture of the couple that had been taken at the White House, and spoke quietly to the Governor alone.

Just as the helicopter was about to take off from Central Park, Johnson decided to run over to the United Nations to see Ambassador Goldberg and UN Secretary General U Thant to press for negotiations to end the war in Vietnam. On the return flight, the President was exhilarated by the welcome he had received in St. Patrick's and the support he had received from U Thant. As we arrived on the south lawn of the White House at 6:30 P.M., Johnson was looking forward to a Democratic congressional fundraising dinner in his and the Vice President's honor, where he knew he'd be greeted by a crowd as thunderously cheering as any he'd faced since the 1964 campaign. And he was savoring flash reports that the next day a Lou Harris poll would reveal a complete reversal in his rating: from 57 percent disapproval before the March 31 speech to 57 percent approval after it.

Johnson Withdrew to Preserve His Historical Reputation

Doris Kearns

Doris Kearns was a staff assistant to Johnson during his administration. The following essay is excerpted from her book *Lyndon Johnson and the American Dream*. Kearns writes that in the early months of 1968, a series of events left Johnson feeling harried, despairing, and trapped in a losing war and a failing presidency. Johnson's decisions both to deescalate the war and withdraw from politics were motivated by his realization that he was destined to fail if he continued on his current course. Instead, he sought to be remembered as a president who brought about peace in Southeast Asia and ensured national security. He withdrew from the presidential race to ensure that his peacemaking would be viewed as a noble act and not a political maneuver, Kearns concludes.

███████

ALL HIS LIFE JOHNSON HAD BELIEVED THAT POWER WAS something you obtained if you had the energy and drive to work harder than everyone else. Power, in turn, made good works possible, and good works brought love and gratitude, which then provided the inspiration and vitality for further work. This formula informed Johnson's personal experience: time and again he had been able to parlay his limited resources into substantial political holdings, rising from Congressman to Senator to Majority Leader to Vice President and finally to President. But now, three years after his landslide victory, the American people had, Johnson believed, broken the cycle of power, energy, and good works by denying him the appreciation he deserved for all that he had produced. Indeed, by Johnson's assessment, his administration had produced more than any administration in history, and he could document his claim: he had given more laws, more houses, more medical services, more jobs to more people, than any other President. Surely, he had earned the love and gratitude of the American people. Yet as he looked around him in 1967 Johnson found only paralyzing bitterness. He could not comprehend the nature of the unrest or the cause of his unpopularity.

"How is it possible," Johnson repeatedly asked, "that all these people could be so ungrateful to me after I had given them so much? Take the Negroes. I fought for them from the first day I came into office. I spilled my guts out in getting the Civil Rights Act of 1964 through Congress. I put everything I had into that speech before the joint session in 1965. I tried to make it possible for every child of every color to grow up in a nice house, to eat a solid breakfast, to attend a decent school, and to get a good and lasting job. I asked so little in return. Just a little thanks. Just a little appreciation. That's all. But look at what I got instead. Riots in 175 cities. Looting. Burning. Shooting. It ruined everything. Then take the students. I wanted to help them, too. I fought on their behalf for scholarships and loans and grants. I fought for better teachers and better schools. And look what I got back. Young people by the thousands leaving their universities, marching in the streets, chanting that horrible song about how many kids I had killed that day. And the poor, they, too, turned against me. When Congress cut the funds for the Great Society, they made me Mr. Villain. I remember once going to visit a poor family in Appalachia. They had seven children, all skinny and sick. I promised the mother and father I would make things better for them. I told them all my hopes for their future. They seemed real happy to talk with me, and I felt good about that. But then as I walked toward the door, I noticed two pictures on the shabby wall. One was Jesus Christ on the cross; the other was John Kennedy. I felt as if I'd been slapped in the face."

So strong was Johnson's need for affection, and so vital his need for public gratitude, that he experienced this rejection of his "good works" as an absolute rejection of himself. Denied the appreciation which not only empowered but sustained his self, the love which validated his identity, the anatomy which gave Lyndon Johnson's ego its shape was dissolved. His energy and capacity to direct that energy outward abandoned him. Every presidential responsibility (speeches, conducting meetings, greeting visitors) took inordinate effort. The man who had battened on the goodwill of crowds, accelerating his pace in proportion to the crowd's number and affection, now could not leave the White House without being harassed by demonstrators and pickets. He had once liked to unwind with reporters, Congressmen, and staff, holding forth upon his strategy for the Great Society. But now Vietnam dominated his every word and a savage rain of vituperation fell upon his staff, the Congress, and reporters.

Now he began to marshal all his resources to fashion a defense, and the energies absorbed in this task of defending the self were no longer available for the everyday demands of leadership. Even at small group meetings Johnson now seemed unaware of what those present were thinking or even talking about. He gave the impression of not seeing his audience at all, having lost his sensitivity to the subtleties of tone and emphasis. This was not simply the passive inattention of a tired mind; it was the active inattention of a preoccupied mind, a mind whose focus was increasingly limited in mobility and scope.

Unhappy Days and Nights

Johnson had traversed 1965, 1966, and most of 1967 re-treating into a dreamlike world in which the tide on both the war and the Great Society was just about to turn. By early 1968 this dream had died. Daily contact with the real world—with the evidence of a deepening inflation, with the results of the Tet offensive, and with the challenge of the primaries—was forcing Johnson back to reality. If the days of accomplishment were truly finished, as Johnson suspected, what then was the point? No good works, no love, no self-esteem. Only the endless repetition of sordid, unhappy days. Johnson's enthusiasm and vitality steadily receded. He was really tired, and he knew it.

Hating the days, Johnson hated the nights even more. He began dreaming again the dream of paralysis that had haunted him since early childhood. Only this time he was lying in a bed in the Red Room of the White House, instead of sitting in a chair in the middle of the open plains. His head was still his, but from the neck down his body was the thin, paralyzed body that had been the affliction of both Woodrow Wilson and his own grandmother in their final years. All his presidential assistants were in the next room. He could hear them actively fighting with one another to di-vide up his power. . . . He could hear them, but he could not command them, for he could neither talk nor walk. He was sick and stilled, but not a single aide tried to protect him.

The dream terrified Johnson, waking from his sleep. Lying in the dark, he could find no peace until he got out of bed, and, by the light of a small flashlight, walked the halls of the White House to the place where Woodrow Wil-son's portrait hung. He found something soothing in the act of touching Wilson's picture; he could sleep again. He was still Lyndon Johnson, and he was still alive and mov-ing; it was Woodrow Wilson who was dead. This ritual, however, brought little lasting peace; when morning came, Johnson's mind was again filled with fears. Only gradually did he recognize the resemblance between this dream and the stampede dream of his boyhood. [As a child, Johnson had a recurring nightmare in which he was sitting in a chair on a plain, paralyzed, as a stampede of cattle came toward him.] Making the connection, his fears intensified; he was certain now that paralysis was his inevitable fate. Remembering his family's history of early strokes, he convinced himself that he, too, would suffer a stroke in his next term. Immobilized, still in office nominally, yet not actually in control: this seemed to Johnson the worst situation imaginable. He could not rid himself of the suspicion that a mean God had set out to torture him in the cruelest manner possible. His suffering now no longer consisted of his usual melancholy; it was an acute throbbing pain, and he craved relief. More than anything he wanted peace and quiet. An end to the pain.

Chased by Stampedes

Through the fall and winter of 1967, Johnson later reported, the decision to withdraw from politics took hold. He discussed it, he wrote in a section of his memoirs that reads as if it were a defense attorney's brief, with a number of people. . . . He claimed he had considered announcing it at the end of the State of the Union message in early January, 1968; he had asked [aide] Horace Busby to write a draft statement. But when he got to the Capitol that night—and his explanation is not entirely convincing from this man of meticulous detail—he reached into his pocket and discovered that he had forgotten to bring it with him. The announcement was not made. Then between the end of January and the middle of March came the Tet offensive, [Senator Eugene] McCarthy's victory [in the New Hampshire primary], the collapse of the gold market, the publication of the Riot Commission Report, and, most importantly, Robert Kennedy's entrance into the presidential race.

"I felt," Johnson said, "that I was being chased on all sides by a giant stampede coming at me from all directions. On one side, the American people were stampeding me to do something about Vietnam. On another side, the inflationary economy was booming out of control. Up ahead were dozens of danger signs pointing to another summer of riots in the cities. I was being forced over the edge by rioting blacks, demonstrating students, marching welfare mothers, squawking professors, and hysterical reporters. And then the final straw. The thing I feared from the first day of my Presidency was actually coming true. Robert Kennedy had openly announced his intention to reclaim the throne in the memory of his brother. And the American people, swayed by the magic of the name, were dancing in the streets. The whole situation was unbearable for me. After thirty-seven years of public service, I deserved something more than being left alone in the middle of the plain, chased by stampedes on every side."

All his life Johnson had held before himself the image of the daring cowboy, the man with the capacity to outrun the wild herd, riding at a dead run in the dark of the night, knowing there were prairie dog holes all around. It was this definition of manly courage, opposed to what he saw as a feminine tendency to run away from responsibility, that had deterred Johnson in August, 1964, from abandoning the Presidency—and at that point the only stampede he faced was his own fear that the memorial film of John F. Kennedy would provoke a rush of delegates to Robert F. Kennedy. How much more difficult it would be for him now—when the stampede had already started—to justify his running away!

So Johnson found himself in an untenable position in early 1968. It was impossible to quit and impossible to stay. If he left office and went back to Texas, he would be acting like a coward; if he stayed for another four years, he would be paralyzed before his term was out. . . . No matter how

Mocking Freedom

This excerpt from a speech by Paul Potter, president of the radical protest group Students for a Democratic Society, provides an example of the intense criticism Johnson faced for his handling of the Vietnam War.

The President says that we are defending freedom in Vietnam. Whose freedom? Not the freedom of the Vietnamese. . . .

The pattern of repression and destruction that we have developed and justified in the war is so thorough that it can only be called "cultural genocide." I am not simply talking about napalm or gas or crop destruction or torture hurled indiscriminantly on women and children, insurgent and neutral, upon the first suspicion of rebel activity. That in itself is horrendous and incredible beyond belief. But it is only part of a large pattern of destruction to the very fabric of the country. We have uprooted the people from the land and imprisoned them in concentration camps called "sunrise villages." Through conscription and direct political intervention and control we have broken or destroyed local customs and tra-

hard he tried to think it out, he got nowhere. One line of action was as bad as the other. No matter how hectic his activity, he could not drive the demons away. But then, Johnson explained, one day—exactly what day is not clear—he realized the total impossibility of his situation. The realization came to him in a dream. In the dream he saw himself swimming in a river. He was swimming from the center toward one shore. He swam and swam, but he never seemed to get any closer. He turned around to swim to the other shore, but again he got nowhere. He was simply going round and round in circles. The dream remind-

ditions, trampled upon those things of value which give dignity and purpose to life. . . .

Not even the President can say that this is war to defend the freedom of the Vietnamese people. Perhaps what the President means when he speaks of freedom is the freedom of the Americans.

What in fact has the war done for freedom in America? It has led to even more vigorous governmental efforts to control information, manipulate the press and pressure and persuade the public through distorted or downright dishonest documents. . . .

The President mocks freedom if he insists that the war in Vietnam is a defense of American freedom. Perhaps the only freedom that this war protects is the freedom of the warhawks in the Pentagon and the State Department to "experiment" with "counter-insurgency" and guerrilla warfare in Vietnam. Vietnam, we may say, is a "laboratory" run by a new breed of gamesmen who approach war as a kind of rational exercise in international power politics.

Paul Potter, "The Incredible War," Speech at the Washington Antiwar March, April 17, 1965.

ed Johnson of his grandfather's story about driving the cattle across the river, where they, too, got caught in a whirl, circling round and round in the same spot.

The Verdict of History

Aware now of the bind he was in, Johnson finally found a way to extricate himself. He ingeniously reasoned that he could withdraw from politics without being seen as a coward. To follow his reasoning, we must understand the intensity of his concern for the verdict of history. The desire to leave something permanent behind as evidence of the work of a lifetime had been with him from the days of his youth, but never had it been so preoccupying a force as it was in the spring of 1968. At a time when the present was filled with unhappiness, Johnson turned to the future for uplift. Widen the constituency, flee once again from the pain of intimacy, multiply your resources. Looking ahead to posterity, Johnson began thinking that his current difficulties might prove to be a blessing in disguise. There was still the opportunity to restore his reputation if he acted nobly at this critical moment. "If the American people don't love me, their descendants will."

Eyes fixed on the future, Johnson believed he would be judged by history for his success or failure in fulfilling three presidential functions: providing domestic peace and tranquillity, providing for the national security, and providing for the general welfare. In each area, he saw a conflict between his role as President of all the people and his role as candidate of the Democratic Party. In each area, he reasoned, he would be more likely to reach his goals if he was not a candidate, but a chief of state above the partisan battle.

First, on questions of national security. . . .

In finally offering an end to the air war against the North, Johnson was not forced to see himself as a coward, running away from Vietnam. To the contrary, he convinced himself that he was the same man of courage, determined to save South Vietnam, daring a new initiative in a continuing course. Moreover, by coupling this initiative with withdrawal from the presidential race, he made sure that it would not be read as a political trick. If, on the other hand, it failed to produce negotiations, then at least Johnson had laid the groundwork for further escalation. If the situation in South Vietnam was as good as the military claimed, then it was just possible that Hanoi would finally come to the peace table. And if that happened, then Johnson believed that he would be honored by history for hav-

ing mapped out a policy in Southeast Asia that had ensured America's national security for years to come.

The General Welfare and Domestic Peace

If concern for the future affected Johnson's decisions about
"national security," it also affected his thinking about "the
general welfare." By the spring of 1968 the tax surcharge
had become the most pressing domestic issue. Without the
surtax the American economy was in danger and Johnson
knew it. And the situation at home was substantially exacerbated by deepening financial problems abroad. British
devaluation of the pound in late 1967 had triggered a general deterioration in the gold market and a crisis of confidence in the dollar. By the middle of March the gold market was in a state of panic. Speculation was rampant that
the United States, too, might be forced to devalue.

Johnson saw the deepest fears of his generation reflected in this situation. He believed that the stalemate on taxes
was being interpreted abroad as a failure of the democratic process and a clear indication that America had neither
the will nor the ability to control its economic affairs. The
specter of 1929 haunted him daily; he worried that if the
economy collapsed, history would subject Lyndon Johnson
to endless abuse. Yet as long as he was a candidate, Johnson
was convinced, the Republicans in Congress would stall
the surtax, so they could campaign in the fall against
"Johnson's inflation" as well as "Johnson's war." Therefore,
in this case, too, withdrawing from the race was the only
answer. Here, too, posterity would see his abdication as an
act of courage, not cowardice.

Withdrawing would also strengthen the President in
his search for domestic peace. Johnson looked back to the
previous summer and recalled the accusation that he had
chosen a partisan course during the Detroit riots. If he reacted strongly to civil disorders, he would be accused of
currying favor on the right; if he reacted temperately, he

would be vulnerable to the opposite charge. Either charge might reduce his reputation in the annals of history. Johnson wanted to be remembered as the preserver of domestic peace, a man who had enforced the law with equity and fairness to all. But here, too, as with Vietnam and the tax bill, the favorable judgment of history could be better secured only by withdrawing from politics.

Abdication was thus the last remaining way to restore control, to turn rout into dignity, collapse into order. It served to advance Johnson's immediate purposes and his long-term goals. As the situation stood, Johnson was about to lose the Wisconsin primary and the forecasts looked equally dim for the primaries in Oregon, Indiana, and California. To win the nomination under these circumstances would have been—though possible—a Pyrrhic victory. It would have torn the nation apart. Johnson recognized this. His concerns for the present and the future, for national unity and posterity, for the war and the economy, joined together. He decided to retreat with honor.

APPENDIX OF DOCUMENTS

Document 1: "Let Us Continue"

On November 27, 1963, five days after John Kennedy's assassination, Johnson entreated the Congress to cooperate with him in implementing Kennedy's legislative agenda.

All I have I would have given gladly not to be standing here today.

The greatest leader of our time has been struck down by the foulest deed of our time. Today John Fitzgerald Kennedy lives on in the immortal words and works that he left behind. He lives on in the mind and memories of mankind. He lives on in the hearts of his countrymen.

No words are sad enough to express our sense of loss. No words are strong enough to express our determination to continue the forward thrust of America that he began.

The dream of conquering the vastness of space—the dream of partnership across the Atlantic—and across the Pacific as well—the dream of a Peace Corps in less developed nations—the dream of education for all of our children—the dream of jobs for all who seek them and need them—the dream of care for our elderly—the dream of an all-out attack on mental illness—and above all, the dream of equal rights for all Americans, whatever their race or color—these and other American dreams have been vitalized by his drive and by his dedication.

And now the ideas and the ideals which he so nobly represented must and will be translated into effective action. . . .

On the 20th day of January, in 1961, John F. Kennedy told his countrymen that our national work would not be finished "in the first thousand days, nor in the life of this administration, nor even perhaps in our lifetime on this planet. But," he said, "let us begin."

Today, in this moment of new resolve, I would say to all my fellow Americans, let us continue.

This is our challenge—not to hesitate, not to pause, not to turn about and linger over this evil moment, but to continue on our course so that we may fulfill the destiny that history has set for us. Our most immediate tasks are here on this Hill.

First, no memorial oration or eulogy could more eloquently honor President Kennedy's memory than the earliest possible passage of the civil rights bill for which he fought so long. We have talked long enough in this country about equal rights. We have talked for one hundred years or more. It is time now to write the next chapter, and to write it in the books of law.

I urge you again, as I did in 1957 and again in 1960, to enact a civil rights law so that we can move forward to eliminate from this Nation every trace of discrimination and oppression that is based upon race or color. There could be no greater source of strength to this Nation both at home and abroad.

And second, no act of ours could more fittingly continue the work of President Kennedy than the early passage of the tax bill for which he fought all this long year. This is a bill designed to increase our national income and Federal revenues, and to provide insurance against recession. That bill, if passed without delay, means more security for those now working, more jobs for those now without them, and more incentive for our economy.

In short, this is no time for delay. It is a time for action—strong, forward-looking action on the pending education bills to help bring the light of learning to every home and hamlet in America—strong, forward-looking action on youth employment opportunities; strong, forward-looking action on the pending foreign aid bill, making clear that we are not forfeiting our responsibilities to this hemisphere or to the world, nor erasing Executive flexibility in the conduct of our foreign affairs—and strong, prompt, and forward-looking action on the remaining appropriation bills. . . .

We meet in grief, but let us also meet in renewed dedication and renewed vigor. Let us meet in action, in tolerance, and in mutual understanding. John Kennedy's death commands what his life conveyed—that America must move forward. The time has come for Americans of all races and creeds and political beliefs to understand and to respect one another. So let us put an end to the teaching and the preaching of hate and evil and violence. Let us turn away from the fanatics of the far left and the far right, from the apostles of bitterness and bigotry, from those defiant of law, and those who pour venom into our Nation's bloodstream.

I profoundly hope that the tragedy and the torment of these terrible days will bind us together in new fellowship, making us one people in our hour of sorrow. So let us here highly resolve that John Fitzgerald Kennedy did not live—or die—in vain.

Lyndon B. Johnson, Address before a joint session of Congress, November 27, 1963.

Document 2: Announcing the War on Poverty

Johnson outlined his proposal for "an unconditional war on poverty" in his 1964 State of the Union Address.

Unfortunately, many Americans live on the outskirts of hope—some because of their poverty, and some because of their color, and all too many because of both. Our task is to help replace their despair with opportunity.

This administration today, here and now, declares unconditional war on poverty in America. I urge this Congress and all Americans to join with me in that effort.

It will not be a short or easy struggle, no single weapon or strategy will suffice, but we shall not rest until that war is won. The richest Nation on earth can afford to win it. We cannot afford to lose it. One thousand dollars invested in salvaging an unemployable youth today can return $40,000 or more in his lifetime.

Poverty is a national problem, requiring improved national organization and support. But this attack, to be effective, must also be organized at the State and the local level and must be supported and directed by State and local efforts.

For the war against poverty will not be won here in Washington. It must be won in the field, in every private home, in every public office, from the courthouse to the White House.

The program I shall propose will emphasize this cooperative approach to help that one-fifth of all American families with incomes too small to even meet their basic needs.

Our chief weapons in a more pinpointed attack will be better schools, and better health, and better homes, and better training, and better job opportunities to help more Americans, especially young Americans, escape from squalor and misery and unemployment rolls where other citizens help to carry them.

Very often a lack of jobs and money is not the cause of poverty, but the symptom. The cause may lie deeper in our failure to give our fellow citizens a fair chance to develop their own capacities, in a lack of education and training, in a lack of medical care and housing, in a lack of decent communities in which to live and bring up their children.

But whatever the cause, our joint Federal-local effort must pursue poverty, pursue it wherever it exists—in city slums and small towns, in sharecropper shacks or in migrant worker camps, on Indian Reservations, among whites as well as Negroes, among the young as well as the aged, in the boom towns and in the depressed areas.

Our aim is not only to relieve the symptom of poverty, but to cure it and, above all, to prevent it. No single piece of legislation, however, is going to suffice.

We will launch a special effort in the chronically distressed areas of Appalachia.

We must expand our small but our successful area redevelopment program.

We must enact youth employment legislation to put jobless, aimless, hopeless youngsters to work on useful projects.

We must distribute more food to the needy through a broader food stamp program.

We must create a National Service Corps to help the economically handicapped of our own country as the Peace Corps now helps those abroad.

We must modernize our unemployment insurance and establish a high-level commission on automation. If we have the brain power to invent these machines, we have the brain power to make certain that they are a boon and not a bane to humanity.

We must extend the coverage of our minimum wage laws to more than 2 million workers now lacking this basic protection of purchasing power.

We must, by including special school aid funds as part of our education program, improve the quality of teaching, training, and counseling in our hardest hit areas.

We must build more libraries in every area and more hospitals and nursing homes under the Hill-Burton Act, and train more nurses to staff them.

We must provide hospital insurance for our older citizens financed by every worker and his employer under Social Security, contributing no more than $1 a month during the employee's working career to protect him in his old age in a dignified manner without cost to the Treasury, against the devastating hardship of prolonged or repeated illness.

We must, as a part of a revised housing and urban renewal program, give more help to those displaced by slum clearance, provide more housing for our poor and our elderly, and seek as our ultimate goal in our free enterprise system a decent home for every American family.

We must help obtain more modern mass transit within our communities as well as low-cost transportation between them.

Above all, we must release $11 billion of tax reduction into the private spending stream to create new jobs and new markets in every area of this land.

Lyndon B. Johnson, Annual message to the Congress on the State of the Union, January 8, 1964.

Document 3: The Civil Rights Act of 1964

Prior to signing the Civil Rights Act of 1964, Johnson addressed the na-
tion from the East Room at the White House.

I am about to sign into law the Civil Rights Act of 1964. I want to
take this occasion to talk to you about what that law means to every
American. . . .

Americans of every race and color have died in battle to protect our
freedom. Americans of every race and color have worked to build a nation of widening opportunities. Now our generation of Americans has
been called on to continue the unending search for justice within our
own borders.

We believe that all men are created equal. Yet many are denied equal
treatment.

We believe that all men have certain unalienable rights. Yet many
Americans do not enjoy those rights.

We believe that all men are entitled to the blessings of liberty. Yet
millions are being deprived of those blessings—not because of their
own failures, but because of the color of their skin.

The reasons are deeply imbedded in history and tradition and the
nature of man. We can understand—without rancor or hatred—how
this all happened.

But it cannot continue. Our Constitution, the foundation of our
Republic, forbids it. The principles of our freedom forbid it. Morality
forbids it. And the law I will sign tonight forbids it. . . .

The purpose of the law is simple.

It does not restrict the freedom of any American, so long as he respects the rights of others.

It does not give special treatment to any citizen.

It does say the only limit to a man's hope for happiness, and for the
future of his children, shall be his own ability.

It does say that those who are equal before God shall now also be
equal in the polling booths, in the classrooms, in the factories, and in
hotels, restaurants, movie theaters, and other places that provide service to the public. . . .

This Civil Rights Act is a challenge to all of us to go to work in our
communities and our States, in our homes and in our hearts, to eliminate the last vestiges of injustice in our beloved country.

So tonight I urge every public official, every religious leader, every
business and professional man, every workingman, every housewife—
I urge every American—to join in this effort to bring justice and hope

to all our people—and to bring peace to our land.

My fellow citizens, we have come now to a time of testing. We must not fail.

Let us close the springs of racial poison. Let us pray for wise and understanding hearts. Let us lay aside irrelevant differences and make our Nation whole. Let us hasten that day when our unmeasured strength and our unbounded spirit will be free to do the great works ordained for this Nation by the just and wise God who is the Father of us all.

Lyndon B. Johnson, Radio and television remarks upon signing the Civil Rights Bill, July 2, 1964.

Document 4: The Gulf of Tonkin Incident

On August 4, 1964, Johnson ordered air strikes against North Vietnamese targets in response to reported attacks on American ships in the Gulf of Tonkin. The following day he asked Congress to support his efforts to protect South Vietnam from Communist aggression.

Last night I announced to the American people that the North Vietnamese regime had conducted further deliberate attacks against U.S. naval vessels operating in international waters, and I had therefore directed air action against gunboats and supporting facilities used in these hostile operations. This air action has now been carried out with substantial damage to the boats and facilities. Two U.S. aircraft were lost in the action.

After consultation with the leaders of both parties in the Congress, I further announced a decision to ask the Congress for a resolution expressing the unity and determination of the United States in supporting freedom and in protecting peace in southeast Asia.

These latest actions of the North Vietnamese regime have given a new and grave turn to the already serious situation in southeast Asia. Our commitments in that area are well known to the Congress. They were first made in 1954 by President Eisenhower. They were further defined in the Southeast Asia Collective Defense Treaty approved by the Senate in February 1955.

This treaty with its accompanying protocol obligates the United States and other members to act in accordance with their constitutional processes to meet Communist aggression against any of the parties or protocol states.

Our policy in southeast Asia has been consistent and unchanged since 1954. I summarized it on June 2 in four simple propositions:

1. America keeps her word. Here as elsewhere, we must and shall honor our commitments.

2. The issue is the future of southeast Asia as a whole. A threat to any nation in that region is a threat to all, and a threat to us.

3. Our purpose is peace. We have no military, political, or territorial ambitions in the area.

4. This is not just a jungle war, but a struggle for freedom on every front of human activity. Our military and economic assistance to South Vietnam and Laos in particular has the purpose of helping these countries to repel aggression and strengthen their independence.

The threat to the free nations of southeast Asia has long been clear. The North Vietnamese regime has constantly sought to take over South Vietnam and Laos. This Communist regime has violated the Geneva accords for Vietnam. It has systematically conducted a campaign of subversion, which includes the direction, training, and supply of personnel and arms for the conduct of guerrilla warfare in South Vietnamese territory. In Laos, the North Vietnamese regime has maintained military forces, used Laotian territory for infiltration into South Vietnam, and most recently carried out combat operations—all in direct violation of the Geneva Agreements of 1962.

In recent months, the actions of the North Vietnamese regime have become steadily more threatening. . . .

As President of the United States I have concluded that I should now ask the Congress, on its part, to join in affirming the national determination that all such attacks will be met, and that the United States will continue in its basic policy of assisting the free nations of the area to defend their freedom.

As I have repeatedly made clear, the United States intends no rashness, and seeks no wider war. We must make it clear to all that the United States is united in its determination to bring about the end of Communist subversion and aggression in the area. We seek the full and effective restoration of the international agreements signed in Geneva in 1954, with respect to South Vietnam, and again in Geneva in 1962, with respect to Laos.

Lyndon B. Johnson, Message to Congress, August 5, 1964.

Document 5: The Gulf of Tonkin Resolution

The Gulf of Tonkin Resolution authorized Johnson to use armed force to defend U.S. forces and uphold America's treaty obligations in Southeast Asia. The document was overwhelmingly approved by a vote of 88 to 2 in the Senate and 416 to 0 in the House. Critics contend that Johnson's actions in Vietnam went beyond the defensive use of force authorized by the resolution.

To promote the maintenance of international peace and security in southeast Asia.

Whereas naval units of the Communist regime in Vietnam, in violation of the principles of the Charter of the United Nations and of international law, have deliberately and repeatedly attacked United States naval vessels lawfully present in international waters, and have thereby created a serious threat to international peace; and

Whereas these attacks are part of a deliberate and systematic campaign of aggression that the Communist regime in North Vietnam has been waging against its neighbors and the nations joined with them in the collective defense of their freedom; and

Whereas the United States is assisting the peoples of southeast Asia to protect their freedom and has no territorial, military or political ambitions in the area, but desires only that these peoples should be left in peace to work out their own destinies in their own way: Now, therefore, be it

Resolved by the Senate and House of Representatives of the United States of America in Congress assembled, That the Congress approves and supports the determination of the President, as Commander in Chief, to take all necessary measures to repel any armed attack against the forces of the United States and to prevent further aggression.

Section 2. The United States regards as vital to its national interest and to world peace the maintenance of international peace and security in southeast Asia. Consonant with the Constitution of the United States and the Charter of the United Nations and in accordance with its obligations under the Southeast Asia Collective Defense Treaty, the United States is, therefore, prepared, as the President determines, to take all necessary steps, including the use of armed force, to assist any member or protocol state of the Southeast Asia Collective Defense Treaty requesting assistance in defense of its freedom.

Section 3. This resolution shall expire when the President shall determine that the peace and security of the area is reasonably assured by international conditions created by action of the United Nations or otherwise, except that it may be terminated earlier by concurrent resolution of the Congress.

Southeast Asia Resolution (H.J. Res. 1145 August 7, 1964).

Document 6: "We Shall Overcome"

On March 7, 1965, state police attacked peaceful demonstrators marching for voting rights in Selma, Alabama. Eight days later, Johnson invoked

the rallying cry of the civil rights movement as he called on Congress to pass voting rights legislation.

This was the first nation in the history of the world to be founded with a purpose. The great phrases of that purpose still sound in every American heart, North and South: "All men are created equal"—"government by consent of the governed"—"give me liberty or give me death." Well, those are not just clever words, or those are not just empty theories. In their name Americans have fought and died for two centuries, and tonight around the world they stand there as guardians of our liberty, risking their lives.

Those words are a promise to every citizen that he shall share in the dignity of man. This dignity cannot be found in a man's possessions; it cannot be found in his power, or in his position. It really rests on his right to be treated as a man equal in opportunity to all others. It says that he shall share in freedom, he shall choose his leaders, educate his children, and provide for his family according to his ability and his merits as a human being.

To apply any other test—to deny a man his hopes because of his color or race, his religion or the place of his birth—is not only to do injustice, it is to deny America and to dishonor the dead who gave their lives for American freedom.

Our fathers believed that if this noble view of the rights of man was to flourish, it must be rooted in democracy. The most basic right of all was the right to choose your own leaders. The history of this country, in large measure, is the history of the expansion of that right to all of our people. . . .

Yet the harsh fact is that in many places in this country men and women are kept from voting simply because they are Negroes.

Every device of which human ingenuity is capable has been used to deny this right. The Negro citizen may go to register only to be told that the day is wrong, or the hour is late, or the official in charge is absent. And if he persists, and if he manages to present himself to the registrar, he may be disqualified because he did not spell out his middle name or because he abbreviated a word on the application.

And if he manages to fill out an application he is given a test. The registrar is the sole judge of whether he passes this test. He may be asked to recite the entire Constitution, or explain the most complex provisions of State law. And even a college degree cannot be used to prove that he can read and write.

For the fact is that the only way to pass these barriers is to show a white skin.

Experience has clearly shown that the existing process of law cannot overcome systematic and ingenious discrimination. No law that we now have on the books—and I have helped to put three of them there—can ensure the right to vote when local officials are determined to deny it.

In such a case our duty must be clear to all of us. The Constitution says that no person shall be kept from voting because of his race or his color. We have all sworn an oath before God to support and to defend that Constitution. We must now act in obedience to that oath.

Wednesday I will send to Congress a law designed to eliminate illegal barriers to the right to vote. . . .

But even if we pass this bill, the battle will not be over. What happened in Selma is part of a far larger movement which reaches into every section and State of America. It is the effort of American Negroes to secure for themselves the full blessings of American life.

Their cause must be our cause too. Because it is not just Negroes, but really it is all of us, who must overcome the crippling legacy of bigotry and injustice.

And we shall overcome.

As a man whose roots go deeply into Southern soil I know how agonizing racial feelings are. I know how difficult it is to reshape the attitudes and the structure of our society.

But a century has passed, more than a hundred years, since the Negro was freed. And he is not fully free tonight.

It was more than a hundred years ago that Abraham Lincoln, a great President of another party, signed the Emancipation Proclamation, but emancipation is a proclamation and not a fact.

A century has passed, more than a hundred years, since equality was promised. And yet the Negro is not equal.

A century has passed since the day of promise. And the promise is unkept.

The time of justice has now come. I tell you that I believe sincerely that no force can hold it back. It is right in the eyes of man and God that it should come. And when it does, I think that day will brighten the lives of every American.

For Negroes are not the only victims. How many white children have gone uneducated, how many white families have lived in stark poverty, how many white lives have been scarred by fear, because we have wasted our energy and our substance to maintain the barriers of hatred and terror?

So I say to all of you here, and to all in the Nation tonight, that those who appeal to you to hold on to the past do so at the cost of denying you your future.

This great, rich, restless country can offer opportunity and education and hope to all: black and white, North and South, sharecropper and city dweller. These are the enemies: poverty, ignorance, disease. They are the enemies and not our fellow man, not our neighbor. And these enemies too, poverty, disease and ignorance, we shall overcome.

Lyndon B. Johnson, Special message to the Congress, March 15, 1965.

Document 7: Why We Are in Vietnam

In the following excerpts from an April 1965 speech at Johns Hopkins University, Johnson outlines the rationale and objectives of the U.S. military intervention in Vietnam.

Viet-Nam is far away from this quiet campus. We have no territory there, nor do we seek any. The war is dirty and brutal and difficult. And some 400 young men, born into an America that is bursting with opportunity and promise, have ended their lives on Viet-Nam's steaming soil.

Why must we take this painful road? . . .

The first reality is that North Viet-Nam has attacked the independent nation of South Viet-Nam. Its object is total conquest.

Of course, some of the people of South Viet-Nam are participating in attack on their own government. But trained men and supplies, orders and arms, flow in a constant stream from north to south.

This support is the heartbeat of the war.

And it is a war of unparalleled brutality. Simple farmers are the targets of assassination and kidnapping. Women and children are strangled in the night because their men are loyal to their government. And helpless villages are ravaged by sneak attacks. Large-scale raids are conducted on towns, and terror strikes in the heart of cities.

The confused nature of this conflict cannot mask the fact that it is the new face of an old enemy.

Over this war—and all Asia—is another reality: the deepening shadow of Communist China. The rulers in Hanoi are urged on by Peking. This is a regime which has destroyed freedom in Tibet, which has attacked India, and has been condemned by the United Nations for aggression in Korea. It is a nation which is helping the forces of violence in almost every continent. The contest in Viet-Nam is part of a wider pattern of aggressive purposes.

Why are these realities our concern? Why are we in South Viet-Nam? We are there because we have a promise to keep. Since 1954 every

American President has offered support to the people of South Viet-Nam. We have helped to build, and we have helped to defend. Thus, over many years, we have made a national pledge to help South Viet-Nam defend its independence.

And I intend to keep that promise.

To dishonor that pledge, to abandon this small and brave nation to its enemies, and to the terror that must follow, would be an unforgivable wrong.

We are also there to strengthen world order. Around the globe, from Berlin to Thailand, are people whose well-being rests, in part, on the belief that they can count on us if they are attacked. To leave Viet-Nam to its fate would shake the confidence of all these people in the value of an American commitment and in the value of America's word. The result would be increased unrest and instability, and even wider war.

We are also there because there are great stakes in the balance. Let no one think for a moment that retreat from Viet-Nam would bring an end to conflict. The battle would be renewed in one country and then another. The central lesson of our time is that the appetite of aggression is never satisfied. To withdraw from one battlefield means only to prepare for the next. We must say in southeast Asia—as we did in Europe—in the words of the Bible: "Hitherto shalt thou come, but no further."

There are those who say that all our effort there will be futile—that China's power is such that it is bound to dominate all southeast Asia. But there is no end to that argument until all of the nations of Asia are swallowed up.

There are those who wonder why we have a responsibility there. Well, we have it there for the same reason that we have a responsibility for the defense of Europe. World War II was fought in both Europe and Asia, and when it ended we found ourselves with continued responsibility for the defense of freedom.

Our objective is the independence of South Viet-Nam, and its freedom from attack. We want nothing for ourselves—only that the people of South Viet-Nam be allowed to guide their own country in their own way.

We will do everything necessary to reach that objective. And we will do only what is absolutely necessary. . . .

We hope that peace will come swiftly. But that is in the hands of others besides ourselves. And we must be prepared for a long continued conflict. It will require patience as well as bravery, the will to endure as well as the will to resist.

I wish it were possible to convince others with words of what we now find it necessary to say with guns and planes: Armed hostility is futile. Our resources are equal to any challenge. Because we fight for values and we fight for principles, rather than territory or colonies, our patience and our determination are unending.

Once this is clear, then it should also be clear that the only path for reasonable men is the path of peaceful settlement. . . .

And until that bright and necessary day of peace we will try to keep conflict from spreading. We have no desire to see thousands die in battle—Asians or Americans. We have no desire to devastate that which the people of North Viet-Nam have built with toil and sacrifice. We will use our power with restraint and with all the wisdom that we can command.

But we will use it.

Lyndon B. Johnson, Address at Johns Hopkins University, April 7, 1965.

Document 8: Education: "The Guardian Genius of Democracy"

Improving the nation's education system was a key goal of Johnson's Great Society agenda. In April 1965, Johnson traveled to the site of his boyhood elementary school to sign a new education bill.

From our very beginnings as a nation, we have felt a fierce commitment to the ideal of education for everyone. It fixed itself into our democratic creed.

Over a century and a quarter ago, the President of the Republic of Texas, Mirabeau B. Lamar, proclaimed education as "the guardian genius of democracy . . . the only dictator that free men acknowledge and the only security that free men desire."

But President Lamar made the mistaken prophecy that education would be an issue "in which no jarring interests are involved and no acrimonious political feelings excited." For too long, political acrimony held up our progress. For too long, children suffered while jarring interests caused stalemate in the efforts to improve our schools. Since 1946 Congress tried repeatedly, and failed repeatedly, to enact measures for elementary and secondary education.

Now, within the past 3 weeks, the House of Representatives, by a vote of 263 to 153, and the Senate, by a vote of 73 to 18, have passed the most sweeping educational bill ever to come before Congress. It represents a major new commitment of the Federal Government to quality and equality in the schooling that we offer our young people. I predict that all of those of both parties of Congress who supported the enactment of this legislation will be remembered in history as men and women who began a new day of greatness in American society. . . .

By passing this bill, we bridge the gap between helplessness and hope for more than 5 million educationally deprived children.

We put into the hands of our youth more than 30 million new books, and into many of our schools their first libraries.

We reduce the terrible time lag in bringing new teaching techniques into the Nation's classrooms.

We strengthen State and local agencies which bear the burden and the challenge of better education.

And we rekindle the revolution—the revolution of the spirit against the tyranny of ignorance.

As a son of a tenant farmer, I know that education is the only valid passport from poverty.

As a former teacher—and, I hope, a future one—I have great expectations of what this law will mean for all of our young people.

As President of the United States, I believe deeply no law I have signed or will ever sign means more to the future of America.

Lyndon B. Johnson, Remarks upon signing the Elementary and Secondary Education Bill, April 11, 1965.

Document 9: "Freedom Is Not Enough"

In a commencement address at Howard University, Johnson declared that laws guaranteeing equality of opportunity did not go far enough in ensuring equality for blacks. In advocating measures to ensure "equality as a result," Johnson launched the era of affirmative action.

We have seen the high court of the country declare that discrimination based on race was repugnant to the Constitution, and therefore void. We have seen in 1957, and 1960, and again in 1964, the first civil rights legislation in this Nation in almost an entire century.

As majority leader of the United States Senate, I helped to guide two of these bills through the Senate. And, as your President, I was proud to sign the third. And now very soon we will have the fourth—a new law guaranteeing every American the right to vote.

No act of my entire administration will give me greater satisfaction than the day when my signature makes this bill, too, the law of this land.

The voting rights bill will be the latest, and among the most important, in a long series of victories. But this victory—as Winston Churchill said of another triumph for freedom—"is not the end. It is not even the beginning of the end. But it is, perhaps, the end of the beginning."

That beginning is freedom; and the barriers to that freedom are tumbling down. Freedom is the right to share, share fully and equally, in American society—to vote, to hold a job, to enter a public place, to go to school. It is the right to be treated in every part of our national life as a person equal in dignity and promise to all others.

But freedom is not enough. You do not wipe away the scars of centuries by saying: Now you are free to go where you want, and do as you desire, and choose the leaders you please.

You do not take a person who, for years, has been hobbled by chains and liberate him, bring him up to the starting line of a race and then say, "you are free to compete with all the others," and still justly believe that you have been completely fair.

Thus it is not enough just to open the gates of opportunity. All our citizens must have the ability to walk through those gates.

This is the next and the more profound stage of the battle for civil rights. We seek not just freedom but opportunity. We seek not just legal equity but human ability, not just equality as a right and a theory but equality as a fact and equality as a result.

For the task is to give 20 million Negroes the same chance as every other American to learn and grow, to work and share in society, to develop their abilities—physical, mental and spiritual, and to pursue their individual happiness.

To this end equal opportunity is essential, but not enough, not enough. Men and women of all races are born with the same range of abilities. But ability is not just the product of birth. Ability is stretched or stunted by the family that you live with, and the neighborhood you live in—by the school you go to and the poverty or the richness of your surroundings. It is the product of a hundred unseen forces playing upon the little infant, the child, and finally the man.

Lyndon B. Johnson, Commencement address at Howard University, June 4, 1965.

Document 10: Nature: A Neglected Part of America's Heritage

As First Lady, Lady Bird Johnson made it her cause to beautify the nation. One outcome of this effort was legislation designed to limit advertising and junkyards along the nation's highways. At the signing of the bill, Lyndon Johnson reminisced about his childhood in rural Texas.

When I was growing up, the land itself was life. And when the day seemed particularly harsh and bitter, the land was always there just as nature had left it—wild, rugged, beautiful, and changing, always changing.

And really, how do you measure the excitement and the happiness that comes to a boy from the old swimming hole in the happy days of yore, when I used to lean above it; the old sycamore, the baiting of a hook that is tossed into the stream to catch a wily fish, or looking at a graceful deer that leaps with hardly a quiver over a rock fence that was put down by some settler a hundred years or more ago?

How do you really put a value on the view of the night that is caught in a boy's eyes while he is stretched out in the thick grass watching the million stars that we never see in these crowded cities, breathing the sounds of the night and the birds and the pure, fresh air while in his ears are the crickets and the wind?

Well, in recent years I think America has sadly neglected this part of America's national heritage. We have placed a wall of civilization between us and between the beauty of our land and of our countryside. In our eagerness to expand and to improve, we have relegated nature to a weekend role, and we have banished it from our daily lives.

Well, I think that we are a poorer Nation because of it, and it is something I am not proud of. And it is something I am going to do something about. Because as long as I am your President, by choice of your people, I do not choose to preside over the destiny of this country and to hide from view what God has gladly given it.

And that is why today there is a great deal of real joy within me, and within my family, as we meet here in this historic East Room to sign the Highway Beautification Act of 1965.

Now, this bill does more than control advertising and junkyards along the billions of dollars of highways that the people have built with their money—public money, not private money. It does more than give us the tools just to landscape some of those highways.

This bill will bring the wonders of nature back into our daily lives.

This bill will enrich our spirits and restore a small measure of our national greatness.

Lyndon B. Johnson, Remarks at the signing of the Highway Beautification Act of 1965, October 22, 1965.

Document 11: Guns and Butter

In his 1966 State of the Union Address, Johnson vowed to continue to develop the Great Society while fighting the war in Vietnam.

Because of Vietnam we cannot do all that we should, or all that we would like to do. We will ruthlessly attack waste and inefficiency. We will make sure that every dollar is spent with the thrift and with the commonsense which recognizes how hard the taxpayer worked in order to earn it.

We will continue to meet the needs of our people by continuing to develop the Great Society.

Last year alone the wealth that we produced increased $47 billion, and it will soar again this year to a total over $720 billion.

Because our economic policies have produced rising revenues, if you approve every program that I recommend tonight, our total budget deficit will be one of the lowest in many years. It will be only $1.8 billion next year. Total spending in the administrative budget will be $112.8 billion. Revenues next year will be $111 billion.

On a cash basis—which is the way that you and I keep our family budget—the Federal budget next year will actually show a surplus. That is to say, if we include all the money that your Government will take in and all the money that your Government will spend, your Government next year will collect one-half billion dollars more than it will spend in the year 1967.

I have not come here tonight to ask for pleasant luxuries or for idle pleasures. I have come here to recommend that you, the representatives of the richest Nation on earth, you, the elected servants of a people who live in abundance unmatched on this globe, you bring the most urgent decencies of life to all of your fellow Americans.

There are men who cry out: We must sacrifice. Well, let us rather ask them: Who will they sacrifice? Are they going to sacrifice the children who seek the learning, or the sick who need medical care, or the families who dwell in squalor now brightened by the hope of home? Will they sacrifice opportunity for the distressed, the beauty of our land, the hope of our poor?

Time may require further sacrifices. And if it does, then we will make them.

But we will not heed those who wring it from the hopes of the unfortunate here in a land of plenty.

I believe that we can continue the Great Society while we fight in Vietnam. But if there are some who do not believe this, then, in the name of justice, let them call for the contribution of those who live in the fullness of our blessing, rather than try to strip it from the hands of those that are most in need.

Lyndon B. Johnson, Annual message to the Congress on the State of the Union, January 12, 1966.

Document 12: Waging War for Profit

In his 1967 book The Accidental President, *journalist Robert Sherrill wrote that Johnson's motives for escalating the Vietnam War were less than noble.*

Knowing from long experience that the best way to pay off campaign backers is via the military pork barrel, [Johnson] went instinctively to the biggest pork barrel of them all, war, to keep a nation working and prosperous and content with his administration.

It was the natural thing for him to do. If you were a cactus-patch politician who had moved into the Washington stream during the days when FDR [Franklin Delano Roosevelt] was proving the invincibility of a combined welfare-war program; if you were the shrewd kind of mechanic who quickly caught on to the gimmickry of the Roosevelt program without picking up the philosophy behind it; if you, further-more, were convinced, and wisely so, that this nation would put up with anything but joblessness; if your long experience in office had convinced you that the easiest way to prime the pump was through de-fense spending; and if coupled to that was a basic disposition to "shove it down the throats" of your selected victim—wouldn't you probably hunt up a nicely paced drawn-out war as just the ticket to prosperity? A war too far removed from sight and understanding to be successful-ly criticized by more than the intellectuals; with a race of people that is unknown to most Americans and therefore unlikely to attract much sympathy; rising out of a dispute that was fuzzed and clouded by old, esoteric treaty alliances? Vietnam was perfect.

Johnson needed a war that would last a while. . . . He needed a war that could be held in check, yet stretched to any desirable term, esca-lated and de-escalated at will. . . .

The manipulative quality of the Vietnam conflict is the only logical reason for our being there. It is ridiculous to think that Johnson would go half way around the world to imbed the nation in the muck of a militarily hopeless war—as his administration has conceded it to be—simply to save from some nebulous brand of Communism a piece of real estate that has been of little exploitative value (not, of course, our reason for wanting to save an Asian or South American country) to anybody but rubber companies. . . .

If Johnson is so terribly eager to save some little patch from Com-munism why does he start with one that requires de-mothballing a hundred Liberty ships? Why not start with one that is only 90 miles away? Or how about Mexico, a wadeable distance, which has a great many socialistic traits and, since it virtually disbanded its army years ago, would be easy to conquer, despoil and rebuild? . . .

There are many more convenient places for Johnson, Global Re-former, to begin; but of course Vietnam is much more preferable *be-cause* it is so far away, so difficult to deal with, so difficult, with its bogs and jungles, to fight over and through.

Further indication of the mercenary motive behind Johnson's desire to save Vietnam is that it did not come about until he was President. If a country was worth saving from Communism in 1964, it must have been worth saving in 1954, yet in that earlier year, when [Dwight] Eisenhower was confronted with the proposal that he send troops to Vietnam, he said he would not do it without support from Congress. Johnson advised him against it. If salvation in 1964, why not in 1961? Robert Trumbull's report to *The New York Times* of Vice-President Johnson's trip to Asia that year records that "according to accounts of Mr. Johnson's conferences by persons who were present, the idea of sending American troops to fight on behalf of the governments under siege by the Communists in South Vietnam and Thailand never came up for discussion.". . .

If he advised Eisenhower against sending troops, and as Kennedy's emissary did not even bother to discuss sending troops, why did a massive buildup suddenly become so appealing? Idealism cannot supply the answer. Johnson has never been known to act out of idealism. He ballooned the war for a practical political reason: because now *he* had a personal interest in keeping the industrial-military pot boiling with profits. But first, the election. He had learned the method from Roosevelt: the promise not to send troops before the election, the plunge after. "We are not about to send American boys 9,000 or 10,000 miles away from home to do what Asian boys ought to be doing for themselves," he had said thirteen days before votes were cast in 1964. In three months he was bombing North Vietnam, the buildup was under way and a lasting prosperity was just around the corner. . . .

It was his very own war, his by creation and by bluff, and he deserved credit for the prosperity. One could sense his contentment. It was a rare speech thereafter that did not refer to the "longest period of uninterrupted prosperity in our history." There were still nuisance criticisms to deflect; it was unfortunate that 20 per cent of the Americans in Vietnam in 1965 came down with a venereal disease; it was regrettable that his construction friends had wasted an estimated $150 million; it was discouraging that an estimated 20 to 40 per cent of our aid supplies to Vietnam were stolen and wound up either on the black market or in the hands of the enemy; it was an inescapable unhappiness that four Vietnam civilians were killed by our troops for each Vietcong. But we reimburse, we recompense: an average of $35 per Vietnam killed, up to $85 for each rubber tree killed. Anyway, as anyone who is not "callous or timid" must know, these things are just the normal tediousness that one must put up with to save a country.

And, he promised, if Vietnam would hold still for the despoliation, he would later be around with the second-stage, the equally profitable stage of rebuilding, and he would make "the Mekong Delta bloom like the Tennessee Valley." Like the god Shiva, Johnson is both the destroyer and the preserver—acting on the omnipotence that there is pucka profit in both.

Robert Sherrill, *The Accidental President*. New York: Grossman Publishers, 1967.

Document 13: Reclaiming Fresh Air and Clean Sky

The massive Great Society legislation included bills to protect the environment. Upon signing the Air Quality Act of 1967, Johnson foresaw America becoming "a nation in gas masks" unless efforts were taken to reduce air pollution.

I would like to begin this morning by reading you a little weather report: ". . . dirty water and black snow pour from the dismal air to . . .the putrid slush that waits for them below."

Now that is not a description of Boston, Chicago, New York, or even Washington, D.C. It is from Dante's "Inferno," a 600-year-old vision of damnation.

But doesn't it sound familiar?

Isn't it a forecast that fits almost any large American city today? . . .

Don't we really risk our own damnation every day by destroying the air that gives us life?

I think we do. We have done it with our science, our industry, and our progress. Above all, we have really done it with our own carelessness—our own continued indifference and our own repeated negligence.

Contaminated air began in this country as a big-city problem. But in just a few years, the gray pall of pollution has spread throughout the Nation. Today its threat hangs everywhere—and it is still spreading.

Today we are pouring at least 130 million tons of poison into the air each year. That is two-thirds of a ton for every man, woman, and child that lives in America.

And tomorrow the picture looks even blacker. By 1980, we will have a third more people living in our cities than are living there today. We will have 40 percent more automobiles and trucks. And we will be burning half again as much fuel.

That leaves us, according to my evaluation, only one real choice. Either we stop poisoning our air—or we become a nation in gas masks, groping our way through the dying cities and a wilderness of ghost towns that the people have evacuated.

We make our choice with the bill that we are going to sign very shortly. It is not the first clean air bill—but it is, I think, the best. . . .

In the next 3 years, it will authorize more funds to combat air pollution—more funds in the next 3 years to combat air pollution—than we have spent on this subject in the entire Nation's history of 180 years.

It will give us scientific answers to our most baffling problem: how to get the sulphur out of our fuel—and how to keep it out of our air.

It will give Secretary Gardner new power to stop pollution before it chokes our children and before it strangles our elderly—before it drives us into a hospital bed.

It will help our States fight pollution in the only practical way—by regional airshed controls—by giving the Federal Government standby power to intervene if and when States rights do not always function efficiently.

It will help our States to control the number one source of pollution—our automobiles.

But for all that it will do, the Air Quality Act will never end pollution. It is a law—and not a magic wand to wave that will cleanse our skies. It is a law whose ultimate power and final effectiveness really rests out there with the people of this land—on our seeing the damnation that awaits us if the people do not act responsibly to avoid it and to curb it. . . .

Let our children say, when they look back on this day, that it was here that a sleeping giant—it was here that their Nation awoke. It was here that America turned away from damnation, and found salvation in reclaiming God's blessings of fresh air and clean sky.

Lyndon B. Johnson, Remarks upon signing the Air Quality Act of 1967, November 21, 1967.

CHRONOLOGY

AUGUST 27, 1908
Lyndon Baines Johnson is born near Stonewall, Texas, in a small farmhouse on the Pedernales River.

1913
The Johnson family moves to Johnson City, Texas.

1924
Johnson graduates from high school and drives with friends to California, where he spends the next year performing odd jobs.

1927
Johnson enrolls at Southwest Texas State Teachers College in San Marcos, Texas.

1928–29
Johnson interrupts his studies to serve as principal and teacher at Welhausen School, a Mexican-American school in the south Texas town of Cotulla.

1929
The Great Depression begins.

JULY 1930
Johnson delivers his first political speech in Henly, Texas. State Legislator Welly Hopkins is impressed and hires Johnson to manage his campaign for the state senate.

AUGUST 1930
Johnson graduates with a B.S. degree in education and history.

1931
Congressman Richard Kleberg hires Johnson as his congressional secretary; Johnson moves to Washington, DC.

1933

Franklin D. Roosevelt becomes president.

SEPTEMBER 1934

Johnson meets Claudia Alta ("Lady Bird") Taylor.

NOVEMBER 17, 1934

Lyndon and Lady Bird are married.

1935

Johnson takes post as Texas state director of the National Youth Administration.

APRIL 1937

Johnson is elected as Representative of the 10th congressional district of Texas in a special election.

1938

Johnson is reelected to the Congress.

1939

World War II begins when Germany invades Poland.

JUNE 1941

Johnson is narrowly defeated in a bid for a seat in the U.S. Senate.

DECEMBER 1941

Japan attacks Pearl Harbor; the U.S. enters World War II; Johnson volunteers for active duty in the U.S. Navy.

JUNE 1942

Johnson is awarded the Silver Star for gallantry in action after participating in an aerial combat mission in New Guinea on June 9.

JULY 1942

Johnson is released from active duty and returns to Congress.

MARCH 19, 1944

Johnson's first daughter, Lynda Bird, is born.

APRIL 1945
Franklin D. Roosevelt dies; Harry S. Truman becomes president.

AUGUST 1945
The U.S. drops atomic bombs on Hiroshima and Nagasaki, ending World War II.

SEPTEMBER 1945
Ho Chi Minh declares Vietnam independent from French rule.

JULY 2, 1947
Johnson's second daughter, Luci Baines, is born.

1948
Johnson is dubbed "Landslide Lyndon" after defeating Coke Stevenson for a seat in the U.S. Senate by 87 votes in a contested runoff election.

JUNE 1950
The U.S. begins fighting in Korea.

1951
Johnson is elected majority whip of the U.S. Senate.

JANUARY 1953
Johnson is elected minority leader of the U.S. Senate.

JULY 1953
The Korean War ends.

APRIL 1954
The French are defeated by Vietnamese rebels at Dien Bien Phu.

MAY 1954
The U.S. Supreme Court decision of *Brown v. Board of Education* declares segregated schools unconstitutional.

NOVEMBER 1954
Johnson is reelected to the Senate by a wide margin.

JANUARY 1955

Johnson becomes minority leader of the Senate.

JULY 1955

Johnson suffers a severe heart attack.

1957

Johnson steers the Civil Rights Act of 1957 through Congress.

OCTOBER 4, 1957

The Soviet Union launches the satellite *Sputnik I*.

1960

Johnson is elected vice president to John F. Kennedy.

MARCH 1961

Johnson is made chairman of the President's Committee on Equal Employment Opportunity.

MAY 1961

Johnson visits Vietnam.

NOVEMBER 22, 1963

Kennedy is assassinated; Johnson is sworn in as president of the United States.

NOVEMBER 27, 1963

Johnson implores Congress to support him in enacting Kennedy's legislative agenda.

MAY 22, 1964

Johnson presents his vision of a Great Society at a speech at the University of Michigan.

JULY 2, 1964

Johnson signs the Civil Rights Act of 1964.

AUGUST 2, 1964

The U.S. destroyer *Maddox* is fired on by North Vietnamese in the Gulf of Tonkin off North Vietnam.

AUGUST 4, 1964

U.S. destroyers in the Gulf of Tonkin report coming under attack by North Vietnamese forces; Johnson orders a bombing raid of North Vietnam in response.

AUGUST 7, 1964

Congress passes the Gulf of Tonkin Resolution.

AUGUST 20, 1964

Johnson signs the Economic Opportunity Act, initiating his War on Poverty.

NOVEMBER 1964

Johnson is elected president by a wide margin; Hubert Humphrey is his vice president.

FEBRUARY 6, 1965

Eight American servicemen are killed in Pleiku when a U.S. military barracks is attacked by Vietnamese guerrillas; Johnson orders a retaliatory bombing of North Vietnam, which gradually evolves into a sustained bombing campaign named Rolling Thunder.

MARCH 7, 1965

Civil rights marchers are attacked by state troopers in Selma, Alabama.

APRIL 1965

Johnson signs the Elementary and Secondary Education Act.

JULY 28, 1965

Johnson announces his decision to escalate U.S. involvement in Vietnam by increasing the number of troops there to 125,000 with more to follow if needed.

AUGUST 6, 1965

Johnson signs the Voting Rights Act.

NOVEMBER 1966

Midterm congressional elections result in large losses for Democrats.

JULY 1967
Race riots take place in Detroit and Newark.

AUGUST 1967
Johnson proposes a tax increase to fund the war effort.

JANUARY 1968
The Vietcong carries out the Tet offensive.

MARCH 31, 1968
Johnson announces his decision to de-escalate the Vietnam War and step out of the presidential race.

APRIL 4, 1968
Martin Luther King Jr. is assassinated.

APRIL 11, 1968
Johnson signs the Civil Rights Act of 1968.

JUNE 5, 1968
Robert F. Kennedy is assassinated.

AUGUST 1968
Hubert H. Humphrey is nominated as the Democratic presidential candidate.

NOVEMBER 1968
Richard M. Nixon defeats Humphrey to become president.

1969
Johnson retires to his ranch in Texas.

JANUARY 22, 1973
Johnson dies of a heart attack.

JANUARY 23, 1973
Nixon announces an end to the Vietnam War.

1975
North Vietnamese raise their flag over Saigon and rename it Ho Chi Minh City as the last remaining U.S. officials depart.

FOR FURTHER RESEARCH

JOHNSON AND HIS PRESIDENCY

IRVING BERNSTEIN, *Guns or Butter: The Presidency of Lyndon Johnson.* New York: Oxford University Press, 1996.

VAUGHN DAVIS BORNET, *The Presidency of Lyndon B. Johnson.* Lawrence: University Press of Kansas, 1983.

H.W. BRANDS, *The Wages of Globalism: Lyndon Johnson and the Limits of American Power.* New York: Oxford University Press, 1995.

JOSEPH A. CALIFANO JR., *The Triumph and Tragedy of Lyndon Johnson: The White House Years.* New York: Simon and Schuster, 1991.

ROBERT A. CARO, *The Years of Lyndon Johnson.* New York: Alfred A. Knopf, 1982.

GEORGE CHRISTIAN, *The President Steps Down: A Personal Memoir of the Transfer of Power.* New York: Macmillan, 1970.

WARREN I. COHEN AND NANCY BERNKOPF TUCKER, eds., *Lyndon Johnson Confronts the World: American Foreign Policy, 1963–1968.* New York: Cambridge University Press, 1994.

PAUL K. CONKIN, *Big Daddy from the Pedernales: Lyndon Baines Johnson.* Boston: Twayne, 1986.

FRANK CORMIER, *LBJ: The Way He Was.* Garden City, NY: Doubleday, 1977.

ROBERT DALLEK, *Lone Star Rising: Lyndon Johnson and His Times, 1908–1960.* New York: Oxford University Press, 1991.

———, *Flawed Giant: Lyndon Johnson and His Times, 1961–1973.* New York: Oxford University Press, 1998.

JAMES DEAKIN, *Lyndon Johnson's Credibility Gap.* Washington, DC: Public Affairs Press, 1968.

ROBERT A. DIVINE, ed., *The Johnson Years, Volume One: Foreign Policy, the Great Society, and the White House*. Lawrence: University Press of Kansas, 1987.

———, *The Johnson Years, Volume Two: Vietnam, the Environment, and Science*. Lawrence: University Press of Kansas, 1987.

ROWLAND EVANS AND ROBERT NOVAK, *Lyndon B. Johnson: The Exercise of Power*. New York: New American Library, 1966.

BERNARD J. FIRESTONE, ed., *Lyndon Baines Johnson and the Uses of Power*. New York: Greenwood, 1988.

ERIC F. GOLDMAN, *The Tragedy of Lyndon Johnson*. New York: Alfred A. Knopf, 1969.

PAUL Y. HAMMOND, *LBJ and the Presidential Management of Foreign Relations*. Austin: University Press of Texas, 1992.

DORIS KEARNS, *Lyndon Johnson and the American Dream*. New York: Harper and Row, 1976.

MERLE MILLER, *Lyndon: An Oral Biography*. New York: Putnam, 1980.

BOOTH MOONEY, *LBJ: An Irreverent Chronicle*. New York: Thomas Y. Crowell, 1976.

GEORGE REEDY, *Lyndon B. Johnson: A Memoir*. New York: Andrews and McMeel, 1982.

PHILIP REED RULON, *The Compassionate Samaritan: The Life of Lyndon Baines Johnson*. Chicago: Nelson-Hall, 1981.

BRUCE J. SCHULMAN, *Lyndon B. Johnson and American Liberalism: A Brief Biography with Documents*. New York: Bedford Books, 1995.

ROBERT SHERRILL, *The Accidental President*. New York: Grossman, 1967.

HUGH SIDEY, *A Very Personal Presidency: Lyndon Johnson in the White House*. New York: Atheneum, 1968.

ALFRED STEINBERG, *Sam Johnson's Boy: A Close-Up of the President from Texas*. New York: Macmillan, 1968.

KENNETH W. THOMPSON, ed., *The Johnson Presidency: Twenty Intimate Perspectives of Lyndon B. Johnson.* Lanham, MD: University Press of America, 1986.

IRWIN UNGER, *The Best of Intentions: The Triumphs and Failures of the Great Society Under Kennedy, Johnson, and Nixon.* New York: Doubleday, 1996.

JACK VALENTI, *A Very Human President.* New York: W.W. Norton, 1975.

JOHNSON AND THE CIVIL RIGHTS MOVEMENT

JAMES C. HARVEY, *Black Civil Rights During the Johnson Administration.* Jackson: University and College Press of Mississippi, 1973.

ROBERT D. LOEVY, *To End All Segregation: The Politics of the Passage of the Civil Rights Act of 1964.* Lanham, MD: University Press of America, 1990.

ROBERT MANN, *The Walls of Jericho: Lyndon Johnson, Hubert Humphrey, Richard Russell, and the Struggle for Civil Rights.* New York: Harcourt Brace, 1996.

MARK STERN, *Calculating Visions: Kennedy, Johnson, and Civil Rights.* New Brunswick, NJ: Rutgers University Press, 1992.

THE GREAT SOCIETY

JOHN A. ANDREW III, *Lyndon Johnson and the Great Society.* Chicago: Ivan R. Dee, 1998.

MARVIN E. GETTLEMAN AND DAVID MERMELSTEIN, eds., *The Great Society Reader: The Failure of American Liberalism.* New York: Random House, 1967.

ELI GINZBERG AND ROBERT M. SOLOW, eds., *The Great Society: Lessons for the Future.* New York: BasicBooks, 1974.

MEL G. GRINSPAN, ed., *The Great Society Revisited: Success, Failure, or Remorse?* Memphis, TN: Rhodes College, 1993.

BERTRAM M. GROSS, ed., *A Great Society?* New York: BasicBooks, 1968.

Marshall Kaplan and Peggy L. Cuciti, eds., *The Great Society and Its Legacy: Twenty Years of U.S. Social Policy*. Durham, NC: Duke University Press, 1986.

Johnson and the Vietnam War

Moya Ann Ball, *Vietnam-on-the-Potomac*. New York: Praeger, 1992.

David M. Barrett, *Uncertain Warriors: Lyndon Johnson and His Vietnam Advisers*. Lawrence: University Press of Kansas, 1993.

Larry Berman, *Lyndon Johnson's War: the Road to Stalemate in Vietnam*. New York: W.W. Norton, 1989.

———, *Planning a Tragedy: The Americanization of the War in Vietnam*. New York: W.W. Norton, 1982.

Robert W. Crawford, *Call Retreat: The Johnson Administration's Vietnam Policy, March 1967 to March 1968*. Washington, DC: Washington Institute for Values in Public Policy, 1987.

Lloyd C. Gardner, *Pay Any Price: Lyndon Johnson and the Wars for Vietnam*. Chicago: Ivan R. Dee, 1995.

Henry F. Graff, *The Tuesday Cabinet: Deliberation and Decision on Peace and War Under Lyndon B. Johnson*. Englewood Cliffs, NJ: Prentice-Hall, 1970.

David Halberstam, *The Best and the Brightest*. New York: Random House, 1972.

George C. Herring, *LBJ and Vietnam: A Different Kind of War*. Austin: University of Texas Press, 1994.

Michael H. Hunt, *Lyndon Johnson's War: America's Cold War Crusade in Vietnam, 1945–1968*. New York: Hill and Wang, 1996.

Fredrik Logevall, *Choosing War: The Lost Chance for Peace and the Escalation of War in Vietnam*. Berkeley: University of California Press, 1999.

H.R. McMaster, *Dereliction of Duty: Lyndon Johnson, Robert McNamara, the Joint Chiefs of Staff, and the Lies That Led to Vietnam*. New York: HarperCollins, 1997.

ROBERT S. MCNAMARA, *In Retrospect: The Tragedy and Lessons of Vietnam*. New York: Times Books, 1995.

ROBERT S. MCNAMARA, JAMES G. BLIGHT, AND ROBERT K. BRIGHAM, *Argument Without End: In Search of Answers to the Vietnam Tragedy*. New York: Public Affairs, 1999.

HERBERT Y. SCHANDLER, *The Unmaking of a President: Lyndon Johnson and Vietnam*. New Jersey: Princeton University Press, 1977.

ORRIN SCHWAB, *Defending the Free World: John F. Kennedy, Lyndon Johnson, and the Vietnam War, 1961–1965*. Westport, CT: Praeger, 1998.

KATHLEEN J. TURNER, *Lyndon Johnson's Dual War: Vietnam and the Press*. Chicago: University of Chicago Press, 1985.

BRIAN VANDEMARK, *Into the Quagmire: Lyndon Johnson and the Escalation of the Vietnam War*. New York: Oxford University Press, 1991.

FRANK E. VANDIVER, *Shadows of Vietnam: Lyndon Johnson's Wars*. College Station: Texas A&M University Press, 1997.

INDEX

Humphrey's role in, 124
Johnson's implementation of, 150
Johnson's support for, 41, 75–76, 116–18, 132–34, 140, 145–46
Johnson's votes against, 111–17, 133
opposition to, 28, 33–34, 149–50
public opinion on, 123
states' rights in, 149–50
was politically expedient for Johnson, 112, 123, 133
was risky for Johnson, 124, 131, 137–38
see also Civil Rights Act of 1964; voting rights
civil rights movement
assaults on, 31, 136
committed to Johnson's election, 136
demonstrations of, 31, 46, 122, 133, 136
efforts to control, 138–39, 141
media coverage of, 136–37
militancy of, 11, 32, 34, 46, 47
sought equality of results, 32, 34, 46–47
success of, 46, 136–37, 147–48
white backlash to, 137–40, 141
Clean Water Restoration Act of 1966, 65
Clifford, Clark, 193, 215–17
appointed secretary of defense, 194–195
did not support U.S. troop buildup in Vietnam, 166
Clinton, Bill, 47
Cloward, Richard A., 84
Cold War, 178, 185, 203
influenced Vietnam policies, 36, 163, 177–78
Communists, 169, 203
see also Cold War; North Vietnam; Vietcong
Community Action Programs, 31, 48, 84–85, 100–101
Congress. *See* House of Representatives; Senate
Congressional Quarterly, 70
Congress of Racial Equality (CORE), 136, 138
Connally, John, 78
Connor, "Bull," 134
conservatives, 45
on Great Society, 45, 53, 87
on Vietnam War, 66, 191
see also Republican Party
Cooke, Terence, 222–23
Cronkite, Walter, 133
Cuciti, Peggy, 53

Dallek, Robert, 16, 119
on Johnson's personality, 15, 17, 19, 20
Dean, Arthur, 197
Democratic Party, 92, 180
civil rights legislation of, 116, 123, 126, 130

see also liberals
desegregation. *See* segregation
Diem, Ngo Dinh, 35–36
Dillon, Douglas, 197
Dirksen, Everett, 129–30
discrimination. *See* segregation; voting rights
Dodd, Tom, 78
Du Bois, W.E.B., 86

Eastland, James, 114
Economic Opportunity Act (1964), 28, 30, 70, 102
economics, 73
free enterprise, 76–77
gold standard, 233
inflation, 62–64, 94, 227
taxes, 28, 61–63, 65–66, 70, 233
of Vietnam War, 63–64, 164–65, 193
see also unemployment
education policies, 30, 71, 88–89, 102, 214
Eisenhower, Dwight, 24, 77, 105–106, 179, 199
Elementary and Secondary Education Act, 30
Engle, Clair, 130
Equal Employment Opportunity Commission, 25, 33, 149
Evans, Rowland, 23

Fair Employment Practices Commission (FEPC), 111–12, 114
Fair Housing Act of 1968, 146
farmers, 82, 111
Farm Security Administration (FSA), 111
Field Foundation, 86–87
Ford Motor Company, 76–77
foreign policy advisers, 169, 171–73, 175–79, 184–86
Ball, George, 153–55, 161–63, 178, 197
Bundy, William, 157–58, 178
on democracy for South Vietnam, 176, 178
favored·de-escalation of war, 195–97, 201–202, 215–17
favored troop increases, 37, 197
saw war as hopeless, 39–40
see also Bundy, McGeorge; Cold War; McNamara, Robert; Rusk, Dean
Fortas, Abe, 166
Fowler, Henry (Joe), 212
France, 35, 154
Fulbright, J. William, 184, 188, 191, 219

Gaither, Jim, 221
Gardner, John, 55
Garrow, David, 136–37
Gelb, Leslie H., 207
Gelfand, Mark I., 86–87

Goebbels, Joseph, 196
Goering, Hermann, 196
Goldman, Eric, 138, 140, 141
Goldwater, Barry, 29, 70, 78, 135, 180
Goodwin, Richard, 51, 74
Graham, Hugh Davis, 50
Great Society legislation, 29–30, 58, 91–92
    attempted to redistribute wealth, 93
    created advancement for blacks, 76–77, 94,
        101–102
    criticism of, 45–46, 72, 92, 94, 100
    did not acknowledge moral inequality,
        87–88, 89
    evolution of, 45–47, 65, 213
    Johnson's commitment to, 40–41, 56–57,
        59, 65, 74–75, 213–15, 220
    maximum feasible participation in, 31,
        100–101
    passed during economic growth, 62, 70, 73
    public support for, 30, 44–45, 52–55, 92, 95
    undermined by
        black militancy, 46
        economic conditions, 45, 49, 62–64
        implementation strategies, 30, 45,
            49–50, 53, 92
        Johnson's lack of leadership, 59–61,
            73–74, 79–80, 149–51
        lack of funding, 31, 45, 51–52, 151
        political ideologies, 53, 54–55
        Vietnam War, 41, 51, 59, 62–63, 65–66,
            76, 151, 180–81
    was response to complex problems, 94–95
    see also civil rights legislation; economics;
        War on Poverty
Greene, Wallace M., 165
Gregory, Dick, 151
Griggs v. Duke Power Co., 47
Guns or Butter: The Presidency of Lyndon
    Johnson (Bernstein), 196–97

Halleck, Charlie, 126
Harriman, Averell, 198
Harvey, James C., 138, 144
Hayden, Carl, 130
Head Start, 30, 76
health care. See Medicare program
Heckling Hare (airplane), 22
Heineman, Ben, 50
Ho Chi Minh, 35, 170, 219
Hoover, J. Edgar, 122
Hopkins, Welly, 17
House of Representatives, 70, 71, 79, 188–89
    on civil rights legislation, 126, 149
    on Kennedy's civil rights bill, 125, 135, 148
    see also Democratic Party; Republican
        Party
Housing and Urban Development
    Department, 30, 52–53, 71

housing programs, 71, 72, 92, 100, 110–11,
    145
Humphrey, Hubert, 29, 72, 185
    civil rights work of, 124, 129–30, 150

immigrants, 30, 71, 82
Indochina, 169, 178
inflation, 62–64, 94, 227

Job Corps, 30–31, 73
Johnson, Harold, 191, 193–94
Johnson, Josefa (sister), 12
Johnson, Lady Bird, 11, 18–19
Johnson, Lucia (sister), 12
Johnson, Lyndon Baines, 11, 25–26, 29–30
    childhood of, 12, 14–15, 107–108, 227–28
    communication style of, 69, 73–80
    concealed details of Vietnam War, 62–64,
        67, 180–81
    as Congressman, 20–21, 23–25, 58–60, 73,
        77, 110–17, 133
    decides not to seek reelection, 40, 44, 198,
        205, 218–22, 228–34
    disillusionment of, 183, 225–27, 229
    on dissenting opinions, 38, 135–41,
        185–86, 208
    dominating style of, 17–18, 20, 27, 179,
        185–86
    economic policies of, 57, 62–67, 69,
        212–13, 222, 233
    education of, 14, 15, 16, 108
    failed to administer Great Society
        programs, 59–61, 65, 150–51
    failed to mobilize public support, 50–52,
        65–67, 69, 72–73
    feared a Third World War, 172–73,
        187–88, 190, 194, 206, 207
    foreign policy of. See foreign policy
        advisers
    on Kennedy's agenda, 26, 28, 119, 121,
        134, 135
    as Kleberg's secretary, 17–19, 58–59
    legacy of, 40–41, 132–33, 143
    military service of, 22
    with the National Youth Association,
        19–20, 58–59, 108–109
    obsessed with Vietnam War, 64–65, 179,
        226
    personality of, 14, 15, 23, 69, 172–73,
        184–85, 226
    personal life of, 12–14, 18–19, 26–27, 40,
        68–69, 227–31
    political campaigns of, 20–24, 28–29,
        78–79, 110, 113–14, 234
    political philosophy of, 13, 16, 33, 121,
        131, 224–25
    public opinion of, 40, 67, 71, 78–79, 207,
        221–23

209, 216, 218
military capabilities of, 189, 192–93, 195,
208, 213–14
military objectives of, 189, 199
see also Cold War; Communists; Vietcong
Novak, Robert, 23

O'Brien, Larry, 71, 125, 126
O'Daniel, W. Lee (Pappy), 21
O'Donnell, Kenny, 128
Office of Economic Opportunity, 84
Ohlin, Lloyd, 53

Pearson, Lester, 183, 185
Piven, Frances Fox, 84
Political Science Quarterly, 172–73
pollution legislation, 30, 52, 65, 71
Potter, Paul, 230–31
poverty
citizens living in, 49, 81, 90
affected by "new minimalism," 54
community action programs, 31, 84–85,
100–101
demonstrations of, 84
did not benefit from civil rights
legislation, 147, 151
moral inequality of, 87–89
status distinctions among, 82, 83, 90
as victims, 83–85, 89
see also unemployment; War on Poverty;
welfare system
Powell, Adam Clayton, 111
Protest at Selma (Garrow), 136
public works projects, 20–21
Pueblo (ship), 213

race relations. *See* civil rights
Randolph, A. Philip, 138
Reedy, George, 116
Republican Party
and civil rights legislation, 47, 126, 128–30
on Great Society, 45, 52–53
see also conservatives
Rivers, Mendel, 190
Robson, John, 221
Rockefeller, Nelson and Happy, 223
Roosevelt, Franklin Delano, 18, 19, 20, 35,
105
Roosevelt, Teddy, 79
Rostow, Walt, 177–78, 215–17
Ruether, Walter, 73
Rusk, Dean, 155, 175–76, 193, 215, 217
on de-escalation, 198, 216
on Vietnam War objectives, 158–59, 163,
177–78
Russell, Richard, 120, 123–24, 131, 160, 190
Rustin, Bayard, 138

Safire, William, 196
Schandler, Herbert J., 201
Schulman, Bruce J., 21, 23, 25, 27–28, 38
Schultze, Charles, 52, 63–64
segregation, 24, 100, 108
bans on, 28, 144
separated South from nation, 122–23
Southern Manifesto on, 24, 115
Senate, 70, 71, 79
civil rights debate, 127–30, 135, 149
cloture vote in, 129–30
on escalation of Vietnam War, 188–89, 217
after Johnson's reelection decision, 222
see also Democratic Party; Republican
Party
Sheppard, Morris, 21
Sherrill, Robert, 112
Sidey, Hugh, 68
Smith, Donald H., 167
Smith, Howard, 126
Social Security system, 71, 96–97
Southeast Asia, 169–70
see also Cambodia; Laos; North Vietnam;
South Vietnam
Southern Christian Leadership Conference
(SCLC), 139
South Vietnam, 198, 230–31
Johnson's commitment to, 181, 183, 185,
206
U.S. advisers on, 154–55, 161–62, 176
U.S. troop strength in, 36, 37, 41, 166, 191,
201–202, 207, 209
see also Vietnam War
Stennis, John, 121–22, 160
Stevenson, Coke, 22–23
Student Nonviolent Coordinating
Committee (SNCC), 136, 138
Supplemental Security Income, 96
Supreme Court, 92, 166
on affirmative action, 47
on election results, 23
on segregation, 24, 115
*Swann v. Charlotte-Mecklenburg County
School District,* 47

Taggart, Robert, 91
Tax Reduction Act of 1964, 62
Taylor, Claudia Alta. *See* Johnson, Lady Bird
Taylor, Maxwell, 175–76, 188, 197
Tet offensive, 38–39, 192, 213
reaction to, 192–94, 202, 211, 216–17
Texas politics, 12, 21, 22
Transportation Department, 30, 71
Truman, Harry, 35, 105, 112–14, 196, 199

unemployment, 94–95
acceptability of, 90
compensation, 96

moral distinctions of, 82–83
United Negro College Fund, 145
Urban League, 139
U Thant, 223

Valenti, Jack, 120, 126, 167
Vance, Cyrus, 159–60, 197
Vandenberg, Arthur, 129
Vietcong
  military capabilities of, 37–38, 155–56,
    213–14
  South Vietnamese as, 35, 189
  see also North Vietnam
Vietnam War
  affected Great Society programs, 31, 41,
    51, 59, 62, 63, 65–66, 76, 151, 180–81
  affected image of Democratic Party, 177,
    180–81
  affected U.S. economy, 62–63, 66, 164–65,
    193
  bombing pauses in, 189, 198, 218, 232
  costs of, 63–64, 193, 203, 207–209
  deaths from, 36, 41, 192
  de-escalation of, 198–99, 201–202,
    204–205, 210–11
  domino theory of, 35, 159, 163, 169–70,
    204–206
  escalation of, 11–12, 36–37, 41, 153,
    165–66, 189, 190–91, 206–207
  failed strategies of, 37, 202–10
  fought for U.S. credibility, 170–71, 176–79,
    190, 203–204, 206
  fought for U.S. national security, 165, 174,
    232–33
  fought to protect Johnson's credibility,
    180, 181–86
  with the French, 154
  funding for, 159–60, 164–65
  Gulf of Tonkin Resolution in, 36
  Johnson's compromising policies on, 189,
    190, 191, 196–97
  Johnson's deception concerning, 37, 38,
    39, 41, 165–66
  Johnson's objectives in, 199, 206–207, 209
  Johnson's skepticism of, 183
  objectives redefined for, 201–202, 209
  peace initiatives in, 40, 183, 189, 198–99,
    201–202, 204, 211, 223
  public opinion on, 190, 192–93, 196, 202,
    207, 209–11, 213–14
  Rolling Thunder campaign in, 36–37
  Tet offensive in, 38–39, 192–94, 202, 211,
    213, 216–17
  U.S. presidential support for, 168, 169–70
  U.S. troop increase in, 36, 37, 41, 166, 191,
    207, 209
  see also antiwar movement; Communists;
    military leaders; North Vietnam

voting rights, 30, 31–32, 57–58, 100, 134
  controlled by states, 111
  support for, 31, 52
Voting Rights Act of 1965, 11, 46, 71,
    144–45, 148
  provisions of, 32, 106, 140
  support for, 52, 136–37

Wabash Cannonball (airplane), 22
Walker, Alice, 147–48
Wallace, George, 135, 214, 215
Walton, Hanes, Jr., 149–50
War on Poverty, 11, 28, 70
  community action programs, 31, 84–85,
    100–101
  did not benefit all blacks, 49, 147, 151
  did not challenge existing economic
    power, 48–49, 50, 53
  Head Start, 30, 76
  health care programs, 30, 57–58, 71, 76,
    77, 98–99
  housing programs, 71, 72, 92, 100, 110–11,
    145
  ideological evaluations of, 86–87
  Job Corps, 30–31, 73
  legal services, 48, 100
  minimum wage increase, 30
  public opinion on, 52, 83
  was successful, 77, 94, 97–98, 102–103
  see also welfare system
Washington Post, 221
Water Quality Act of 1965, 65
welfare system
  destroys obligation to be self-sufficient,
    82–83, 90
  eligibility for, 84–85, 97
  eliminates unworthiness, 84–88
  female-headed families in, 97, 98
  forced marital separations, 97
  is unjustly criticized, 93, 96–98
  means testing in, 89–90
  and Medicaid, 99
Westmoreland, William, 159, 160, 166, 193,
    208–209
Wheeler, Earle, 164, 166
  favored escalation of war, 191, 193, 217,
    218
White, Lee, 120–21, 128, 130, 141
Wicker, Tom, 134
Wiley, George, 84
Wilkins, Roy, 121–22, 128–29, 138
Williams, T. Harry, 134, 142
Wilson, Harold, 183
Witt, Edgar, 17
Wright, Zephyr, 121–22

Young, Andrew, 124
Young, Whitney, 138